Master Olof, Creditors, To Damascus (Part I)

Only recently has Strindberg begun to receive the recognition he deserves. His obsessional treatments of insanity, sexual domination and the psychological warfare between men and women provoked incomprehension and abhorrence during his lifetime. But now his plays have taken on a new relevance and directness. He is rightly acclaimed a pioneer of twentieth-century theatre and one of the world's great dramatists.

This volume contains: Strindberg's first great play, *Master Olof* 'Michael Meyer's agile translation of a flawed idealist who shrinks from the logic of his own actions and puts compromise before martyrdom' (Michael Billington, *Guardian*); *Creditors* 'is a masterpiece of concentrated passion' (Jane Edwardes, *Time Out*); and *To Damascus* (Part I) 'A play so packed with ideas and invective that it makes most contemporary dramas seem trivial' (Allen Wright, *Scotsman*).

Michael Meyer's translations of Strindberg are well-known and widely performed, and in 1964 they won him the Gold Medal of the Swedish Academy, the first time that award had ever been bestowed on an Englishman. Meyer has also provided introductions tracing the origins and background of each play. He is the author of a definitive biography of Strindberg and has written a critically acclaimed play about his life, *Lunatic and Lover*.

also by August Strindberg in the World Dramatists series
translated and introduced by Michael Meyer

PLAYS: ONE
The Father, Miss Julie, The Ghost Sonata

PLAYS: TWO
The Dance of Death, A Dream Play, The Stronger

AUGUST STRINDBERG
Plays: Three

Master Olof
Creditors
To Damascus (Part I)

Translated from the Swedish
with introductions by
MICHAEL MEYER

Methuen Drama

METHUEN'S WORLD DRAMATISTS

This collection fist published as a paperback original in Great Britain in 1991 by Methuen Drama, Michelin House, 81 Fulham Road, London SW3 6RB.

Master Olof copyright © 1991 by Michael Meyer
Creditors copyright © 1991 by Michael Meyer
To Damascus (Part I) first published by Secker & Warburg Ltd.
copyright © 1971, 1973, 1975 by Michael Meyer
This collection copyright © 1991 by Michael Meyer
Introductions copyright © 1991 by Michael Meyer
Michael Meyer has asserted his moral rights.

ISBN 0-413-64840-0

A CIP catalogue record for this book may be obtained from The British Library.

The front cover shows a detail from Edvard Munch's painting *Aften på Karl Johan*, 1892, from the Rasmus Meyer Collection, Bergen, Norway. The back cover portrait of Strindberg is also by Munch (1892) from Moderna Museet, Stockholm, reproduced by kind permission of Oslo Kommunes Kunstsamlinger, Munch-Museet.

Printed and bound in Great Britain by Cox & Wyman Ltd, Cardiff Road, Reading

Contents

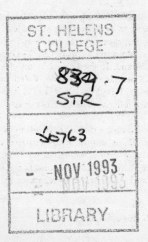

Johan August Strindberg

22 January 1849	Born in Stockholm, the fourth child of a shipping merchant and his former maid-servant.
1853	His father goes bankrupt.
1862	His mother dies. The next year his father marries his housekeeper.
1867	Goes to Uppsala University, where he decides to become a doctor.
1869	Fails preliminary examination, leaves University and goes on the stage. Fails at that. Writes his first plays, *A Nameday Gift* and *The Freethinker*.
1870	Returns to Uppsala to study modern languages and political science. His fourth play, *In Rome*, is performed briefly at the Royal Theatre in Stockholm.
1872	Leaves Uppsala and settles in Stockholm. Tries to go on the stage again, and fails again. Writes first major play, *Master Olof*, but it is not performed for nine years.
1872–4	Journalist in Stockholm.
1874–82	Librarian in Stockholm.
1877	Marries Finnish actress Siri von Essen.
1879	Established himself as an author with autobiographical novel, *The Red Room*.
1880–2	Writes historical and pseudo-historical prose works; also *The New Kingdom*, a provocative book for which he is venomously attacked.
1883	Leaves Sweden (partly because of these attacks) to spend the next six years abroad in France, Switzerland, Germany and Denmark. First theatrical success with *Lucky Peter's Journey* (his ninth play).

1884	Published volume of short stories, *Getting Married;* is prosecuted for blasphemy; returns to Sweden to face trial; is acquitted.
1886	Writes novel about his childhood, *The Son of a Servant*.
1887	Writes *The Father* in Bavaria. It has a small success in Denmark but fails in Sweden. Also writes rustic novel, *The People of Hemsö*, and, in French, *A Madman's Defence*, an account of his marriage.
1888	*The Father* staged by Freie Bühne in Berlin; Strindberg becomes known in Germany. He writes *Miss Julie* and *Creditors*, both in Denmark. *Miss Julie* attacked on publication for immorality.
1889	Starts own experimental theatre in Denmark; *Miss Julie* and *Creditors* are staged there, and fail. Theatre goes bankrupt. Strindberg returns to Sweden.
1891	Divorces Siri.
1892	Writes *Playing With Fire* and *The Bond*, his last play for six years. Leaves Sweden for Germany.
1893	Marries Austrian journalist, Frida Uhl. Visits England.
1893–7	Writes many pseudo-scientific articles for alchemistical and other journals, in French.
1894	Leaves Frida and settles in Paris. *Creditors* and *The Father* are staged there, and are well received. Strindberg is lionized but, as always, makes little money.
1894–6	Poor and alone in Paris. Scientific experiments; dabbles in alchemy and tries to make gold. *Inferno* crisis; hovers on brink of insanity.
1896	Emerges from mental crisis and returns to Sweden.
1897	Writes *Inferno* in French, the account of his years of near-madness.

1898	Writes Parts I and II of his dramatic trilogy, *To Damascus*. In the next eleven years he writes thirty-five plays.
1899	Writes *There Are Crimes and Crimes* and *Erik the Fourteenth*, his best historical play.
1900	Meets Norwegian actress, Harriet Bosse, twenty-nine years his junior. Writes *Easter* and *The Dance of Death*, Parts I and II.
1901	Writes *To Damascus*, Part III, and *A Dream Play*. Marries Harriet. She leaves him before the end of the year; returns briefly; then moves away for good (though they remain in contact).
1904–6	He writes no plays. His reputation in decline.
1907	Founds his own Intimate Theatre in Stockholm. Writes four chamber plays for it: *Storm*, *The Burnt House*, *The Ghost Sonata*, *The Pelican*, the first three all within ten weeks. They are coldly received.
1909	Writes last play, *The Great Highway*.
1909–12	Devotes last three years of his life to writing pamphlets on politics, sociology and philosophy.
14 May 1912	Dies in Stockholm of stomach cancer, aged sixty-three.

THE PLAYS OF STRINDBERG
(1849–1912)
with their dates of composition

PRE-INFERNO

1869   A Nameday Gift (lost)
      The Freethinker
187C   Hermione
      In Rome
1871   The Outlaw
1872–1877   Master Olof
1876–1877   Anno 48
1880   The Secret of the Guild
1882   Lucky Peter's Journey
      Sir Bengt's Wife
1886–1887   The Robbers (The
      Comrades)
1887   The Father
1888   Miss Julie
      Creditors
1888–1889   The Stronger
1889   Pariah
      The People of Hemsö
      Simoom
1892   The Keys of Heaven
      The First Warning
      Debit and Credit
      In the Face of Death
      A Mother's Love
      Playing with Fire
      The Bond

POST-INFERNO

1898   To Damascus, *Part I*
      To Damascus, *Part II*
      Advent
1899   There are Crimes and
      Crimes
      The Saga of the Folkungs
      Gustav Vasa
      Erik the Fourteenth

1900   Gustav Adolf
      Midsummer
      Casper's Shrove Tuesday
      Easter
      The Dance of Death,
      Part I
      The Dance of Death,
      Part II
1901   The Virgin Bride
      Swanwhite
      Charles XII
      To Damascus, *Part III*
      Engelbrekt
      Queen Christina
      A Dream Play
1902   Gustav III
      The Dutchman (frag-
      ment)
      The Nightingale of
      Wittenberg
1903   Exodus (Moses)
      Hellas (Socrates)
      The Lamb and the
      Beast (Christ)
1907   Storm
      The Burnt House
      The Ghost Sonata
      Toten-Insel (fragment)
      The Pelican
1908   The Last Knight
      Abu Casem's Slippers
      The Protector
      The Earl of Bjälbo
1909   The Black Glove
      The Great Highway

Master Olof

(1872)

Introduction to

MASTER OLOF

Master Olof was Strindberg's first great play. He wrote three
separate versions, completing the first, which is that most
commonly performed in Sweden and is by general agreement
the best, by the age of 23. He began it in 1871 in Uppsala, to
which he had returned to complete his university studies after
a two year absence trying to make his name as an author and
actor, and finished it the following summer in the Stockholm
skerries, employing, in his own words, 'simple, everyday
speech such as people use off the stage'. Olaus Petri
(1493–1552) was a disciple of Martin Luther and the man
most responsible for introducing Lutheranism into Sweden
and breaking the power of Rome over the Swedish Church.
Into the character of the troubled young priest, Strindberg
poured his own problems: the dilemma of the young who wish
to revolutionize society and pull down what is old and dead,
yet who shrink from violence and from a violent death. It is
an unashamed self-portrait; in a letter to the Danish critic
Georg Brandes on 29 July 1880, Strindberg called it 'the story
of my life'. 'You were born to make men angry', says Olof's
brother to him in the opening scene. 'You were born to fight.'
Olof, aged 30 when the play begins, defies the might of the
established Church. The young King, Gustav Vasa, three
years Olof's junior, recruits him as a weapon against that
establishment. But in his new position, Olof finds the King an
establishment figure against whom he feels compelled to
rebel, as against the Church, and when Gert, a seasoned old
revolutionary who is Olof's father-in-law, plans to assassinate
the King, Olof joins the conspiracy. They are discovered and
condemned to death. Gert welcomes martyrdom as the best
way to advance the cause of radicalism, but Olof allows
himself to be persuaded that he can achieve more as a living
new Luther (as, historically, he did). In the magnificent final

scene a young follower, ignorant that Olof has recanted, kneels to him in the pillory and blesses him for, as he supposes, choosing martyrdom.

Master Olof is arguably as astounding a play as was ever written by a dramatist of 23 (always excepting Büchner's *Woyzeck and Danton's Death*), vividly characterized, sharply written and told in a series of swift and powerful scenes rising to a superb climax. Played uncut, even at a modern pace, it would run for upwards of four hours; and for non-Swedish audiences it presents a problem that was to recur in all Strindberg's historical plays, the presupposition of a basic background knowledge which few non-Swedes, and by no means all Swedes, possess. But it is full of fire and eloquence, in a different class to Strindberg's four surviving earlier plays, *The Freethinker, Hermione, In Rome* and *The Outlaw*, none of which is nowadays ever staged in Sweden. The minor characters are all sharply drawn, which cannot always be said of his more mature works, and in its use of ordinary everyday prose it anticipated Ibsen's 'contemporary' plays, for it was written five years before *The Pillars of Society* and seven years before *A Doll's House*. Had it been accepted and adequately performed, what plays might Strindberg not have written in the next decade and a half? As things turned out, its rejection turned him away from the drama towards the novel and the short story, and it was to be fifteen years before he wrote another play of lasting merit, *The Father*.

It is not surprising that the Royal Theatre of Stockholm, which had staged *In Rome* and *The Outlaw*, rejected *Master Olof*. The qualities that make it admired today, the sharp modernity of its dialogue and characterization, were regarded as unsuitable for a play about ancient heroes. Admittedly Ibsen had demonstrated precisely these qualities in his historical play *The Pretenders* nine years earlier, but *The Pretenders*, though a success in Norway, was not seen in Sweden until 1879. Poetry was still regarded as the only possible medium for stage tragedy throughout the western world. *Master Olof* lacked the declamatory monologues which audiences, and actors, expected, and the humanity, the

five-foot-six quality of the famous historical figures, bothered
them. They wanted to see, and act, giants. The subtle
relationships, too, needed the kind of acting that would
emerge later in the century with Stanislavsky and Duse.
Although Strindberg rewrote it twice in an effort to
compromise with popular taste, the play had to wait nine
years before it was staged, and then, ironically enough, in the
original version. It was an experience with which Strindberg
was to become increasingly familiar; several of his finest plays
were to meet a similar, or worse fate.

His first rewrite, in prose, took him over two years; he
delivered it to the Royal Theatre in December 1874. Seldom
can any revision have been so inferior to the original. If the
theatre had given it to one of their hack dramatists and asked
him to remodel it to suit their audiences, the result would
have approximated to what Strindberg now produced. The
passion and originality are gone, replaced by heavy
platitudinous moralizing, and the sharp outlines of the
characters have become blurred. It is as though Strindberg
had deliberately set out to show the debilitating effects of
abandoning one's beliefs. Again the Royal Theatre rejected it,
as did the New Theatre. He then wrote a third version, this
time mainly in verse in obedience to the prevailing dogma
regarding stage tragedies, and it too was rejected. An old
Uppsala friend of Strindberg, Anton Stuxberg, a zoologist,
generously paid for this version to be printed, but, not
surprisingly, it attracted little notice. One newspaper
complained of 'the pessimistic viewpoint borrowed from
abroad', though admitting 'traces of a genuine if in some
respects misguided originality'.

In 1881, having made his name with a novel, *The Red Room*,
Strindberg offered his verse version of *Master Olof* to Ludvig
Josephson, a Swedish Jew who five years earlier had given
Ibsen's *Peer Gynt* its first production in Christiania and had
now taken over the New Theatre in Stockholm. Josephson
rejected it, but he evidently did so sympathetically, for
Strindberg then sent him the original prose version,
suggesting that an actable text might be made from a

combination of the two texts. Josephson reacted enthusiast-
ically. Only three days later he replied: 'On re-reading *Master
Olof* in its original form, I hasten to say that I have not for
many years read a play which has made such an
overwhelming impression on me. I say plainly that there can
never have been a more short-sighted, insensitive, lazy and
un-Swedish [!] theatre board than that which refused to
accept this piece for production.' On 30 December 1881 it
duly received its première, directed by a young actor, August
Lindberg, who two years later was to direct and play Oswald
in the European première of *Ghosts*. The performance lasted
for over five hours, and the audience showed signs of
restlessness, but the reviews were favourable. 'With all its
faults and its many qualities', wrote *Ny Illustrerad Tidning*, 'it is
one of the finest Swedish plays to have appeared', and even
Card David af Wirsén, a very conservative critic who was to
become one of Strindberg's (and Ibsen's) worst enemies,
praised it as being 'constructed with great assurance and full
of dramatic life'. Strindberg, who had suffered what sounds
like a psychosomatic illness on the afternoon of the
performance (to the end of his life he hated, and if possible
avoided, seeing his own plays with an audience), wrote to
Josephson the next day: 'After a dreadful evening and night of
rheumatic agony I have gradually returned to life and begin
to understand from various signs that the play last night
achieved a certain success.' It achieved twelve performances,
a fair run for so long and demanding a work in a city as small
as Stockholm was then. A year later, on 26 January 1883, it
was staged in Gothenburg, where it was equally successful;
the respected critic Karl Warburg, after noting that it had
received twenty curtain calls, praised it for what others had
criticized as a fault, its relevance to contemporary life as well
as to the Middle Ages. Gert, he wrote, would have been 'in
the 18th century a Jacobin, today a nihilist or anarchist . . . It
cannot fail to stimulate debate'. It achieved eleven
performances, most of them to full houses, but brought
Strindberg no financial reward, for the theatre promptly went
bankrupt and could pay him nothing.

In 1890, by which time Strindberg had moved on to modern plays such as *The Father, Miss Julie* and *Creditors*, the Royal Theatre of Stockholm (by then renamed the Dramatic Theatre and known as Dramaten) staged the verse version of *Master Olof* which they had urged him to write eighteen years earlier and had then rejected. Strindberg, for once attending a première, was called six times, garlanded with two laurel wreaths and entertained as a guest of honour at a public supper attended by 150 people. Eighteen years later Dramaten revived this version to open their new, present building. Ivar Nilsson, who was rehearsing the title role, wrote to Strindberg for advice. 'He is no poetic Hamlet', Strindberg replied (16 February 1908), 'but an angry man. It says so in the play: "The pale cleric", sharp in logic, thinks much, etc. "To fight with such a man required Satan himself!" And M. O. says of himself: "I have lived on a war footing and slept on my sword. And I had the strength to defy a world".* Brazen – very young! He is as proud as a king. He is snappish, vitriolic and sullen . . . Many have played your role, mostly like Hamlet . . . Let us now see my Master Olof, our Luther! for the first time! . . . a man of cast iron with an extraordinary assurance who is not sympathetic and does not bother to be. Most actors have ended by playing him with warmth instead of fire . . . His manner of speech is always arrogant, whether he is addressing bishop, king or peasant.' This production, too, was a success, and for more than a decade Dramaten revived the verse version to open its autumn seasons. But the original prose version has by now rightly superseded it.

The ultimate triumph of *Master Olof* did not remove Strindberg's bitterness at its early rejection. As late as 1899, after several successful revivals, he wrote to the painter Carl Larsson: 'My life is a cripple lacking a foot of spine. The years between 20 and 30 are missing; the best years . . . Imagine yourself painting enormous canvases which never get

---

* These quotations are from the verse version, and do not figure in the text translated here.

accepted for exhibition but which you must roll up and carry
to the attic where they must lie until they grow old-fashioned.
That is what I have had to do repeatedly.' *Miss Julie* had had
to wait eighteen years for its Stockholm première, and the
pattern was to continue; *A Dream Play* had to wait five years,
The Dance of Death nine years.

Like most of Strindberg's historical plays, *Master Olof* is
virtually unknown outside Scandinavia. Its first English
performance was on 8 January 1986 on radio, in a production
by Martin Jenkins starring Miles Anderson and Alfred Burke;
and on 3 May 1989, 117 years after it was written, it received
its English stage première when Peter Casterton directed it in
the appropriate setting of Christ Church, Spitalfields,
London. 'Pillars, galleries, doors and surrounding empty
spaces', wrote Katharine Worth in the *Times Literary
Supplement*, 'provide a natural framework in which stage
properties such as medieval tombs and a huge crucifix acquire
a disturbing reality. It only needs the stage crowd to batter
for admittance on the great central door of the real church for
it to become the door of the cathedral at Strängnäs, locked
against their flock by the bishops (the act which initiates
Olof's rebellion). Or it could be the door that opens to show
the approach, through lurid light and smoke, of the plague
cart, symbol of God's wrath, as some in the play see it.'

In 1899, twenty-seven years after *Master Olof*, Strindberg
wrote *Gustav Vasa*, in which he portrays both the King and
Olof as they approach middle age. The fiery young King has
become the father of his people, a mixture, like most great
kings, of benevolence and ruthlessness. Olof has changed even
more and has become a skilful politician, an obedient servant
of his master and a devious spinner of webs. In a moving sub-
plot, Olof sees his early self in his young son who wants to
'tear down like Luther'; when he learns that Luther is dead,
the son cries that he will tear down the universe, then himself.
Olof tells him: 'Begin with yourself; the universe will always
be here . . . When I was your age, I thought I knew and
understood everything. Now I know nothing and understand
nothing, so I limit myself to doing my duty and patiently

enduring.' If *Gustav Vasa* has a message, it is that even the greatest must see much of their labour wasted, endure ingratitude and the meanness of small men, and often be compelled to act against their consciences; and (as in *To Damascus* and *Easter*, both written around the same time) that just punishment is a necessary condition of grace, a lesson that Strindberg had learned during his spiritual crisis in Paris in 1895–6 which he described so memorably in *Inferno*.

Master Olof needs considerable cutting and some adaptation, notably in the clarification of historical background, to make it intelligible to a non-Swedish audience (some of the historical references, such as 'Remember the murders at Käpplinge', 'Thomas Münzer has established a new Kingdom of the Spirit in Mülhausen' and 'What was Däcke if not a defender of the oppressed?' would baffle most modern Swedes). The text offered here is basically that which I made with Martin Jenkins for the 1986 radio production, though I have cut some lines which were added for the special requirements of radio. The main differences from Strindberg's 1872 text are as follows.

I have introduced thirteen lines of dialogue at the beginning of Act One to establish the background, and have reduced the long opening to Act Two, Scene 1, in the alehouse, in which a German, a Dane, Windrank (a merchant skipper) and a Swedish farmer debate political matters at enormous length, to a much shorter discussion between Windrank and the two Blackfriars, Martin and Nils, combining the two characters of Windrank and the farmer. I have completely cut the 'Interlude' which follows in the Cathedral (an irrelevant scene between the Verger, his Wife and Windrank, in which the Wife mistakes the drunken Windrank for a ghost), and in the following scene (p. 53) in the sacristy, where Strindberg has Olof offstage 'speaking powerfully, though we cannot distinguish the words', I have invented a short passage from his sermon. In Act Three, Scene 1, I have cut the irrelevant character of the Chancellor Lars Andreae, as well as a good deal of the loquacious

Nobleman and the final dialogue between Gert and the Attendant. In Act Three, Scene 2, the opening pages of dialogue between Olof and Kristina have been cut, as they tell us nothing that does not emerge in the rest of their conversation. In Act Five, I have cut the opening dialogue between Nils and Windrank; all references to Olof's brother Lars as one of the conspirators (Strindberg has him incomprehensibly pardoned by the King, which much weakens his final appeal to Olof to recant); Lars's few lines early in Act Five; a good deal of Windrank's drunken rambling; and much of the Earl Marshal's address to Olof in the final scene. I have also taken a liberty with the last line of the play. In the original, Gert, offstage, cries 'Apostate!' on hearing of Olof's recantation. Many members of the audience will not immediately understand what this word means, and unfamiliar offstage words are notoriously difficult to catch. I have therefore altered the word to 'Traitor', and have put it into the mouth of Vilhelm, the young scholar, the only character left onstage with Olof. Finally, I have thinned out the dialogue throughout (Strindberg told the director of the first Swedish production of *The Father*: 'Cut . . . what doesn't work'), though less than might be expected for so youthful a play. In all I have reduced the text by about one-fifth, mostly through the long cuts detailed above. With a single interval, a performance should last around three hours. Because of the additions, rewrites and occasional transpositions, it has not been practicable to print Strindberg's full text and indicate cuts by square brackets as I have done with other translations in this series.

A note on pronunciation: Gert is pronounced Yeert (but as a short syllable), Måns is Mawns, Strängnäs Strengness, and Linköping is Lin-cherping.

Master Olof

(1872)

CHARACTERS

MASTER OLOF (OLAUS PETRI)
GERT THE PRINTER
KING GUSTAV ERIKSSON VASA
HANS BRASK, BISHOP OF LINKÖPING
MÅNS SOMMAR, BISHOP OF STRAÄNGNÄS
LARS SIGGESON, EARL MARSHAL
LARS PETRI, OLOF's brother
WINDRANK, a farmer
BISHOP'S SECRETARY
KNIPPERDOLLINK
MARTIN, a Blackfriar
NILS, a Blackfriar
LANDLORD OF THE ALEHOUSE
A CORPSE-BEARER
VILHELM, a scholar
PETER, a scholar
VERGER
COURT ATTENDANT
A FOREMAN
A NOBLEMAN
OLOF's mother
KRISTINA, GERT's daughter
A WHORE
VERGER'S WIFE
ABBESS
A FEMALE CITIZEN
and supporting characters

This translation of *Master Olof* was commissioned by the BBC and was first broadcast on Radio 3 on 8 January 1986 and repeated on 29 January 1988. The cast was:

MASTER OLOF	Miles Anderson
GERT THE PRINTER	Alfred Burke
KING GUSTAV VASA	Geoffrey Collins
BISHOP BRASK	Cyril Luckham
BISHOP MÅNS	Manning Wilson
EARL MARSHAL	Bernard Brown
LARS PETRI	Anthony Jackson
WINDRANK	John Hollis
BISHOP'S SECRETARY	Trevor Nichols
KNIPPERDOLLINK	Mark Straker
BROTHER MARTIN	Jim Norton
BROTHER NILS	Tony Robinson
LANDLORD	Trevor Nichols
CORPSE-BEARER	Brian Smith
VILHELM	David Lonsdale
PETER	Mark Straker
VERGER	Alan Thompson
COURT ATTENDANT	Manning Wilson
FOREMAN	Trevor Nichols
NOBLEMAN	John Webb
OLOF'S MOTHER	Dilys Hamlett
KRISTINA	Kathryn Hurlbutt
WHORE	Helena Breck
VERGER'S WIFE	Anne Jameson
ABBESS	Tessa Worsley

Directed by Martin Jenkins

This translation was first staged by the European Stage Company at Christ Church, Spitalfields, London, on 3 May 1989. The cast was:

MASTER OLOF	Jake Nightingale
GERT THE PRINTER	Richard Gofton
KING GUSTAV VASA	Samuel Lathem
BISHOP BRASK	Dalibor Satalic
BISHOP MÅNS	James Pegg
EARL MARSHAL	Peter Neathey
LARS PETRI	Michael Gould
WINDRANK	Peter Neathey
BISHOP'S SECRETARY	Mark Dyson
KNIPPERDOLLINK	Michael Gould
BROTHER MARTIN	Mark Dyson
BROTHER NILS	Samuel Lathem
LANDLORD	Dalibor Satalic
CORPSE-BEARER	Dalibor Satalic
VILHELM	Julia Bell
PETER	Louise Bangay
VERGER	James Pegg
COURT ATTENDANT	Michael Gould
FOREMAN	Michael Gould
NOBLEMAN	James Pegg
OLOF'S MOTHER	Sydnee Blake
KRISTINA	Louise Bangay
WHORE	Julia Bell
VERGER'S WIFE	Julia Bell
ABBESS	Julia Bell

Designed by Bruce Gallup
Costumes by Monika Frelin
Directed by Peter Casterton

ACT ONE

STRÄNGNÄS

A cloister outside the Scholars' Garden, with trees. Beyond, the Abbey. In the background, a wall, above which fruit trees in flower can be seen. OLOF is seated on a stone bench. In front of him the scholars sit reading their parts in the 'Comedy of Tobias'.

FIRST SCHOLAR (VILHELM):
Now we are caught in the web of our enemies.
Alas, unhappy children of Israel.

SECOND SCHOLAR (PETER):
Alas, dear brothers, what boots it to wail?
Now our days of sorrow are come.
Our land and goods are taken from us,
Now we can never expect anything good.
I have long spoken and dreamed of this,
That Abraham's promise has long since been forgotten.

OLOF [*interrupts them*]: No, no. You're all too serious. This is meant to be a comedy.

VILHELM: Master Olof, surely it is a tragedy.

OLOF: The theme is tragic, Vilhelm, but the mood should be light.

VILHELM: The Abbot said it was a tragedy.

PETER: He does not like us to be light-hearted about holy matters.

OLOF: I know.

VILHELM: He says there is no place for laughter in the life of a monk.

OLOF: Yes. He said that to me when I was a novice. I was often punished for it.

VILHELM: You, Master Olof? But you are the most learned of our teachers.

PETER: They say you will become an abbot yourself soon. The youngest in Sweden.

OLOF: I doubt it, Peter. The Church doesn't like rebels. You know what they did to Martin Luther. [*The* SCHOLARS *gasp.*] Why do you cross yourselves?

VILHELM: The Abbot says Luther is an Antichrist. Do you think he – ?

OLOF [*defensively*]: Never mind what I feel.

LARS PETRI *enters.*

VILHELM [*softly*]: Here is your brother.

OLOF [*joyfully*]: Lars! Welcome!

LARS: Hullo, Olof. What are you doing?

OLOF: Rehearsing a play.

LARS: A play?

OLOF: A little comedy about the children of Israel and their captivity in Babylon.

LARS: Have you nothing better to do? Greater work awaits you, Olof.

OLOF: I am still too young.

LARS: Don't say that.

OLOF: No – I suppose too many people make that excuse.

LARS [*quotes*]: 'The Lord said: "Thou shalt go to all to whom I send thee, and whatsoever I command thee, thou shalt speak. For I shall make thee this day an iron pillar against the Kings of Judah, against the princes and the priests thereof. And they shall fight against thee; but they shall not prevail against thee; For I am with thee", saith the Lord, "to deliver thee".'

OLOF [*starts up*]: Did the Lord say that?

LARS [*continues*]: ' "Therefore gird up thy loins and arise, and speak unto them all whatsoever I shall command thee" '.

OLOF: Why don't you go, brother?

LARS: I am too old.

OLOF: You are a coward.

LARS: Yes, I have not the strength. But you have. May God now give you the faith.

OLOF: Ah, yes. Once I had the flame of faith and it burned gloriously. But the monks quenched it with their holy water, when they sought to pray the Devil out of my body.

LARS: That was a fire of straw which would soon have burned out. But now the Lord will kindle in you a greater fire, which will consume the seed of the Philistines. Do you know what you want, Olof?

OLOF: No. But I seem to suffocate when I think of these poor people sighing for liberation. They cry for water, living water. What does the Church in Sweden care for the people? They pay taxes to the Pope in Rome, and what does he give them in return? The Bishops ride through the land with trains of a hundred followers demanding food and lodging from peasants who can scarcely feed themselves. Bishop Brask of Linköping is the richest man in Sweden, richer than the King.

LARS: Then pull down the old, rotten house. You can! The Lord will build a new one.

OLOF: How long will that take? And meanwhile the people will have no roof over their heads.

LARS: At least they will get fresh air.

OLOF: But to rob a people of their faith! They will cry out against me, revile me and drag me before their masters.

LARS: Are you afraid?

OLOF: No, but to provoke –

LARS: Olof! You were born to provoke. You were born to fight. As a boy you fought against everything Mother stood for.

OLOF: What storms you have awoken in my soul! A moment ago I sat playing in the shadow of these trees, and it was Whitsun Eve, it was spring, and peace. And now – why don't the trees shake and the heavens darken? Feel my forehead, feel how the blood begins to pulse. Don't leave me, Lars. I see an angel walking towards me with a cup. She walks there in the evening sky, her path is red like blood and she bears a cross in her hand. No, I have not the strength, I must go back to the calm valley. Let others fight, I shall look on. No, I shall follow after them and heal the wounded, I shall whisper peace in the ears of the dying. Peace! No, I shall fight with them, but in the rearmost ranks. Why must I lead them?

LARS: Because you are the boldest.

OLOF: Not the strongest?

LARS: The strong follow. And you have the strongest on your side: He Who exhorts you to battle.

OLOF: Help me, God. I go.

LARS: Amen.

OLOF: And you will come with me?

LARS: You must go alone with God.

OLOF: Why do you shrink?

LARS: I was not born for battle, Olof. But I shall be your armourer. God's pure words shall be your weapons, and you will set them in the hands of the people. For now the Church must crumble and the door of the Pope's armoury be broken open. Everyone who calls himself a man must wage his own war to free his spirit.

OLOF: But where are my enemies? I burn to fight, but see no one to fight with.

LARS: Revolution is in the air. Listen! Look at the crowd approaching the church.

OLOF: Why have they come?

LARS: You will learn. Farewell. God be with you.

He goes. A group of citizens with women and children approach the church door. They stop there, remove their hats and cross themselves.

GERT THE PRINTER [*disguised as a* CITIZEN]: They have not rung the bells for vespers on Whitsun Eve. That is most unusual, friends.

1ST CITIZEN: And the church door is shut. Perhaps the priest is sick.

GERT: Or is still abed.

1ST CITIZEN: What are you saying?

GERT: I mean he is sick.

2ND CITIZEN: But he has enough pupils for one of them to say a mass for us in his place.

GERT: They're probably all busy.

1ST CITIZEN: Doing what?

GERT: It's best not to know.

1ST CITIZEN: Take care, my good man. You speak like a Lutheran. Bishop Brask is in town, and the King too.

GERT: Is Brask here?

3RD CITIZEN: Indeed he is. But let us try the door and see if the church is shut.

GERT [*runs up on to the step and beats on the door*]: God's house is shut on Whitsun Eve. The holy priests will not grant audience to God today, so the humble people must go home to bed without their mass. We are prevented from entering and celebrating divine service this evening, we who have toiled six days making shoes and coats, we who all week have brewed and baked and butchered for our revered priests so that on the seventh day they might have the strength to conduct God's service for us. In saying this I in no way reproach our revered priests, for they are but men, and only God had the strength to work for six days and rest on the seventh.

1ST CITIZEN: You blaspheme against God!

GERT: God can't hear when the door's shut.

1ST WOMAN: Jesus Maria! He is an Antichrist!

GERT [*bangs on the door*]: Do you hear how empty it sounds!

1ST CITIZEN: Woe to thee, Luther, for such thou art! We have sinned, and therefore the Lord has closed His house.

2ND WOMAN: Who is this man? Do not go near him. He is possessed by the Devil.

2ND CITIZEN: Down with him, down with him!

They rush towards GERT. *The children scream.*

GERT: Do not touch me! In this place I stand under the protection of God's hand.

2ND CITIZEN: God does not protect the outcast angel.

GERT: If God does not, the holy church does, and I stand within her consecrated walls.

3RD CITIZEN: Drag him outside, then!

2ND WOMAN: It is his unclean spirit which has bewitched the church!

2ND CITIZEN: Yes, yes! God will not open His church to the Devil! Drag him from the door!

They rush at GERT.

BISHOP'S SECRETARY (*enters*): Silence!

1ST WOMAN: Who is that?

4TH CITIZEN: Bishop Måns's secretary.

SECRETARY [*reads*]: 'Whereas this cathedral city of Strängnäs has not paid its dues to the Bishopric, and since the aforesaid city remains obstinate in this, the Cathedral Chapter has decided in accordance with its prerogative as confirmed by Parliament to close the doors of the church and cease holding mass and all divine services forthwith, reminding all who do not hereafter mend their ways of our displeasure.'

He hammers the proclamation on the door, and goes. The people crowd around.

1ST WOMAN: They have closed our church.

GERT: What say you to this, good people?

1ST CITIZEN: No mass on Whitsun Eve! It is a scandal.

GERT: Take care. Speak no ill of the priests, it is surely not their fault.

1ST CITIZEN: Whose fault is it?

GERT: Rome's! That invisible, that almighty body! It is the Pope, don't you see, who has shut the church.

The people murmur their displeasure.

OLOF [*comes forward and rings the vesper bell with a rope which hangs from the tower*]: If you want a service, I will say a mass for you.

1ST CITIZEN: Thank you, Master Olof. But don't you know what consequences this may bring?

OLOF: Let us fear God, not men. [*The people kneel.*] My dear
friends, brothers and sisters in Jesus Christ. Since we are
gathered here –

1ST CITIZEN: Master Olof –

OLOF: What is it?

1ST CITIZEN: We want to have our proper mass, nothing
new-fangled.

Murmurs of agreement.

GERT: Good Master Olof, it must be in Latin. Otherwise we
won't understand what you say.

1ST CITIZEN: Yes. It must be in the holy tongue, otherwise
anyone could say mass.

OLOF: And that, my friend, is how it must be. Each man for
himself, and with God.

CITIZENS: A Luther! A Luther! Antichrist!

1ST CITIZEN: Master Olof, you are young and hot-blooded. I
am an old man, and have seen the world. Turn while you
are yet young. Do as we wish and say the old mass.

OLOF: No. You should worship in truth, not in words which
you do not understand.

1ST CITIZEN: Do you not believe, my young friend, that our
Lord understands Latin?

GERT: Do you think he can't understand Swedish?

1ST CITIZEN: Master Olof! Don't you see how the people
long for their God? Sacrifice your sinful desire, and do not
let us go as though we had no shepherd.

OLOF: You call my wish sinful?

1ST CITIZEN: You are a hard man.

OLOF: Do not say so.

GERT: This is the tocsin that sounds the call to battle. Soon the bells of Stockholm will answer, and the blood of a thousand peasants will drown the Popes and the princes.

2ND WOMAN: Alas! What madness is this?

1ST CITIZEN: Do you know this man, Master Olof?

OLOF: No.

GERT: Olof! You know me. Do not deny me. These poor unfortunate people do not want what is best for them – they have never heard the word freedom.

OLOF: Your face is veiled but I know your voice. Who are you?

GERT: If I tell you, you will tremble. You must tremble, to wake from your sleep. I am the outcast angel who shall walk again. I am the liberator who came too early, I am called Satan, I was called Luther, now I am called Anabaptist.

CITIZENS [*huddle together and cross themselves*]: Anabaptist!

GERT [*uncovers himself and is seen to be much older*]: Do you know me now, Olof?

OLOF: Father Gert!

2ND CITIZEN: He calls him father!

1ST WOMAN: It is the printer.

3RD CITIZEN: Gert the printer.

1ST CITIZEN: The man who printed Luther!

2ND WOMAN: Alas for us and for our city! Woe on our priests when they walk with Antichrist!

2ND CITIZEN: He denies the baptism!

1ST WOMAN: He denies God!

1ST CITIZEN: I smell sulphur here. We must leave this place.

Murmurs of agreement. The people go.

OLOF: Those were dangerous words you spoke.

GERT: You believe they were dangerous, Olof? God bless you for that.

OLOF: Dangerous for you, I mean.

GERT: For no one else?

OLOF: Let us hope not. [*Gently.*] How is Kristina?

GERT: My daughter is safe. [*Pause.*] You heard Luther preach in Germany?

OLOF: Oh, yes! I met him. Now I want to do his work.

GERT: Is that all?

OLOF: What do you mean?

GERT: It is too little. We must go further, you and I.

OLOF: Where will you lead me?

GERT: Far, Olof. Far.

OLOF: You frighten me.

GERT: Yes! You will be frightened, for I want to lead you up on to a high mountain whence you will look out over the world. Mark, Olof, it is Whitsun. That was when the Holy Ghost descended upon the Apostles – upon all mankind. You can receive the Holy Ghost, I have received the Holy Ghost, for I believed in it. God's spirit had descended on me, I feel it, and that is why they imprisoned me as a madman, but now I am free, now I shall preach the word, for see, Olof, now we stand on the mountain! Do you not see the people crawl on their knees towards two men seated on their thrones? The stronger has two keys in one hand, a thunderbolt in the other. That is the Pope. Now he raises his thunderbolt condemning thousands of souls to damnation while the others kiss his foot and sing Glory be to God. And he on his throne turns and smiles. Now look at

the other. He holds a sword and a sceptre. Bow to the
sceptre or the sword will bite. He frowns and all the people
tremble. Then he turns to his neighbour on the other
throne and both smile. They are twin statues of Baal.

OLOF: Do you mean the Holy Roman Emperor? Or our King
Gustav?

GERT: All kings are alike. Now a noise is heard in the air like
the sighing of people. 'Who complains?' cries the Pope.
'Who murmurs?' asks the Emperor. No one replies. But the
whisper of complaint lingers in the air. 'Think!' And the
Pope starts and the Emperor pales and asks: 'Who cried
"Think"? Bring him forth and I shall take his life'. And the
Pope cries: 'Bring him hither and I shall take his soul'. It
was the air that cried, but the voice will grow louder and a
mighty wind will rush across the Alps and stir up the Baltic
and echo against our shores, and the cry goes out over
Sweden: 'Freedom! Freedom!' And the Pope will cast his
keys into the sea and the Emperor will sheath his sword, for
they are powerless against this cry. Olof, you want to strike
at the Pope, but you forget the Kings – the Kings who
murder their people without counting them, because they
dare to sigh when they are crushed and trampled. You
want to strike at the Pope of Rome, but you only want like
Luther to give them a different kind of Pope. Listen, Olof,
listen! Do not seek to bind the spirit with any chains. Do
not forget your great goal – spiritual life and full spiritual
freedom.

OLOF *remains silent*.

Do I dazzle you?

OLOF *is still silent*.

You must aim for the impossible.

OLOF: You will bring ruin on yourself and this land. You
would provoke a civil war! It is against God.

GERT: No. The knife is already in the flesh. Cut boldly and the body may be saved.

OLOF: I shall denounce you as a traitor.

GERT: You should not do that. You have today irretrievably defied the Church. Besides –

OLOF: Go on.

GERT: I must tell you a secret. The day after tomorrow Stockholm will rise against the King.

OLOF: What! Who?

GERT: The Anabaptists.

OLOF [*fearfully*]: The Anabaptists?

GERT: Yes. Led by two simple men, a furrier and a grocer, whose only crime is to deny the validity of baptizing an infant who can neither speak nor think.

OLOF: There's something else, isn't there?

GERT: What?

OLOF: They are possessed.

GERT: By the spirit of freedom. That is the storm that rages through them. Beware of standing in its way.

OLOF: They must be stopped. I shall go to the King.

GERT: Olof! Your mother lives in Stockholm, doesn't she? And is a devout Catholic?

OLOF: You know she is.

GERT: Do you know that my daughter Kristina is living with her?

OLOF: Kristina? With my mother?

GERT: For the moment. If we win, your mother will be safe with my daughter. If the Catholics win, my daughter will be safe with your mother.

OLOF: Do not try to stop me.

GERT: Do you still love Kristina?

OLOF: Gert! Where did you learn such cunning?

GERT: In the madhouse.

OLOF: Get away from me. You will lead me to disaster.

GERT: Yes, if you call it a disaster to lose all earthly fortune, to be cast into prison, to suffer poverty, to be mocked and reviled for the sake of the truth. I thought you would understand me. I counted on your help. You still have the fire within you.

OLOF: No man can recreate the world.

GERT: Luther did.

OLOF: One cannot swim against the tide.

GERT: We are the tide. You will lead us. You will be a Daniel, you will speak truth to the princes, they will seek your life, but the Lord will protect you. Now I can go in peace, for I see the lightning flash in your eye and the tongue of fire quiver over your head. But Kristina must know nothing of this. That you must promise.

OLOF: I promise.

GERT: Happy Whitsun, Olof.

OLOF: Jesus help me.

BISHOP HANS BRASK *and* BISHOP MÅNS SOMMAR *enter.* MÅNS *approaches* OLOF. BRASK *remains behind, glancing around.*

MÅNS: Who rang the vesper bell?

GERT (*aside to* OLOF): Here comes Bishop Måns, the King of Flies. Do not let him sully your pure soul. (*Goes.*)

MÅNS: Who rang the bell?

OLOF [*quietly but firmly*]: I did, your Grace.

MÅNS: Were you not aware of the King's command?

OLOF: I knew of the ban.

MÅNS: And you dared defy it?

OLOF: Yes. When the people were left with no shepherd, I thought it right to gather them.

MÅNS: You seem to question the authority of the Church. You are audacious.

OLOF: The truth is always audacious.

MANS: You have ideas above your station, young man. You will get no thanks for this.

OLOF: I want no thanks.

MÅNS: Keep your truths to yourself. They won't go far in the market.

OLOF [*vehemently*]: A counsel worthy of the Father of Lies! [*Pause. Softly.*] Forgive me.

MÅNS: Do you know to whom you are talking?

OLOF [*hotly*]: To the slave of slaves, Bishop Måns!

BRASK [*comes forward*]: Who is this young man?

MÅNS: He belongs to the church here, your Grace.

BRASK: What is his name? [*Pause.*] Are you Master Olof? I like you. By the way, I am Bishop Brask. Will you be my secretary?

OLOF: I thank your Grace, but I am not qualified.

MÅNS: Your Grace!

BRASK: Bishop Måns? What were you about to say?

MÅNS: He is said to have won much praise from Dr Luther.

BRASK: So I have heard. It is but the heat of youth. We shall educate him.

OLOF: I fear it is too late.

BRASK: A young sapling can be straightened.

MÅNS: Your Grace, we cannot employ a heretic. Today this man dared to defy our injunction.

BRASK: Indeed?

MÅNS: We ordered the suspension of mass on perfectly legal grounds, and he dared to offer mass and, what is worse, a Lutheran mass, thereby provoking the people.

BRASK: Have a care, young man. Do you know that the penalty for preaching Luther is excommunication?

OLOF: I fear no God but God.

BRASK: Do think what you are saying. I am trying to help you and you defy me.

OLOF: You are trying to save the Catholic Church. It is an ailing cause. Do not try to silence me by locking me in an asylum. You did that with Gert the printer. It has not silenced him.

BRASK: Do you know this Gert, Bishop Måns?

MÅNS: No, your Grace.

BRASK: A madman who used my press to publish Lutheran writings after I had ordered him to print tracts denouncing Luther. He started raving and had to be silenced. Have you seen him, Olof?

OLOF: He was here now.

BRASK: Has he been released?

OLOF: Soon he will be in Stockholm. Then you will hear from him. Think, my Lord Bishop.

BRASK [laughs]: There is no danger.

OLOF: The Anabaptists are in Stockholm.

BRASK: What!

OLOF: The Anabaptists.

KING GUSTAV VASA *enters quickly*.

KING GUSTAV: What is happening? The city is in an uproar. The people are gathering in the streets demanding mass. What does it mean?

BRASK: Mischief, your Majesty.

KING GUSTAV: Why are they demanding mass? Why is this cathedral closed?

MÅNS: This city has not paid its levy to the Church

KING GUSTAV: And for that you refuse to allow them to worship God? Death and – !

BRASK: Your Majesty should reflect that –

KING GUSTAV: Let Bishop Måns answer!

MÅNS: Your Majesty should reflect that matters such as these come under the jurisdiction of the Church –

KING GUSTAV: I order you to do your duty as a churchman.

BRASK: The Bishops of Sweden accept orders only from our supreme lord, the Pope.

KING GUSTAV [*sobered*]: I know that. But if the Pope does not know what is happening?

BRASK: Then we decide.

KING GUSTAV [*flares up*]: You – ! [*Calms himself.*] You are quite right, my Lord. You shall decide.

BRASK: Stockholm is rumoured to be on the brink of sedition.

KING GUSTAV: Who says so?

MÅNS: Master Olof.

KING GUSTAV: The schoolmaster? Where is he? Is it you?
What is your name?

OLOF: Olof Pederson.

KING GUSTAV: You're a heretic, aren't you? Hatching plans
against the Holy Church? That is dangerous work.

BRASK: He has today thrown off his mask and openly defied
our ordinance forbidding mass. He must be suitably
punished.

KING GUSTAV: That is a matter for the Church, not for me.
What is this sedition you talk of in Stockholm?

OLOF: The Anabaptists.

KING GUSTAV: Is that all?

BRASK: Does your Majesty not know what these madmen
have done in Germany? We suggest that your Majesty
return with all speed to Stockholm.

KING GUSTAV: I shall do as I think best. Olof –

OLOF: Your Majesty?

KING GUSTAV: I name you Secretary to the City Council in
Stockholm. Go there at once. Speak to the people. I rely
upon you. Well?

Pause.

BRASK: In the interests of the fatherland your Majesty must
consider the folly of trying to reason with madmen.

KING GUSTAV: And you must consider, my Lord, that the
spirit of freedom cannot be quelled by the sword.

BRASK: The Church has never –

KING GUSTAV: Nor by locking doors. Olof, go to my
Chancellor. He will give you the necessary authority.

BRASK: I would advise this young man to wait.

KING GUSTAV: Our Secretary is not subject to your commands.

BRASK: The rights of the Church must be exacted first. Olof Pedersen –

KING GUSTAV [*corrects him*]: Secretary.

BRASK: Secretary Olof Pedersen may not leave this city before the Chapter has passed judgement.

KING GUSTAV: The Chapter will not pass judgement before the accused has been properly examined.

BRASK: That is our business.

KING GUSTAV: It is not your business. Bishop Brask. A priest of this city of Strängnäs cannot be judged by the Bishop of Linköping. Bishop Måns, what have you to say?

MÅNS: In view of what has happened – ahem –

BRASK: There is no need for any further discussion.

KING GUSTAV: Kindly hold your peace, your Grace, or leave us, while I speak privately with Bishop Måns. Privately! Proceed.

MÅNS: I can see no alternative – since his Grace Bishop Brask –

KING GUSTAV: I am speaking of Master Olof, sir, not Bishop Brask! My lords, you can postpone his examination. Be so good as to leave us.

The Bishops go.

KING GUSTAV: Will you be my man?

OLOF: Your Majesty's Secretary?

KING GUSTAV: No. My right-hand man. But you must remember that for the time being, my left hand must not know what my right hand is doing. Go to Stockholm.

OLOF: The Chapter will have me brought back here to Strängnäs, and will excommunicate me.

KING GUSTAV: If they go that far, leave things to me.

Pause.

OLOF: What does your Majesty wish of me?

KING GUSTAV: I want you to talk to these fanatics in Stockholm.

OLOF: And then?

KING GUSTAV: Ah, that is far away! I dare not even think about the future yet. Let them preach, it can't hurt dulled souls to hear something new, even if what they hear is mad. But there must be no violence. Then I have to use the sword. Goodbye, Olof. (*Goes.*)

OLOF [*alone*]: The King rebels against the Pope!

The scholars, who have been waiting in the background, come forward.

VILHELM: Shall we go on with our play now, Master Olof?

OLOF: The time for playing is over, my children.

VILHELM: Are you leaving us, Master Olof?

OLOF: Yes. For ever, I think.

VILHELM: Surely you can stay over Whitsun so that we can perform our comedy?

PETER: And I can act the Angel Gabriel.

VILHELM: Please, Master Olof. You are the only one of our teachers who has ever been kind to us.

PETER: Don't leave us, Master Olof.

OLOF: Children, you do not know what you ask. A day will come when you will thank God that I left you. Oh, no. May that day never come!

Let us make our farewell short. Goodbye, Peter, goodbye, Vilhelm. [*He embraces them.*]

LARS [*comes forward*]: Are you ready to leave now, brother?

VILHELM: Will you never come back, Master Olof?

OLOF [*to the boys*]: No, I shall never come back.

Pause.

PETER: Goodbye, Master Olof.

VILHELM: Do not forget us.

They go. OLOF *gazes after them.*

LARS: I have met the King.

OLOF [*abstractedly*]: Have you?

LARS: Do you know what he said?

OLOF: No.

LARS: 'I have found a dog that will hunt the quarry. But will he come to heel when I whistle?'

OLOF: Look, now they are sitting among the graves and playing, picking flowers and singing Whitsun songs.

LARS [*takes his arm*]: Child!

OLOF [*starts*]: What do you mean?

LARS: Today you have grasped the nettle firmly. It is too late to look back.

OLOF *waves to the scholars.*

LARS: Are you still dreaming?

OLOF: It was the last bright morning dream that faded. Forgive me. Now I am awake.

They go out right. As OLOF *reaches the side of the stage, he turns once more to gaze after the scholars. Where the scholars went out, the Blackfriars,* MARTIN *and* NILS *appear.* OLOF *gives an involuntary cry of astonishment and puts his hand to his forehead.* LARS *leads him out.*

ACT TWO

Scene 1

An alehouse in the wall of Stockholm Cathedral. Upstage, a counter with stoops, jugs of ale, etc. To the right of this counter is a table behind which an iron door can be seen. At the table sit the two Blackfriars, MARTIN and NILS, disguised, drinking beer. At other tables sit soldiers, peasants and sailors. A FIDDLER sits on a barrel. Everyone is noisy and drunk; some are playing dice. Right, the door to the street.

NILS: Who are all these people, Brother Martin?

MARTIN [*contemptuously*]: Peasants, merchants, soldiers. Anyone who's thirsty.

NILS: It's strange they should allow an alehouse in the wall of the cathedral.

MARTIN: It means money for the Chapter.

NILS: You don't mean they share in the profits?

MARTIN: What do you think?

NILS: Of intoxicating liquor? If the Holy Father in Rome knew of this –

MARTIN: The Holy Father shares in the profits of worse things than intoxicating liquor.

NILS: That's true, Brother Martin. He'll take money from anything.

MARTIN: Except heresy, Brother Nils.

NILS: Of course. Except heresy.

MARTIN: That's our task. We Blackfriars seek out heresy and

treason to destroy them. That is why we are here in this alehouse. Men's tongues are loosened here. (*Shouts.*) Landlord! Another jug of schnapps!

WINDRANK [*a farmer, drunk*]: That's the kind of talk I like to hear. May I join you two gentlemen?

MARTIN: Be off with you.

WINDRANK: You think I can't pay? I have money. And I'm going to drink it up, every farthing. You two gentlemen can help me.

LANDLORD: That'll be one crown, gentlemen.

WINDRANK: No, no, let me pay! Skoal!

MARTIN: Skoal!

NILS: Skoal!

MARTIN: What is wrong, my good man? I see something is amiss.

WINDRANK: I am ruined.

NILS: Ruined? By whom?

WINDRANK: By the King.

MARTIN: How?

WINDRANK: He's taxing us out of existence. When he sought our support to put him on the throne, he said he'd be the people's king. [*Scornfully.*] The people's king! He's got no further use for us. All he cares about now is the nobility. They're the ones he needs now.

NILS: Is King Gustav siding with the nobles? I thought he was twisting their arms.

WINDRANK: He? No, he lets them grow fat. They can run around in our forests with their guns and shoot our game just for the fun of it. But if one of us peasants was dying of hunger and snared a deer, he'd hang us. They even say he's going to take away our monks and priests.

MARTIN [*startled*]: Why?

WINDRANK: To please the nobles. Skoal!

MARTIN: Skoal!

NILS: Skoal!

WINDRANK: And that's not all. He's going to take the silver from all the churches. And melt it down for his own use. Mind you, there are some monks we could do without.

MARTIN: Oh? Who?

WINDRANK: Those Blackfriars. They're a treacherous lot. Only out to line their own pockets. And spying for the Pope in Rome. Why should we Swedes pay tax to the Pope in Rome? We could do with a Martin Luther here.

MARTIN: This is heresy.

WINDRANK: Those Anabaptists have got the right ideas.

NILS: You praise the Anabaptists! They break into the churches and destroy our holy images and tear the priests' vestments.

WINDRANK: They say such things show our slavery to the Pope in Rome. They say we simple folk should be brought closer to God. [*Whispers.*] They say we should pray to him in our own language, not the Pope's Latin.

MARTIN: Heresy!

NILS: Heresy!

The door is burst open, knocking over the table at which MARTIN *and* NILS *are sitting, with its jugs and tankards. A* WHORE, *wearing a black and red skirt and a nun's veil over her head, runs in.* GERT *is momentarily seen behind her in the doorway before the door is banged shut again.*

WHORE [*looks round, startled*]: Help me! Please! They want to
  kill me!

WINDRANK: Hey! A whore in nun's clothing!

Everyone laughs.

MARTIN [*crosses himself*]: A harlot! Who brought her into this
  respectable company? Landlord, throw her out, unless you
  want to soil the good name of this house and the sanctity of
  the Church.

WHORE: Will no one save me?

LANDLORD: Come along.

WHORE: Don't turn me over to that mob outside! I only
  wanted to creep into the Lord's house to seek a morsel of
  His grace. I wanted to start a new life – but the monks
  drove me out and incited the people against me. Then
  someone led me here to escape them. But the mob followed
  us.

NILS: You hear what she says! She has defiled God's holy
  place. She seeks to hide the skirt of shame beneath the veil
  of sanctity.

MARTIN [*comes forward to pull off her veil*]: Remove thy mask,
  woman, and show thy hideousness. [*He tears it off and
  gasps.*]

WHORE: Is it you, Martin?

WINDRANK: Old friends!

WHORE: Murderer!

WINDRANK: Murderer?

WHORE: Our child is dead, Martin. Yours and mine.

MARTIN: It is a foul lie. I have never seen this woman before.
  I am Martin the Blackfriar, as my brother Nils here can
  bear witness.

WINDRANK: Blackfriars!

WHORE: Why, Nils! It was you who showed me Martin's letter of absolution, when they drove me from the abbey and let him stay.

NILS: That's true.

MARTIN [*beside himself with rage, grabs* NILS *by the arm*]: You're lying. You too! You can all see that he's drunk.

THE PEOPLE [*indignantly*]: A drunken priest!

WINDRANK: Ah, well. Drunkenness absolves a lie, eh, Brother Martin?

LANDLORD: I can't let my house be the scene of disturbances. I'll lose my customers and get dragged before the Chapter. Get rid of this woman.

MARTIN: Throw her out, or I'll have you all excommunicated! Don't you know we are within the walls of the holy Church, although the Chapter has permitted this building to be used for the bodily refreshment of travellers?

WINDRANK: This is God's house. Drive out the whore.

PEOPLE: Out with her! Put her outside! Out with the harlot!

They drag the WHORE *towards the door.*

WINDRANK: Stone her! Give her to the mob!

WHORE: Jesus Christ, help me!

OLOF *appears in the doorway. He forces his way through the* CROWD, *takes the* WHORE *by the hand and pulls her away from the drunken people who hold her.*

OLOF: Who is this woman? Answer me!

MARTIN: She is no woman, Master Olof.

OLOF: What do you mean?

MARTIN: Nor no man neither, although she is disguised.

OLOF: You say 'she'. Is she then not a woman?

MARTIN: It is a harlot.

OLOF [*amazed, drops her hand*]: A harlot!

LANDLORD: Don't let go of her, Master Olof, or she'll escape.

OLOF: What is her crime?

NILS: She entered the cathedral dressed like that.

WINDRANK: A whore dressed as a nun.

OLOF: I understand. [*Looks around.*]

MARTIN: What are you looking for?

OLOF: A priest. [*Pause.*] Are you one?

MARTIN: I am Brother Martin, a Blackfriar.

OLOF: Yes. I guessed as much. It is you who incited the
people against her.

MARTIN: It is I who protect Holy Church from filth and
would keep it free from vice. This is an excommunicated
woman who plies usury with her body, which should be a
temple of God.

PEOPLE: Stone her!

WHORE [*falls on her knees before* OLOF]: Help me.

OLOF [*takes her hand*]: Look, Blackfriar. I dare to take her
hand and stand with her before you. She had sold her
body, you say. How many souls have you bought, Friar? I
too am a priest. No, I am a human being, for I am not so
bold as to lock the house of God, and as a sinful mortal I
give my hand to this fellow-mortal, who cannot be without
sin. Step forward, any of you that is without sin, and cast
the first stone. [*Pause.*] You, Brother Martin, angel of light,
who clothe yourself in the black robes of innocence and
shave your head that none may see how sin has greyed

your hair. Have you no stone to hand? What have you done with them, what will you offer the people when they ask for bread? [*To* WINDRANK, *who is asleep on the floor.*] And you who roll in your own vomit, have you no stones? And you who lust after her body, have you no stones? And you who swear, curse and blaspheme, have you no stones? (*Silence.*) Do my words make you blush? Cast your stones. If you will not, give her to the mob. If fifty men cannot tear her to pieces, five hundred women will do it. You are silent. Stand up, woman. The people have acquitted you. Go, sin no more, but beware of the priests, for they will hand you to the mob.

MARTIN: Wait. Listen. This man is a heretic. An excommunicate consigned to damnation. [*Takes out a document.*] Read this paper for yourselves. [*Takes a candle from a table and throws it to the floor.*] 'As this light is quenched, so let joy and gladness be quenched in him and every good that he receives from God!'

PEOPLE [*cross themselves and shrink back*]: Anathema!

OLOF *is left alone with the* WHORE *in the middle of the room.*

MARTIN [*to* WHORE]: Now you see the worth of his absolution.

OLOF [*has listened abashed*]: Woman! Dare you still rely on my word? Are you not afraid? Do you not hear the thunderbolt of excommunication hiss around our heads? Why don't you leave me for these righteous men who still stand under the protection of Holy Church? Answer me. Do you believe that God has cast me out, as these people have done?

WHORE: No.

OLOF [*picks up the poster of excommunication*]: Very well. The great Bishop Brask has sold my soul to Satan for the term of my life – his power extends no further – because I bade the people turn to God when he had forbidden it. As the Church by this has condemned me to hell, so I free myself from it – and from the Church's excommunication. [*Tears the parchment.*] God's mercy on me, amen.

PEOPLE [*howl*]: Anathema!

OLOF: You hear, woman? The devils howl for their prey. Do not touch me, any of you!

MARTIN: Seize him! Beat him! He is excommunicate!

The iron door is burst open, and the ANABAPTISTS, *led by* KNIPPERDOLLINK, *rush in shrieking, with broken crucifixes and images of saints, and torn vestments. Everyone else crowds towards the other door.*

KNIPPERDOLLINK: This way, my brothers! You see an alehouse in the temple. Abomination has so multiplied that the very churches themselves are defiled. And those within are all sinners.

NILS: The Anabaptists!

PEOPLE: They are mad! Mad!

KNIPPERDOLLINK: This place shall be cleansed with fire. Cast all the images upon the pyre.

OLOF: Consider what you do.

KNIPPERDOLLINK: Do you fear the ale-casks will burst with the heat, O Belial? Are you a papist innkeeper, that you dare set up a chapel of vice in the wall of the Cathedral?

OLOF: As Secretary of the City Council, I command you to respect the law in the King's name.

KNIPPERDOLLINK: So – you're the man the King has sent to resist our holy war? Seize him, that we may cleanse the Lord's house of idolatry!

MARTIN: Seize him, good people, he is a heretic and excommunicate.

KNIPPERDOLLINK: Heretic? Then you are not a papist?

OLOF: Now that I am excommunicate, I no longer belong to the Church.

KNIPPERDOLLINK: Then you are on our side! [OLOF *is silent.*] Answer! Are you with us or against us?

MARTIN: This is Olof Pedersen, sent forth by the King.

KNIPPERDOLLINK: Are you Master Olof?

OLOF: Yes.

KNIPPERDOLLINK: And a heretic?

OLOF: I pride myself I am.

KNIPPERDOLLINK: But in service with the King?

OLOF: Yes.

KNIPPERDOLLINK: Then you are against us. Take him!

The ANABAPTISTS *scream and surround* OLOF. GERT *rushes in through the iron door.*

GERT: Stop! What are you doing? Release him, friends. These men are the devil's emissaries. Olof is ours.

He points at MARTIN *and* NILS, *who run out through the door. The* ANABAPTISTS *run after them, raining blows on them.* GERT *turns at the door to* OLOF. *The* WHORE *has shrunk into a corner.* WINDRANK *is still asleep beneath the table.* OLOF *stands pensively in the middle of the room.*

GERT: This is hard work, Olof.

OLOF: What have you done?

GERT: Some cleansing. As a start. The city is in uproar. The Anabaptists are inflaming the people against the Church and the King. [*Pause.*] Olof, has the King sent you to work against us?

OLOF: Yes.

GERT: That was clever of him.

OLOF: Tomorrow I am to preach in the new pulpit. Bring your brothers to church tomorrow.

GERT: What will you preach to us? A high papal sermon?

OLOF: Today I have been excommunicated.

GERT [*leaps up and clasps* OLOF *to his breast*]: God bless you, Olof! This is the baptism of a new birth for you.

OLOF: I don't understand you. Why do you all rage like wild beasts? Defile holy objects?

GERT: Did Jesus Christ come down to earth and die so that people might worship wooden images? [*Picks up the broken image of a saint.*] Is this thing a God? I can snap it in two. Look. [*He breaks it.*]

OLOF: The people regard it as sacred.

GERT: As they did the golden calf, and Thor. And Odin. But they were cast down. [*Sees the* WHORE.] Who is that woman? Oh, yes, the one I sent to you for safety. Olof! Has the King bought your soul?

OLOF: Leave me, Gert. I hate you. When I stand before you, I become small. Get away from me! I want to do my work, not yours.

GERT: Now, listen –

OLOF: You have cast an invisible net around me. You are linking me with the Anabaptists. How shall I answer to the King?

GERT: Which King?

OLOF: Gustav.

GERT: Oh, him. Goodbye, Olof. Preach boldly tomorrow. Why doesn't that woman go? [*Goes.*]

WHORE [*goes to* OLOF *and falls on her knees*]: You are my master. You have saved my life.

OLOF: Thank only God who has saved your soul. God has forgiven you. Mankind never will.

BROTHER MARTIN *appears through the iron door, accompanied by* OLOF'S MOTHER *and* KRISTINA.

MOTHER: Olof! We have been looking everywhere for you. Brother Martin told me you were here.

OLOF: Mother! Kristina!

KRISTINA: Who is this woman who kneels at your feet? She looks so unhappy.

MOTHER: Can you not see her scarlet skirt? We must leave this house of sin.

KRISTINA: But she wears the holy veil.

MOTHER: Come. Martin will take us home.

OLOF: Mother, listen to me. [*Runs towards the door, which is slammed shut by* MARTIN.] Mother!

Scene 2

The Cathedral sacristy. A door leads out to the main body of the church. Stone steps lead up to the pulpit. 'Prie-dieux' and some smallish chests. The sun shines in through a window. The bells are ringing. A continuous murmuring of prayer is audible from beyond the left wall. The VERGER *is pouring water into a cup. His* WIFE *enters. They talk in whispers.*

VERGER: Have you dusted the robing-room yet?

WIFE: There's no need. It's only that Master Olof preaching today. I don't know how the Chapter allows such a thing.

VERGER: He has been granted permission by the King.

WIFE: There'll be the same trouble as yesterday. I thought

those Anabaptists would burn the place down. Heathen savages!

VERGER: I'd best put this cup of water in the pulpit. He'll need something to wet his gullet with today, poor fellow. [*Goes up steps.*]

WIFE: Fat lot I care.

The rear door of the cathedral opens.

VERGER [*in the pulpit*]: Katrina! Here he comes.

WIFE: Fancy them not having rung the priest bell. No, no, there'll be no priest bell for that one.

OLOF *enters, solemn and formal. He goes to a 'prie-dieu' and kneels. The* VERGER *descends and takes a surplice, which he holds ready for* OLOF.

OLOF [*gets up*]: God's peace be with you.

The WIFE *curtseys and goes. The* VERGER *holds out the surplice.*

OLOF: Put it back on its hook.

VERGER: Aren't you going to wear a surpl – ?

OLOF: No.

VERGER: But it's always done.

OLOF: It's not necessary.

VERGER: Surely –

OLOF: Please leave me, friend.

VERGER: You want me to go? But I usually –

OLOF: Please. [*He walks to the pulpit steps.*]

VERGER: I see. Very good. I've put the missal on the right there as you go up, and a marker to show you where to start, and a cup of water by it. Don't forget to turn the hourglass, so you don't go on too long –

OLOF: Don't worry. Today there will be some who will tell me when to stop. Without an hourglass. (*Pause.*) Verger, what is that sad murmuring?

VERGER: A pious brother reading a prayer for a lost soul. (*Goes.*)

OLOF: 'Abandon thy worldly goods and stand forth and preach to the people all that I command thee'. God help me. [*Throws himself down at a 'prie-dieu'. He finds a paper on it.*] What's this? [*Reads.*] 'Do not go into the pulpit today. Your life is in danger.' The Tempter has written this. [*Tears it up.*]

MOTHER [*enters*]: Yours is a false road, my son.

OLOF: Who knows, Mother?

MOTHER: I know. But as a mother I stretch forth my hand to you.

OLOF: Where would you lead me?

MOTHER: Back to virtue and a fear of God.

OLOF: If you counsel virtue and fear of God, you have come too late.

MOTHER: Olof, it isn't only what you teach. It is the way you live.

OLOF: I know you mean the woman you saw me with last night. I disdain to answer you. And what would be the use?

MOTHER: Oh, that I might be rewarded for the sacrifices I made, so that you might go out into the world and teach.

OLOF: I swear to God, Mother, your sacrifice shall not be in vain. It is thanks to you that I can at last stand forth freely and speak the truth.

MOTHER: You talk of truth? You have made yourself the prophet of lies! Has everything our family lived for, is everything I believe in, to die because of your heresy?

OLOF: What you believe has become a lie, Mother. When you were young, you were right, when I am old I may be wrong.

MOTHER: I don't understand you.

OLOF: That is the great sorrow of my life. Everything I do, from whatever motive, seems to you evil and godless.

MOTHER: Olof! I know your decision, I know the false step you have taken. I cannot change your mind, for you are more learned than I, and God will surely lead you back, but I beg you, do not rush headlong into damnation. Do not cut short your life.

OLOF: My life?

MOTHER: Haven't you heard that Bishop Brask is negotiating with the Pope to bring to this country the law that condemns heretics to the stake?

OLOF: The Inquisition? Here?

MOTHER: Yes. That is its name.

Pause.

OLOF: Leave me, Mother. I must preach today.

MOTHER: No. You preach heresy. You will destroy the people's faith.

OLOF: Nothing will stop me.

MOTHER: I have prayed to God to change your heart. I must tell you – but you must not repeat it – I was weak with age and my knees feeble – I sought out one of the Lord's servants and asked him, who stood closer to God, to say masses for your soul. He refused, because you were excommunicated, but, God pardon my sin, I corrupted his pure conscience with gold, the Devil's gold, just to save you.

OLOF: Mother, what are you saying?

MOTHER: Listen, my son. That is him praying for you in the chapel.

OLOF: So that was the murmuring I heard. Who is it?

MOTHER: Brother Martin.

OLOF: You ask the Devil for pray for me! Forgive me, Mother – I thank you for meaning well, but –

MOTHER [*kneels and weeps*]: Olof! Olof!

OLOF: Do not pray to me. A mother's prayers could tempt the angels themselves to apostasy. I must preach today.

MOTHER: You will bring me to the grave, Olof.

OLOF [*vehemently*]: Then the Lord will raise you again! [*Kisses her hand.*] Speak no more to me.

MOTHER: Listen! Listen! The people are growing restless.

OLOF: The God who held his hand over Daniel in the lions' den will guard me too. I must preach, Mother.

He climbs into the pulpit. During the following scene in the sacristy, his voice is heard speaking powerfully, though we cannot distinguish the words. After the sermon has proceeded for a while, we hear murmurs, which turn to shouts.

KRISTINA [*enters*]: They said you were in here. Did you see him, mother? [*Closes door.*] Did you talk to him?

MOTHER: Kristina! I told you to stay at home.

KRISTINA: Why may I not enter the Lord's house? You are hiding something from me. Why are you not in the Cathedral listening to Olof preach?

MOTHER: Go home, Kristina.

KRISTINA: May I not hear him? They are God's words, aren't they? [*The* MOTHER *is silent.*] You don't answer. What does this mean? Why do the people in there look so secretive?

MOTHER: Do not ask me. Go home and thank God for your ignorance.

KRISTINA: Am I a child? Why will no one tell me?

MOTHER: Your soul is still pure and must not be soiled. What have you to do with this war?

KRISTINA: War?

MOTHER: Yes, this is war, so you must keep away. You know our fate when men turn to battle.

KRISTINA: Then let me know what it is all about! I hate this ignorance. All I see is a dreadful darkness, and shadows that scare me. Give me light that I may understand. Perhaps I know these ghosts.

MOTHER: You will tremble when you see what they are.

KRISTINA: Let me tremble, rather than be tortured by this awful calm.

MOTHER: Do not call down the wrath of heaven. It will destroy you.

KRISTINA: You frighten me. But tell me the truth. I must know.

Pause.

MOTHER: Are you resolved to become a nun?

KRISTINA: My father wishes it.

MOTHER: You hesitate. [KRISTINA *is silent.*] Is there something that holds you back?

KRISTINA: You know it.

MOTHER: I know, and you must break it.

KRISTINA: That will soon be impossible.

MOTHER: I will save you, child, for you can still be saved. I shall offer to the Lord my greatest sacrifice if one soul can

be spared damnation. My son has fallen and I must
abandon him.

KRISTINA: Fallen?

MOTHER: He is a prophet of lies. The Devil has seized his
soul.

KRISTINA [*passionately*]: It is not true.

MOTHER: Would God it were not.

KRISTINA: Why do you tell me this now? No, it is a lie. Look,
Mother, there he stands! Is that an evil spirit that speaks
from his mouth, is that a flame from hell burning in his
eyes, do those trembling lips tell lies, can the darkness give
forth light, do you not see the brightness round his head?
You are wrong. I know it. I do not know what doctrine he
proclaims, I do not know what he denies, but he is right.
He is right and God is with him.

MOTHER: You do not know the world, child, you do not
know the Devil's cunning. Take care. [*Pulls* KRISTINA *from
the door.*] You must not listen to him, your soul is weak,
Olof is the apostle of Antichrist – a Lutheran!

KRISTINA: You have never told me who Luther is, but if Olof
is his apostle, then Luther must be great.

MOTHER: Luther is of the Devil.

KRISTINA: Why did no one tell me this before? Now I cannot
believe it.

MOTHER: I tell you now. Alas, I wanted to protect you from
the evil of this world, so I kept you in ignorance –

KRISTINA: I do not believe you! Let me go, I must see him, I
must hear him. He does not speak like other men.

MOTHER: Blessed Jesus! You too are possessed by the
unclean spirit.

KRISTINA [*opens door to the church*]: Listen to him, mother. Listen.

OLOF [*is heard preaching*]: Rome has bound your souls. You believe everything the Pope and his Bishops tell you, but theirs is not the voice of the true God. You are not blind slaves. Do not bind the spirit. You are free, for God has made you free.

The CONGREGATION's *anger turns to fear.*

You do not want freedom. Woe on you, woe, that is the sin against the Holy Ghost.

Furious reaction.

KRISTINA [*excitedly*]: Did you hear him!

VERGER [*enters*]: Ladies, you should not remain here. [*He closes the door.*] The people are growing restless. This will not end well for Master Olof.

MOTHER: Jesus Maria! What are you saying?

KRISTINA: Don't be afraid, mother. God's spirit is with him.

VERGER: I don't know about that, but he is an inspiring preacher. Old sinner as I am, I couldn't help weeping as I sat up in the organ loft. I don't understand how a heretic and an Antichrist can speak like that. Oh, that Luther! [*Cries are heard from the church.*] Oh dear, now something terrible is going to happen again, and the King away!

MOTHER: Let us leave this place. If God is with him, no harm can come to him. If it is the Devil – then Thy will be done, O Lord, but forgive him. Come, child.

KRISTINA: I shall wait for him.

MOTHER: God help you both.

She goes. OLOF's *voice is heard more strongly than ever, broken by shouts and the throwing of stones.* KRISTINA *throws herself down against a 'prie-dieu'. Heavy blows are heard on the door, and tumult from the church. Then silence, and* OLOF *descends with blood on his forehead, looking distraught.*

OLOF: It was all in vain! They do not want it. I free the prisoner from his chains, and he strikes me. I say: 'You are free!', and he does not believe me. Is the word so huge that there is not space for it in a human brain? Oh, if there was only one who believed in me! To be so alone – a madman whom no one understands –

KRISTINA [*comes forward*]: I believe in you.

OLOF: Kristina!

KRISTINA: You are right.

OLOF: How do you know?

KRISTINA: I do not know it, but I feel it. I heard you just now.

OLOF: And you do not curse me, Kristina?

KRISTINA: It is God's word that you preach, isn't it?

OLOF: Yes.

KRISTINA: Why has no one told us this before? Why do people speak a language we do not understand?

OLOF: Who put these words into your mouth? Your father?

KRISTINA: He wants me to become a nun.

OLOF: The man who wants everyone to be free would lock you up in a convent? [*Pause.*] What do you want?

KRISTINA: Olof, your forehead is bleeding. Let me bandage the wound.

OLOF [*sits*]: Kristina, have I shaken your faith?

KRISTINA: Sit still. Is there any water?

OLOF: Over there.

KRISTINA: Give me your handkerchief. My faith? I don't

understand you. Tell me, who is Luther? [OLOF *is silent.*]
Always the same silence. My father will not tell me, nor
your mother, and now you. Dare no one tell me the truth?
Is the truth so dangerous?

OLOF: You see what it has made the people do to me.

KRISTINA: Do you want me to be locked away in a convent
to live in ignorance a life that is no life? [OLOF *is silent.*] Do
you want me to weep away my life, my youth, and pray
long unending prayers until my soul falls asleep? No. I will
not. Now I have woken. Men fight around me, suffer and
despair. I see it but I may not join them. I must not even
watch, I may not know what they are fighting for. You
would all have me sleep like a beast. Don't you think I
have a soul which cannot be satisfied with bread and dry
bones? 'Do not bind the spirit', you said. Oh, if you knew
how those words excited me! The dawn broke and those
wild cries of horror were like the morning song of birds –

OLOF: Kristina! You are a woman! You were not born to
fight.

KRISTINA: If I cannot fight, then in God's name at least let
me suffer. God has opened my eyes, in spite of you all. You
would never have dared to tell me who Luther was. When
your mother frightened me by saying you were a Luther,
then I blessed Luther. Whether he was a heretic or a
believer, I don't know and I don't care. Neither Luther nor
the Pope nor Antichrist can satisfy my immortal soul, if I
have no faith in the everlasting God.

OLOF: Kristina! Will you fight with me? You can help me.
You are the only one who can.

KRISTINA: Now I can answer you with an open heart. Yes! I
know what I want, and I do not need to ask my father, for
I am free. My spirit is free!

OLOF: Think what kind of life awaits you.

KRISTINA: I know it now. And you will not be destroying

any false dreams. They are gone. Oh, Olof, I did dream –
of a knight who would come and offer me a kingdom, and
speak of flowers and love. Olof, I want to be your wife.
Here is my hand. But I must tell you, you were never the
knight of my dreams, and I thank God he never came, for
had he done so he would have gone – like a dream.

OLOF: Kristina, when I was downcast or tempted, I saw you
beside me. You were the maiden of my dreams, and now
my dream has come true. You are mine.

KRISTINA: Beware of dreams, Olof. Don't expect too much of
me.

A knocking is heard on the door.

OLOF: Who is that?

GERT [*offstage*]: Gert!

OLOF: What will he say? I promised him –

KRISTINA: Are you afraid?

OLOF: No. I will let him come in. [*He opens the door.*]

GERT [*enters and starts*]: Kristina! Olof, you have broken your
word.

OLOF: How?

GERT: You promised me you would not involve Kristina.
You have broken your word to me.

KRISTINA: He has not broken his word, Father. I have heard
this morning what you did not want me to hear. My eyes
are open.

GERT: Lord, why hast Thou robbed me of this one joy?

OLOF: The torrent takes its victims where it finds them.

GERT: You have stolen her. My child, my only comfort.

OLOF: Give her to me.

GERT: Never.

OLOF: Is she not free?

GERT: She is my child.

OLOF: Do you not preach freedom? She is mine. God has given her to me, and you cannot take her.

GERT: Remember, Olof, you are a priest and therefore may not enter into marriage.

Pause.

OLOF: But if I should?

GERT: You would dare to do that?

OLOF: Yes.

Pause.

GERT: Will you take a husband who is excommunicate, Kristina?

KRISTINA: I don't know what that means, Father.

OLOF: You see, Gert? You see!

GERT: O God, Thou punishest me cruelly.

OLOF: The truth is for all.

GERT: Your love is greater than mine. Mine was selfishness. God bless you both. Now I stand alone. [*Embraces them.*] There. Go home, Kristina. I want to speak with Olof.

KRISTINA *goes.*

GERT: Now we are one.

OLOF: What?

GERT: You are my son now, Olof. You found my letter?

OLOF: It was you who warned me not to preach!

GERT: I wanted you to preach.

OLOF: I don't understand.

GERT: You are still too young, so you need to be approached cautiously. To a man like you, one says: 'Don't do that', when one wants the opposite.

OLOF: Why weren't you in church with your followers?

GERT: It's only the sick who need medicine, we were busy elsewhere. You have done good work today, and I see you have your reward. I have freed you today, Olof.

OLOF: You?

GERT: The King commanded you to calm the city, to silence the rebellion, and what have you done? The opposite!

OLOF: Yes, I have.

GERT: What do you think the King will say to this?

OLOF: I shall speak to him when he returns to Stockholm.

GERT: Good!

OLOF: He will approve of what I have done. He wants to free us from the tyranny of Rome. He wants a reformation but dare not start it himself.

GERT: He is a fool.

OLOF: You still want to set me against my lawful king.

GERT: Olof, how many masters do you think you can serve? [OLOF *is silent*.] The King is already back.

OLOF: And the Anabaptists?

GERT: Rounded up and imprisoned, of course.

OLOF: And you stand here calmly?

GERT: Olof, I am old now. In my time I have raged like you, but I grow tired. The Anabaptists were doomed to fall, that was obvious. They struck the first blows. Nothing more. Now my work really begins.

Drums beat outside in the street.

OLOF: What is that?

GERT: The Anabaptists are being led to prison. Come here, and look.

OLOF *climbs on a bench and looks through the window.*

OLOF: But these are women and children!

GERT: Yes, well, they threw stones at the King's bodyguard, and that's not allowed.

OLOF: Are they to be treated like madmen and locked in prison?

GERT: Olof, there are two kinds of madmen. One kind you lock in the asylum and treat with pills and cold baths, the others you cut off their heads. It's a radical cure, but effective.

OLOF: I am going to the King. He cannot wish such things to happen.

GERT: Watch your head, Olof.

OLOF: And yours, Gert.

GERT: Oh, no danger for me. They already know I am mad. I've been certified.

OLOF: I can't bear to watch this. I shall go to the King at once, even if it costs my life. [*Goes to the door.*]

GERT: This is not a matter for the King. You must appeal to the law.

OLOF: The King is the law.

GERT: Yes, unfortunately. If the horse knew his strength he would not so foolishly bend under the yoke as he does now. But whenever he does break free of his oppressors, he is called mad and has to be destroyed or locked away. Olof, let us pray to God to open the people's eyes. But speak to the King, Olof. You speak to the King.

ACT THREE

Scene 1

A hall in the palace in Stockholm. In the background, a gallery, later divided off by a curtain. An old ATTENDANT *is walking in the gallery, waiting.*

OLOF [*enters*]: Will the King hold audience today?

ATTENDANT: Yes.

OLOF: Can you please tell me why I have been kept waiting here four days?

ATTENDANT: No idea.

OLOF: It seems strange that I have not been admitted.

ATTENDANT: What do you want?

OLOF: That is not your business.

ATTENDANT: No, no. I understand. I just thought I might be able to help.

OLOF: Do you decide to whom the King will speak?

ATTENDANT: No, no. But someone who hears as much as I do knows a bit about most things.

Pause.

OLOF: Will he be long? [*The* ATTENDANT *pretends not to hear.*] Do you know if the King will be here soon?

ATTENDANT [*off-handedly*]: What?

OLOF: Do you know to whom you are talking?

ATTENDANT: No idea.

OLOF: I am the King's Secretary.

ATTENDANT: Good God, are *you* Master Olof? I knew your father, we grew up together. Peter the Smith.

OLOF: Can't you be civil, then?

ATTENDANT: Ah, well. That's how it is when one comes up in the world. One forgets old friends. Ssh! Here comes the Earl Marshal.

He goes. Pause. The EARL MARSHAL, LARS SIGGESON, *enters.*

EARL MARSHAL [*throws* OLOF *his cloak without looking at him*]: Will the King be here soon?

OLOF [*catches the cloak and throws it on the floor*]: I don't know.

EARL MARSHAL: Get me a chair.

OLOF: That isn't my job.

EARL MARSHAL: You're damned impertinent.

OLOF: I am not a servant.

EARL MARSHAL: I don't care what you are. Mind your manners. [OLOF *is silent.*] Well, do something. Have you gone mad?

OLOF: I am sorry, but my duties as the King's Secretary do not include waiting on people.

EARL MARSHAL: What? Master Olof? I see, so you think it is funny to sit by the door and play the servant so that you can suddenly reveal yourself as God. I thought you were a proud man. [*Picks up his cloak meanwhile and puts it on the bench.*]

OLOF: My Lord Marshal –

EARL MARSHAL: You, sir, are a conceited upstart. If you'll excuse me.

Strides off. OLOF *sits. A young* NOBLEMAN *greets him from the gallery.*

NOBLEMAN: Good morning, Mr Secretary. Nobody come yet? Well, how are things in Stockholm? I have just arrived from Malmö.

OLOF: There is much unrest.

NOBLEMAN: Yes, so I have heard. As soon as the King turns his back, the mob causes trouble, as always. And those idiotic priests. Oh, forgive me. You are of course a freethinker, Mr Secretary?

OLOF: I –

NOBLEMAN: Oh, please don't get embarrassed. I was brought up in Paris, you understand. King François, O Saint-Sauveur! There's a man who'll go far. Do you know what he said to me at a *bal masqué* during the recent carnival?

OLOF *is silent.*

'*Monsieur*', he said, '*la religion est morte, morte*', he said. But that doesn't stop him going to mass.

OLOF: Indeed?

NOBLEMAN: And do you know what he said when I asked him why he did so? '*Poésie! Poésie!*', he said. Oh, he is divine.

OLOF: What did you say then?

NOBLEMAN: 'Your Majesty', I said, in French of course, 'happy the land that possesses a king with the vision to see beyond the narrow confines of time, who can perceive the needs and spirit of the age, yet does not importune the sleeping masses to share his vision.' Was not that well said?

OLOF: Very. But it lost everything in the translation. Such things need to be said in French.

NOBLEMAN [*abstractedly*]: You are quite right. I say, you'll go far – should make your fortune, you're very advanced for your age.

OLOF: I don't think I shall 'go far'. My education was sadly neglected – I was in Germany and the Germans do not yet believe that religion is dead.

NOBLEMAN: Yes, yes! Yes, yes! Can you tell me why they bother so much about that Reformation in Germany? Luther is a civilized man, I know, I believe it, but surely he can keep his ideas to himself, or at least not strew sparks among the vulgar masses, pearls before swine. If one studies the main intellectual currents, one sees the great cultural countries are losing their equilibrium. I'm not speaking of Sweden, of course – we have no culture. You see, the centre of gravity of a civilized nation is the nobility. Disturb us and everything flies apart. Why is Germany rent asunder? Because the peasants have risen against the nobility and are chopping off their own heads. Why does France survive? Because France is the nobility, and the nobility is France. Why is Sweden now shaken to its very foundations? Because when the Danes invaded us, they executed eighty of our leading nobles. But now the King is restoring the nobility, the Church will be crushed and Sweden will be saved. Talk of the Devil, here comes Bishop Brask, the wealthiest man in Sweden – and the Earl Marshal – oh, dear! Those two don't love each other.

BISHOP BRASK *enters. The* EARL MARSHAL *returns.*

BRASK: There are a lot of people here today, my Lord Marshal.

EARL MARSHAL [*pointedly*]: Mostly to congratulate His Majesty on his safe return.

BRASK: I can assure you that no one delights in this more than the Church.

EARL MARSHAL: It is good of your Grace to inconvenience yourself by so long a journey, especially when you are so advanced in years. And I hear your Grace's health is not all it should be.

BRASK: We churchmen tend to live long. In that respect we are the envy of many noble families, my Lord.

EARL MARSHAL: To say nothing of your wealth and the size of your private armies. It is said, my Lord Bishop, that your riches exceed those of the King himself.

BRASK: I have heard that rumour.

EARL MARSHAL: Has your Grace also heard the rumour that His Majesty intends to restore the balance?

BRASK: I am sure His Majesty would not be so unwise as to seek a confrontation.

EARL MARSHAL: With your private army, your Grace?

BRASK: With the Holy Father in Rome, Earl Marshal.

ATTENDANT: His Majesty!

KING GUSTAV *enters.*

KING GUSTAV: Gentlemen, welcome.

ALL: Your Majesty.

KING GUSTAV [*sits at a table*]: Now, if you will be so good as to withdraw to the ante-room I shall receive you in turn. The Earl Marshal will stay.

BRASK: Your Majesty!

KING GUSTAV [*raises his voice*]: Earl Marshal!

BRASK *goes. Pause.*

KING GUSTAV: Well, Earl Marshal?

EARL MARSHAL: Your Majesty! The state has lost its main ally, the nobility. This leaves it weak. You have an enemy which has become over-powerful. Raise up the nobility, and crush your enemy, the Church.

KING GUSTAV: I dare not.

EARL MARSHAL: But you must.

KING GUSTAV: What do you mean?

EARL MARSHAL: Brask is conspiring with the Pope to
introduce the Inquisition. The merchants of Lübeck, who
have financed you hitherto, are stubborn in their demands
and threaten war. Our treasury is empty, there is unrest
throughout the land –

KING GUSTAV: But I have the people behind me.

EARL MARSHAL: Not all. The Dalecarlians, who claim to
have done most to put you on the throne, will now rise
against you unless you redress their grievances. Their
arrogance knows no bounds.

KING GUSTAV: What do they say?

EARL MARSHAL [*reads*]: 'Foreign modes of dress, with
gaudy, slashed garments such as have recently been seen at
the court, shall not be permitted.'

KING GUSTAV: God's death! Give that to me. [*He reads.*] 'All
those who eat meat on Fridays or Saturdays shall be
burned at the stake or otherwise executed.' 'No new belief
or Lutheran doctrine shall be introduced.' This is a direct
challenge to my authority! Yet they once proved themselves
loyal.

EARL MARSHAL: When flames threatened their doorstep, of
course they ran to quench them. But how often have they
not broken their sworn word! They even boast of their
impudence. They call it 'good Swedish bluntness'.

KING GUSTAV: You speak as a nobleman.

EARL MARSHAL: Yes. These peasants have driven out the
enemy by the strength of their arms. But their role is over.
Your Majesty! Crush the Church. It is she who holds the
people in chains. Seize the Church's gold and pay the
country's debts. And give back to your loyal nobles what
the Church stole from us.

KING GUSTAV: Tell Bishop Brask to enter.

EARL MARSHAL: Your Majesty – !

KING GUSTAV: Bishop Brask!

The EARL MARSHAL *goes.* BISHOP BRASK *enters.*

KING GUSTAV: Well, my lord Bishop?

BRASK: I wished to convey to you the Church's
congratulations on –

KING GUSTAV: Thank you, my Lord. What else?

BRASK: I regret to inform Your Majesty, complaints have
been reported from certain quarters of your kingdom
regarding loans of silver from the Church which have not
been repaid. Articles of great value borrowed by your
Majesty –

KING GUSTAV: And which you now want back. Do you
really need silver chalices for communion?

BRASK: Yes.

KING GUSTAV: Then the people must drink from pewter,
your Grace.

BRASK: Your Majesty!

KING GUSTAV: Is there anything else?

BRASK: The worst thing of all. Heresy.

KING GUSTAV: That does not concern me. I am not the
Pope.

BRASK: Then I must tell your Majesty that the Church will
take whatever steps are necessary to combat it, even at the
risk of coming into conflict with –

KING GUSTAV: With whom?

BRASK: With the state.

KING GUSTAV: With myself. Then to the Devil with your
Church! Well, now I have said it.

BRASK: I already knew your feelings.

KING GUSTAV: And you were simply waiting to hear the
   words from my mouth?

BRASK: Yes.

KING GUSTAV: Take care. You travel with two hundred
   servants while the people eat husks.

BRASK: Your Majesty over-simplifies.

   Pause.

KING GUSTAV: You know about Luther. You are an
   enlightened man. What is this phenomenon? What do you
   feel about these movements that are shaking Europe?

BRASK: A step backwards. Luther's role is merely to test by
   fire the ancient truths that have withstood the trial of
   centuries, that they may be purified and emerge
   triumphant from their ordeal.

KING GUSTAV: Bishop, I am not interested in learned
   disputations.

BRASK: Yet your Majesty does not hesitate to protect law-
   breakers and infringe the Church's sacred rights. Master
   Olof has grievously outraged the Church.

KING GUSTAV: Excommunicate him, then.

BRASK: We already have, but your Majesty still employs
   him.

KING GUSTAV: What more would you do to him? [*Pause.*]
   Well, Bishop?

BRASK: It is rumoured he has entered into a secret marriage,
   in defiance of canon law.

KING GUSTAV: Indeed? He moves quickly.

BRASK: Your Majesty seems unconcerned. Yet if he should
   incite the people –

KING GUSTAV: That would be my concern. Is there anything else?

BRASK [*after a pause*]: I beg you, sir, do not plunge the country into chaos. It is not yet ripe for unfamiliar doctrines. We mortals are weak reeds that can be bent, but the Church, the faith, never!

KING GUSTAV [*offers his hand*]: You may be right. Let us be enemies, Bishop Brask, rather than false friends.

BRASK: As you wish. But do not do what you will regret. Every stone you wrench from the Church the people will throw at you.

KING GUSTAV: Do not drive me to extremities, Bishop, or the tragedy that they are enacting in Germany will be repeated here. For the last time, will you make concessions should the welfare of my kingdom depend upon it?

BRASK: The Church –

KING GUSTAV: The Church must always come first. Of course. [*Pause.*] Ask the Earl Marshal to return.

BRASK *goes. The* EARL MARSHAL *enters.*

KING GUSTAV: He has confirmed your fears. So that's what he wants. Right. I must find some way of destroying their Church. Find me masons who understand demolition. The walls will stand, the cross will remain on the roof, the bells in the steeple, but their foundations will be destroyed. One must strike at the heart.

EARL MARSHAL: But the people will think we are striking at their faith. We must educate them so that they understand.

KING GUSTAV: We shall send Master Olof to preach to them.

EARL MARSHAL: Olof is a dangerous man.

KING GUSTAV: I need him.

EARL MARSHAL: Instead of preaching against the Anabaptists' revolt he has been raving like one himself.

KING GUSTAV: I know. He will fight them later. Send him in.

EARL MARSHAL: Yes, your Majesty.

He goes. OLOF *enters.*

KING GUSTAV: Well, Olof, have you calmed down yet?

OLOF *is silent.*

I gave you four days to think things over. Have you done what I told you? Have you preached to the people and warned them against the men in Rome?

OLOF [*vehemently*]: I have spoken to them.

KING GUSTAV: Ah, I see. You're still in a fever. And do you still plan to defend these Anabaptist madmen?

OLOF [*boldly*]: Yes.

Pause.

KING GUSTAV: I hear you have married.

OLOF: Yes.

KING GUSTAV: And have been excommunicated.

OLOF: Yes.

KING GUSTAV: Still as bold as ever! Suppose, as one who has incited rebellion, you had to follow these traitors to the gallows, what would you say then?

OLOF: I would regret I had been unable to complete my work, but would thank God for what I have achieved.

KING GUSTAV: Good. Dare you go to Brask and his fellow bishops and tell them that the Pope is not God and that he has no business in my kingdom? Defeat all their arguments. I want them destroyed, utterly.

OLOF: Is that all?

KING GUSTAV: You will also tell them that the Bible alone is God's word.

OLOF: Nothing else?

KING GUSTAV: You must not mention Luther's name.

OLOF [*thinks for a moment*]: No. I won't agree to that.

KING GUSTAV: Would you rather die?

OLOF: You need me.

KING GUSTAV: You know how to exploit my position. Very well, say what you will to them. But I may retract some of it later.

OLOF: One doesn't bargain about the truth.

KING GUSTAV: God's death! [*Changes his tone.*] Do as you wish.

OLOF: I may tell them everything?

KING GUSTAV: Yes.

OLOF: My life will not have been wasted if I can kindle one spark of doubt to wake the people from their sleep. Then we shall have a true Reformation.

KING GUSTAV: Yes!

Pause.

OLOF: What will become of the Anabaptists?

KING GUSTAV: You ask me that? They must die. Tell me, Olof, what do these madmen want?

OLOF: The tragedy is they don't really know. And if I told you –

KING GUSTAV: Tell me.

GERT *runs in, feigning madness.*

GERT: May I humbly beg your Majesty to attest the correctness of this declaration?

KING GUSTAV: Who are you? How dare you force your way in here? Are you an Anabaptist?

GERT: Yes, I did happen to get mixed up with them. But I have here a certificate that I am an inmate of a mental institution, department number three for incurables, cell number seven, and am not responsible for my actions.

KING GUSTAV [*to* OLOF]: Call the guards.

GERT: There's no need. I only want justice, and your guards don't handle that.

KING GUSTAV [*looks at him*]: Weren't you involved in these disturbances in the city churches?

GERT: Of course. No sane person would behave that crazily. We only wanted to make a few formal changes. We thought the roof was stiflingly low.

KING GUSTAV: What exactly did you want?

GERT: Oh! Such a lot – we haven't half done yet. Yes, we want so much, and so fast. Thought can't keep pace with it, that's why we're a little behind schedule. We wanted to take out the windows because the Church smelt musty. And a lot more, but that'll do for the moment.

KING GUSTAV: This is a dangerous madness, Olof. It can't be anything else.

OLOF: Who knows?

KING GUSTAV: I'm tired. You have two weeks to do as I say. Promise you'll help me!

OLOF: I shall do my duty.

KING GUSTAV: Tell them to take those Anabaptists to Malmö.

OLOF: And then?

KING GUSTAV: They can go free. Have this idiot returned to his asylum. [*Goes.*]

GERT [*clenches his fist after* KING GUSTAV]: Shall we go, Olof?

OLOF: Which way?

GERT: Home.

OLOF *is silent.*

Do you want to take your father-in-law to the madhouse, Olof?

OLOF: Want to? It is my duty.

GERT: Aren't there higher duties than obedience to the King?

OLOF: Are you starting all that again?

GERT: What will Kristina say if you leave her father among the insane?

OLOF: Do not tempt me, Gert.

GERT [*laughs*]: You see how hard it is for you to serve the King.

OLOF *is silent.*

Poor boy, I won't make things difficult for you. This paper will absolve your conscience. [*Shows him a paper.*]

OLOF: What is it?

GERT: My certificate of sanity! You see, Olof, one must be mad among the sane but sane among the mad.

Pause.

OLOF: Let's go home.

Scene 2

OLOF'*s study. Windows upstage, through which the sun is shining in. Trees outside.* KRISTINA *stands at a window watering flowers and talking to birds in a cage.* OLOF *sits writing. He looks up from the paper with an expression of impatience and over to* KRISTINA *as though wishing to silence her. This happens several times until* KRISTINA *knocks over a flower-vase.* OLOF *taps lightly on the floor with his foot.*

OLOF [*writing*]: Why are you so happy today, Kristina?

KRISTINA: Shouldn't I be happy? I have ceased to be a slave and have become your wife. Why are you sad?

OLOF: You must forgive me if my happiness is less than yours. It has cost me my mother.

KRISTINA: I know. When your mother learns of our marriage, she will forgive you but curse me. Whose burden will be heavier then? But it doesn't matter, I shall bear it for your sake. I know great battles await you, bold thoughts grow in your head, but I can never·take part in the battles, never help you with advice, or defend you against abuse. I can only look on from my small world, busy with trivialities like cooking and knitting and feeding birds. Olof, I cannot weep with you, so help me by smiling with me, step down from your height to which I cannot climb. Come down sometimes from the war you wage on the mountain – I cannot climb up to you, so come down for a moment to me. You are a man sent by God, I know that, but you are also a human being, and my husband. Are you too great to look at a flower or listen to a bird? Olof, I put flowers on your table to rest your eyes, you told the servant to take them out because they gave you a headache. I wanted to relieve the lonely silence of your work, so I gave you birdsong, but you said it disturbed you. I ask you to eat dinner, you have no time. I want to talk to you, you have no time. You despise my small world of reality, yet it was you who gave it to me. You do not wish to raise me. At least do not crush me.

OLOF [*takes her in his arms and kisses her*]: Kristina! My dear! You are right. Forgive me.

KRISTINA: Olof, the freedom you gave me is difficult. I cannot use it. I need someone to obey.

OLOF: You will use it. But now we must eat.

KRISTINA (*looks out through the window and reacts in surprise*): Go inside and start. I must finish my work.

OLOF: Don't be too long.

He goes. OLOF'S MOTHER *enters through the front door and walks past* KRISTINA *without turning her head.*

MOTHER: Is Master Olof at home?

KRISTINA: No. Please sit down, and he'll come soon.

MOTHER: Thank you. [*Sits. Pause.*] Give me a glass of water. [KRISTINA *does so.*] Now leave me.

KRISTINA: As mistress of the house it is my duty to keep you company.

MOTHER: I was not aware that a priest's housekeeper was entitled to call herself mistress of the house.

KRISTINA: I am Master Olof's wife in the sight of God. You evidently do not know that we are married.

MOTHER: I know that you are a whore.

KRISTINA: I don't understand that word.

MOTHER: You are the kind of woman Master Olof talked to that night in the alehouse.

KRISTINA: The woman who looked so unhappy. Yes, I am not happy.

MOTHER: Get out of my sight, your presence shames me.

KRISTINA [*kneels*]: For your son's sake, do not abuse me.

MOTHER: By a mother's right, I order you out of my son's house, the threshold of which you have stained and dishonoured.

KRISTINA: As mistress of this house I open the door to whom I please. I would have closed it to you had I guessed what you would say.

MOTHER: Fine words! I order you to leave!

KRISTINA: By what right do you order me from my home? You have borne your son, brought him up, as was your duty, your calling in life. You should thank God that He enabled you to fulfil it – not everyone is so fortunate. Now you stand on the edge of the grave. If you want gratitude, seek it in some other way. Do you think it is your child's vocation to sacrifice his life to show you gratitude? Is he to stray from his chosen path to satisfy your private selfishness? Do you think the fact that you gave him life and brought him up demands gratitude? Was not this the purpose of your life, should you not thank God that He gave you so high a calling, or did you do it all just so that half a lifetime later you might claim gratitude? Don't you know that by the use of this word gratitude you destroy what you once built up? And what right do you claim over me? I never swore obedience to you when I married Olof, and I have sufficient respect for my husband not to allow anyone to insult him, even his mother. That is why I have spoken like this.

MOTHER: Now I see the fruits of the heresies my son teaches.

KRISTINA: If you wish to abuse your son, then do so to his face. [Goes to the inner door and calls.] Olof!

MOTHER: You have learned cunning already.

KRISTINA: Already? I have always had it, though I didn't realize until I needed it.

OLOF [enters]: Mother! How good to see you!

MOTHER: Thank you, my son. Goodbye.

OLOF: Are you going? Why? I want to talk to you.

MOTHER: There is no need. She has said everything.

OLOF: Mother, what in God's name are you saying?
Kristina! What is this?

MOTHER [*turns to go*]: Goodbye, Olof. I shall never forgive
you for this.

OLOF [*tries to stop her*]: At least stay and explain.

MOTHER: I shall not demean myself. You left her to tell me
that you owe me nothing and no longer need me. That is
hard, Olof – hard. [*Goes.*]

OLOF: What did you say to her? Kristina?

KRISTINA: I don't remember now. A lot of things I'd never
dared to think, but must have dreamed while my father
kept me in slavery.

OLOF: Were you discourteous?

KRISTINA: I must have been. Do you think I have become
hard, Olof?

OLOF: Did you tell her to go?

KRISTINA: Forgive me, Olof. I was not polite to her.

OLOF: For my sake you might have been kinder. Why didn't
you tell me she was here?

KRISTINA: I wanted to see if I could manage on my own.
Olof, would you abandon me if your mother asked you?

OLOF: I can't answer such a question at once.

KRISTINA: Then let me answer. It pleases you to bow to your
mother's will because you are strong. But it hurts me to do
it because I am weak. I shall never do it.

OLOF: If I begged you to?

KRISTINA: You cannot ask me that. [*Pause.*] Tell me, Olof.
What does whore mean?

OLOF: You ask such strange questions.

KRISTINA: You must tell me. [*Long pause.*] Always this eternal silence! Do you still not dare to tell me everything? Must I still be treated as a child? Then put me in the nursery and make silly noises to me.

OLOF: It means an unfortunate woman.

KRISTINA: No. It means something else.

OLOF: Has someone dared to call you – that? [*Pause.*] Kristina?

KRISTINA [*after a pause*]: No.

OLOF: You are not being truthful, Kristina.

KRISTINA: I am lying, I know. Oh, I have become so sinful since yesterday.

OLOF: Something happened yesterday which you are hiding from me.

KRISTINA: Yes, I thought I could bear everything alone, but I haven't the strength any longer.

OLOF: Tell me, I beg you.

KRISTINA: Yesterday a mob followed me here and shouted this dreadful word which I do not understand. People don't laugh at unfortunate people – do they?

OLOF: Yes, my dear, that is just what people do.

KRISTINA: I did not understand their words. But I understood their gestures.

OLOF: It is a word the mob shouts at someone it seeks to humiliate. You will learn about it soon enough. [*Knock on door.*] Who is that?

MESSENGER [*enters*]: A letter for Master Olof.

OLOF: Who sent you?

MESSENGER: Bishop Brask. [*Goes.*]

OLOF: At last! Read it to me, Kristina. I want to hear the good news from your lips.

KRISTINA [*reads*]: 'You have won, young man. I, your enemy, am the first to tell you, and I do so without humiliation, for when you spoke for the new faith you unsheathed the sword of the spirit. I do not know if you are right, but you deserve a word of advice from an old man. Stay here, for your enemies are gone. Do not go forth to fight with spirits of air, you will cripple your arm and waste away. "Put not your trust in princes" is the counsel of a once powerful man who now steps aside and commends to God's hand the fate of his defeated Church. Johannes Brask.' Olof, you've won!

OLOF [*happily*]: O God, I thank Thee for this moment! [*Pause.*] No, I am afraid, Kristina. This happiness is too great. I am too young to have won the fight. To have nothing to strive for – that is a fearful thought. No more strife. That is death.

KRISTINA: Rest for a while, and be happy it is ended.

OLOF: Can there be an end? An end to this beginning? No, Kristina. Oh, I want to begin again! It wasn't the victory I wanted, it was the fight!

KRISTINA: Do not tempt God, Olof. You will find there is much left to do.

Another knock at the door. It is opened.

NOBLEMAN [*enters*]: Good day, Master Secretary. I bring good news. Er – if I may speak with you privately – ?

KRISTINA: Of course. [*Goes.*]

OLOF: Is your news from the King?

NOBLEMAN: Yes. Now that the Catholic Church is defeated, here are his orders. Briefly: first, mutual agreement to resist and punish all rebellion.

OLOF: Go on.

NOBLEMAN: Secondly: the King claims the right to possess the Bishops' palaces and castles and to limit their income –

OLOF: Thirdly?

NOBLEMAN: Ah, this is the *pièce de resistance*, the kernel of the enterprise. Thirdly: the nobles are granted the right to repossess such of their wealth and property as was previously transferred to the churches and monasteries.

OLOF: Is that all?

NOBLEMAN: Yes. Beautifully simple, don't you think?

OLOF: Nothing else?

NOBLEMAN: A few trifles, but they're not important.

OLOF: Let me hear them.

NOBLEMAN: There's a clause about the right of preachers to proclaim God's word, but they had that before.

OLOF: And?

NOBLEMAN: A register is to be established of the income of all bishops, cathedrals and canons, and the King has the right to determine –

OLOF: Never mind that.

NOBLEMAN: – what proportion they shall keep and what proportion shall be placed at the disposal of the Crown. All clerical appointments – this should interest you – whether of high or low degree, shall henceforth be made only with the King's approval.

OLOF: Please read the paragraph relating to belief.

NOBLEMAN: Belief? There's nothing about belief. Oh, yes, wait a moment. 'The Gospel shall henceforth be read in all schools.'

OLOF: And that is all?

Pause.

NOBLEMAN: No. I have a special command from the King to you, very sensible, that since the people have been upset by recent religious innovations, you must not in any way criticise the old mass, holy water and such established customs, nor commit any impetuous follies, for as from today the King will not close his eyes to your excesses as he did in the past when he had no power to do otherwise.

OLOF: I see. And the new faith which I have been allowed to preach?

NOBLEMAN: It must ripen slowly. It will come. It will come. Just be sensible, Olof, and you will go far. Oh, I nearly forgot the best thing. Your Reverence, I have the honour to congratulate you. Look: here is your letter of commission. Rector of the City Church at an annual salary of three thousand crowns a year. And so young! Well, now you can relax and enjoy life, even if you should rise no higher. It is wonderful to have attained one's goal at so early an age. I congratulate you. Goodbye. [*Goes.*]

OLOF [*throws letter of commission on the floor*]: Is this all I have fought and suffered for? To be Rector of the City Church! I served Belial instead of God. The King has betrayed me. Have I betrayed my life's work for three thousand crowns a year? God in heaven forgive me!

He throws himself on a bench and weeps. KRISTINA *enters with* GERT.

OLOF: Gert! You here?

GERT: Was that letter from the King?

OLOF: Yes.

GERT: What does he say?

OLOF: Read it.

KRISTINA *picks up the letter and reads it.*

KRISTINA: What wonderful news! Look, Father! [*Gives* GERT

the letter.] Oh, my dearest, I am so happy. [*Goes to embrace* OLOF.]

OLOF: Get away from me!

KRISTINA [*distraught*]: Why?

GERT: The Pope is beaten, then. Shall we now cross swords with the temporal power?

OLOF: He destroyed the power of Rome and the Bishops for his own ends. He has simply replaced one tyranny with another.

GERT: At last!

OLOF: You were right, Gert. I am yours. It must be war. But openly, and honourably.

GERT: Until today, Olof, you lived in a world of dreams. But now you see clearly.

OLOF: Now comes the day of judgement.

KRISTINA: Olof, in God's name, wait.

OLOF: You must leave me, child. You will drown in this deluge, and drag me down with you.

GERT: Kristina, my child. What could you do?

KRISTINA *goes. From outside comes the sound of bells, jubilation, music and drums.*

OLOF [*goes to the window*]: Why are the people celebrating?

GERT: The King has ordered a maypole and music outside the North Gate.

OLOF: Do they not know that in place of the rod, the King now rules with the sword?

GERT: Know? If they knew!

OLOF: Unhappy children! They dance to his pipes and march to their death to his drums. Must all die that one may live?

GERT: One must die that all may live.

OLOF *makes a gesture of amazement and horror.*

ACT FOUR

Scene 1

A room in OLOF's MOTHER's *house. To the right, a curtained bed in which the* MOTHER *lies, sick.* KRISTINA *is seated in a chair, asleep.* LARS PETRI *is pouring oil into the night lamp and turning the hourglass.*

LARS: Kristina! [*She starts.*] Go to bed, child. I shall keep watch over her.

KRISTINA: No, Lars, I want to wait. I must talk to her before she dies. Surely Olof will come soon.

LARS: You are keeping awake for his sake.

KRISTINA: Yes. You mustn't tell him I fell asleep. Promise.

LARS: Poor child. You are not happy.

KRISTINA: Who said people should be happy?

LARS: Does Olof know you are here?

KRISTINA: No. He would never allow it. He wants to keep me on a shelf like a holy image. The smaller and weaker he makes me, the more he will enjoy laying his strength at my feet.

MOTHER [*wakes*]: Lars! [KRISTINA *restrains him and goes to her.*] Who is there?

KRISTINA: Your nurse.

MOTHER: Kristina!

KRISTINA: Is there anything you want?

MOTHER: Nothing from you.

KRISTINA: Mother –

MOTHER: Do not embitter my last hour. Leave – leave this house.

LARS: What do you want, Mother?

MOTHER: Take her away! Bring my confessor, I am going to die soon.

LARS: Is Olof not worthy to receive your last confidences?

MOTHER: He is not worthy to hear them. Has Martin come yet?

LARS: Martin is an evil man, Mother.

MOTHER: O God, Thou punishest me too harshly. My children keep Thee from me. Must I be denied the comfort of religion in my last moments? You have taken my life, will you destroy my soul too? Your mother's soul? [*Falls unconscious.*]

LARS: Oh, Kristina! Is she to die cheated by a wretch like Martin, and thank us, or is her last prayer to be a curse? No. They must be allowed in. What do you think, Kristina?

KRISTINA: I dare not think anything.

LARS: I will fetch them. [*Goes out and returns at once.*] Oh, it's horrible! They've fallen asleep among glasses and dice. And these are the men who would prepare my mother for death.

KRISTINA: Tell her the truth, then.

LARS: She won't believe it. She will think we are lying.

MOTHER: My son! Obey your mother's last prayer!

LARS [*goes*]: God forgive me.

MOTHER: Olof would never have done this.

LARS *returns with* MARTIN *and* NILS, *and takes* KRISTINA *out.* NILS *puts a chest on the floor, opens it and takes out holy water vessels, censers, horns of ointment, palm branches and candles.*

MARTIN [*goes to the bed*]: She's asleep.

NILS: Then we may not start work yet.

MARTIN: We've waited so long, we can wait a little longer.
As long as that priest of Satan doesn't come!

NILS: Olof? Do you think he saw anything out there?

MARTIN: I don't care any longer. As long as the old hag
gives us the money. Then I am free.

NILS: You're a dreadful rogue.

MARTIN: Yes, but I'm getting tired of it. I'm beginning to
long for peace. Do you know what life really is?

NILS: No.

MARTIN: Pleasure. The flesh is God. Didn't someone write
that once?

NILS: The Word was made flesh, you mean.

MARTIN: Oh, yes. Yes.

NILS: You should have been something big, with your brains.

MARTIN: Maybe I should. But that was what scared people.
So they whipped the spirit out of my body in the monastery
– yes, I had spirit too, once. But now I'm only flesh, and
the flesh will take its revenge.

NILS: They seem to have whipped out your conscience too.

MARTIN: Pretty well. Tell me the recipe for that mulled
claret which sent us to sleep out there.

NILS: Well, you take a jug of wine, half a pound of
cardamum, well washed –

MARTIN: Hush, she's moving. Bring out the book.

NILS [*reads half-aloud during the following scene*]:
Aufer immensam, Deus aufer iram;
Et cruentatum cohibe flagellum;
Nec scelus nostrum proferes ad aequam
    Pendere lancem.

MOTHER: Is that you, Martin?

MARTIN: It is my brother Nils invoking the Blessed Virgin.

MOTHER: What a blessed comfort to hear the Lord's words in the holy tongue!

MARTIN: No sacrifice is so pleasing to God as the prayers of pious souls.

MOTHER: My heart is kindled like incense by holy prayer.

MARTIN [*sprinkles her with holy water*]: From the pollution of sin thy God doth wash thee clean.

MOTHER: Amen. Martin, I am going. The King's ungodly ordinance forbids me to bestow my earthly goods on the Church, to strengthen her power to save souls. You must take my wealth, holy man, and pray for me and for my children. Pray the Almighty to turn their hearts from heresy, that we may meet in heaven.

MARTIN [*takes her purse*]: Your sacrifice is pleasing to the Lord, and for your sake God will hear my prayers.

MOTHER: Now I want to sleep a little, to gather my strength for the final sacrament.

MARTIN: No one will disturb your last moments. Not even those who were once your children.

MOTHER: That is hard, Brother Martin. But God will have it so.

MARTIN [*opens the purse and kisses the gold coins*]: Oh, Nils! What a wealth of voluptuous pleasure lies in these hard discs of gold!

NILS: Shall we go now?

MARTIN: We could, since we've got what we came for. But it'd be hard on the old hag to let her die in a state of sin.

NILS: A state of sin!

MARTIN: Yes.

NILS: Do you believe that?

MARTIN: One doesn't know what to believe. One man dies saved by one faith, the next by another. They all think they've found the truth.

NILS: Suppose you were to die now, Martin?

MARTIN: I won't.

NILS: But supposing?

MARTIN: I'd go to heaven like all the rest. But I'd just like to settle a little account with Master Olof first. There's only one pleasure more pleasing than all the rest, and that's revenge.

NILS: Revenge? What harm has he done you?

MARTIN: He dared to see through me, he unmasked me, he sees what I think – ah!

NILS: And you hate him for that?

MARTIN: Isn't that cause enough? [*Banging is heard on the outer door.*] Someone's coming. Read, read, you devil!

NILS *gabbles the verses again. The door is opened from without; a key is heard in the lock.* OLOF *enters, looking confused.*

MOTHER [*wakes*]: Is that you, Brother Martin?

OLOF: It is your son, Mother. You didn't let me know you were ill.

MOTHER: Olof, goodbye. I shall forgive the evil you did me if you do not disturb me while I prepare myself for heaven. Brother Martin! Give me the holy unction that I may die in peace.

OLOF: So this was why you didn't send for me! [*Sees the purse which* MARTIN *has been trying to hide and snatches it from him.*]

Do you trade in souls here? And is this the price? Leave
this room and this deathbed. This is my place, not yours.

MARTIN: You seek to hinder us in our holy task.

OLOF: Go!

MARTIN: We act not by the Pope's authority but by that of
the King. He is our master now.

OLOF: I shall cleanse God's Church even if I have to fight
both Pope and King.

MOTHER: Olof! You will consign my soul to damnation, you
will let me die cursing.

OLOF: Mother, you must not die surrounded by false
comfort. Pray to God yourself. He is not as far away as you
suppose.

MARTIN: You must be a prophet of Satan not to want to save
your own mother from the agonies of purgatory.

MOTHER: Blessed Jesus, save my soul.

OLOF [to MARTIN and NILS]: Get out of this room before I
throw you out. And take your trash with you. [Kicks the
things aside.]

MARTIN: If you let us keep the money your mother has given
to the Church, we will go.

MOTHER: Was this why you came, Olof? You want my gold?
Give it to him, Martin. Olof, you may have it all if you
leave me in peace. You shall have more. You shall have
everything!

OLOF [in despair]: In God's name, take the money and go! I
beg you!

MARTIN [grabs the purse and goes with NILS]: Woman! Our
power ends where the Devil walks. You heretics are
damned for eternity. And you who break the law will meet
judgement here. Beware of the King! [They go.]

OLOF [*kneels at his* MOTHER's *bed*]: Mother, listen to me
before you die. [*The* MOTHER *has lost consciousness.*] Mother,
Mother, if you are still alive, speak to your son. Forgive me,
but I cannot do otherwise. I know you have suffered all
your life for my sake, you have prayed God that I should
find Him. The Lord has heard your prayer. I have found
Him. Do you want me now to negate your whole life, do
you want me to destroy what has cost you so much
suffering and tears by rejecting everything I believe?
Forgive me!

MOTHER: Olof! My soul no longer belongs to this world. I
speak to you from the other side of the grave. Turn, break
this unclean bond into which your flesh has entered, leave
Kristina, return to the one true faith I gave you. Then I
shall forgive you.

OLOF [*weeps with despair*]: Mother! Mother!

MOTHER: Swear to me that you will do this.

OLOF [*after a pause*]: No.

MOTHER: God's curse upon you! I see Him, I see God
frowning in anger. Help me, Blessed Virgin!

OLOF: That is not the God of love.

MOTHER: It is the God of vengeance. It is you who have
provoked Him, it is you who have cast me into the fire of
His wrath. Cursed be the hour I bore you! (*Dies.*)

OLOF: Mother! Mother! [*Takes her hand.*] She died
unforgiving. Oh, if your soul still lingers, look down on
your son. I will do as you wish, what is sacred to you shall
be sacred to me. [*Lights the big wax candles which the* MONKS
have left and places them around the bed.] You shall have holy
candles to light you on your journey. [*Puts a palm branch in
each of her hands.*] And with the palms of peace you will
forget your last struggle with mortality. Oh, Mother, if you
see me you will forgive me.

The sun has begun to rise and throws a red glow on the curtains.

OLOF [*leaps to his feet*]: Oh, morning sun, you make my candles pale. You are more loving than I.

LARS [*enters slowly, surprised*]: Olof!

OLOF [*embraces him*]: It is finished.

LARS [*goes to the bed, kneels, then rises*]: She is dead. [*Makes a silent prayer.*] You were alone here!

OLOF: It was you who let the monks in!

LARS: You drove them out?

OLOF: Yes. You should have done that.

LARS: She forgave you?

OLOF: She died cursing me.

Pause.

LARS [*points at the candles*]: Who put those candles around her, and the palms in her hands?

OLOF [*angry and ashamed*]: I was weak for a moment.

LARS: Thank you. It is what she wanted.

OLOF: Do you mock my weakness?

LARS: I praise your humanity.

OLOF: I curse it. God in heaven, is not my way right?

LARS: You are wrong.

KRISTINA [*has entered*]: You are right, Olof.

OLOF: Kristina!

KRISTINA: It was so silent and lonely at home.

OLOF: I told you not to come here.

KRISTINA: I thought I could be of some help, but now I see – Next time I will stay at home.

OLOF: You have stayed awake all night.

KRISTINA: That is not hard. I will go now if you order me to.

OLOF: Go inside and rest while we talk.

She abstractedly puts out the candles.

What are you doing, my dear?

KRISTINA: It is daylight.

LARS *glances at* OLOF.

OLOF: My mother is dead, Kristina.

KRISTINA [*goes to him with gentle yet cold sympathy to receive his kiss on her forehead*]: I commiserate with your grief.

She goes. LARS *and* OLOF *look at* KRISTINA *as she leaves, then at each other.*

LARS: As your brother and friend, Olof, I beg you, do not continue on this dangerous path.

OLOF: The King has betrayed our cause. I shall take it up.

LARS: The King is no fool.

OLOF: He is a traitor, a sycophant fawning to the nobility. First he uses me like a dog, then he kicks me out.

LARS: He is more far-sighted than you. Suppose you now went to three million people and said: 'Your faith is false, believe what I tell you', do you think they would at once throw aside their deepest and most cherished convictions, which have sustained them in sorrow and in joy? No, there would be something wrong with religion if it were that easy to throw out the old beliefs.

OLOF: Lars, you're wrong. The whole nation is beset by doubt, there's hardly a priest who knows what to believe, or even whether he believes at all. The time is ripe for the new faith. It's you who are to blame, you weak men who dare not trust your consciences to cast out doubt where faith is feeble.

LARS: Take care, Olof. You want to play at being God.

OLOF: One must, since He will no longer dwell among us.

LARS: You keep on destroying things, Olof. Soon there will be nothing left. And when men ask what you have to give us in its place, you reply: 'No, not that', 'Nor that', but never 'That'.

OLOF: Lars, how dare any man be so presumptuous? Do you think one can give people a new faith? Has Luther given anything new? No, he has only torn down the shutters that blocked the light. What I want is to sow doubt, doubt about the old faith, not because it is old but because it is rotten.

LARS *indicates their* MOTHER.

I know. She was too old, and I thank God that she died. Now at last I am free. It was God's will that it should happen thus.

LARS: You are out of your mind. Or evil.

OLOF: I respect my mother's memory as much as you do, but if she had not died now I don't know how long I could have gone on. Brother, have you seen how in the spring, last year's fallen leaves cover the ground and threaten to choke the young plants striving to find the light? What do they do? They either push the dry leaves aside or force their way through them, because they must seek life.

LARS: But, Olof, you have broken the laws of the Church at a time of civil disobedience and unrest. What was pardonable before must be punished now. Do not force the King to seem worse than he is. Do not compel him by your disobedience and violence to punish you when he admits he is grateful to you.

OLOF: He governs by violence. He must learn to tolerate it in

others. Why do you argue so strongly for the King? (*Pause.*)
You have entered the King's service. (*Pause.*) Do you
intend to fight against me?

LARS: Yes.

OLOF: Then we are enemies. I need new ones.

LARS: Olof, the ties of blood –

OLOF: I recognize none, except in its source, the heart.

LARS: Yet you wept for your mother.

OLOF: Weakness. And perhaps old affection and gratitude.
But not the ties of blood. What does it mean, anyway?

LARS: You are tired, Olof.

OLOF: Yes, I am worn out. I have been awake all night.

LARS: Why did you come so late?

OLOF: I was away.

LARS: Your work shuns the daylight.

OLOF: Daylight shuns my work.

LARS: Beware of the false apostles of freedom.

OLOF [*fights against sleep and tiredness*]: That is a self-
contradiction. Don't talk to me, I can't stand it any longer.
I've talked so much at the meeting – no, you don't know
about us. We must achieve our Reformation. Gert is a man
of vision – I am so small beside him. Goodnight, Lars.
[*Falls asleep in a chair.*]

LARS [*looks at him sympathetically*]: My poor brother. God
protect you.

Blows are heard on the main door.

What is that? [*Goes to the window.*]

GERT [*outside*]: Open, for God's sake.

LARS [*goes out*]: Gert! Is your life in danger?

GERT: Let me in, in God's name.

KRISTINA [*enters with a blanket*]: Olof! What is all this noise?
He is asleep. [*Wraps the blanket around* OLOF.] Why am I not
asleep, that you might come to me when you rest from the
strife?

The rattle of a heavy cart is heard outside the house.

OLOF [*starts up*]: Is it five o'clock already?

KRISTINA: It's only three.

OLOF: Wasn't that the baker's cart I heard?

KRISTINA: I don't know. It sounds too heavy. [*She goes to the
window.*] Look, Olof. What is it?

OLOF [*goes to window*]: It's the hangman's tumbril. No. It –

KRISTINA: It's full of bodies.

LARS: Olof, the plague has broken loose.

ALL: The plague!

GERT: Kristina, my child, you must leave this house. The
angel of death has set his mark on its door.

OLOF: Who has sent the cart here?

GERT: Whoever marked the black cross on the door. Her
body must not remain in the house a moment longer.

Pause.

OLOF: Martin was your angel of death. So it was all a lie,
everything he said.

GERT: Look out of the window. The cart is full. [*A knock on
the door.*] You hear? They're waiting.

OLOF: Without burial? I will not allow it.

KRISTINA: Without ceremonies, Olof.

LARS [*goes*]: I will let them in.

GERT: Kristina, come with me and leave this dreadful house. I will take you out of the city to where there is sun and light.

KRISTINA: I will stay with Olof. If you had loved me a little less, Father, you would have done less harm.

GERT: Olof, she is your wife. Order her to come with me.

OLOF: I freed her once from your authority, for selfish reasons. She will never return to it now.

GERT: Kristina, at least leave this house.

KRISTINA: Not a step, until Olof orders me to.

OLOF: I do not order you to do anything, Kristina. Remember that.

The Corpse-bearers enter.

CORPSE-BEARER: We've a corpse to collect. Be quick! Stand aside.

OLOF: No.

CORPSE-BEARER: It's the King's command.

LARS: Olof! For heaven's sake. The law –

GERT: We can't waste time, Olof. The people are angry and inflamed against you. This was the first house to be marked. Now they cry: 'God's vengeance on the heretic!'

OLOF [*falls on his knees by the bed*]: Forgive me, mother. [*Gets up.*] Do your duty.

The corpse-bearers go to the body and prepare their equipment.

GERT [*whispers to* OLOF]: But, we cry: 'God's vengeance on the King!'

Scene 2

The churchyard of St Clara's Abbey. Upstage, the half-demolished abbey building, from which workmen are carrying timber and rubble. To the left, a mortuary chapel. Light is visible through its windows; later, when the doors are opened, an image of Christ can be seen, brightly lit above a sarcophagus. Here and there graves lie open. The moon is beginning to rise behind the ruined building. WINDRANK is sitting on guard at the chapel door. Singing is audible from the chapel. NILS enters.

WINDRANK: What do you want here? The King has ordered all the abbeys and monasteries to be torn down.

NILS: The nuns of St Clara are coming to celebrate their Saint's memory for the last time.

WINDRANK: A strange spectacle for this new enlightened age!

NILS: The King has given his permission. The plague started here in this parish, and the people take it for a sign of God's wrath at the King's decision to tear down their ancient and blessed Abbey.

WINDRANK: And now they hope to drive out the plague with song!

NILS: They are to bury the Saint's bones in the sanctuary before the building is levelled to the ground.

The singing has come nearer. A procession of Blackfriars and Franciscan nuns enters, with MARTIN at their head. They stop and sing. The Workmen busy themselves noisily in the background.

PROCESSION:
   Cur super vermes luteos furorem
   Sumis, O magni fabricator orbis!
   Quid sumus quam fex, putris, umbra, pulvis
   Glebaque terrae!

MARTIN [*to the* ABBESS]: You see, Reverend Mother, how they lay waste the dwellings of the Lord.

ABBESS: God who gave us into the hands of the Egyptians
will deliver us in His own time.

MARTIN [*calls to the* WORKMEN]: Our orders are that you
stop your work and do not disturb our holy rites.

FOREMAN: Our orders are to work night and day until this
place is destroyed.

ABBESS: Alack, have even the humblest become so ungodly?

MARTIN: We perform this ritual with the King's authority.
Here is his seal.

FOREMAN [*examines the paper*]: That seems in order.

MARTIN: And I further command you to stop all noise.

FOREMAN: Now, look –

MARTIN: I shall appeal to your men, whom you are forcing
to act thus shamefully. I shall entreat them to respect the
holy –

FOREMAN: You leave my men alone. I'm the one who gives
the orders here. Anyway, they're happy enough to knock
this old place down – they've had to skin their pockets for
its upkeep. And they're grateful for work – any work in
hungry times like these.

MARTIN: Reverend Mother, let us forget the evil and tumult
of this world and enter the sanctuary to pray for them.

ABBESS: Lord, Lord, Thy holy places are laid waste. Zion is
laid waste. Jerusalem is destroyed.

OLOF *enters. At the same time,* GERT *and* OTHER
CONSPIRATORS *emerge from the chapel.*

OLOF: What is this folly?

MARTIN: Make way for the servants of the blessed Saint
Clara.

OLOF: You fools, do you think your idols can ward off the

plague which God has sent to chastise you? Do you think the Lord finds those stumps of bone which you carry so pleasing that he will forgive your loathsome sins? Away with this abomination! [*Snatches chest from the* ABBESS *and throws it into an open grave.*] Dust thou art and to dust shalt thou return!

The Nuns scream.

MARTIN: If you do not fear that which is holy, at least fear your earthly King. [*Shows* OLOF *the paper.*] We perform this sacred rite with his authority.

OLOF: Do you know what the Lord did to the King of the Assyrians when he permitted idolatry? He smote him and his people, the just and the unjust. In the name of the One Almighty God I denounce this Baal-worship. The Pope excommunicated me and sold my soul to Satan, but I tore up the contract, remember? Should I now fear a King who sells his people to Baal? [*Tears up the order.*]

MARTIN [*to his followers*]: I call you all to witness that he reviles the King.

OLOF: I call you to witness before God that I rescue His stricken people from an ungodly King.

MARTIN: Hearken, ye faithful. It is because of this heretic that the Lord smote us with the plague. It was God's vengeance that slew his mother.

OLOF: No, Papists! The Lord chastiseth me because I served Sennacherib against Judah. I shall atone for my crime, I shall lead Judah against the Kings of Egypt and Assyria.

The moon has risen red, and a red light falls over the scene. The PEOPLE *become fearful.*

OLOF [*climbs up on to a grave mound*]: Look! Heaven weeps blood for your sins and your idolatry. You will be punished for the sins of those who lead you. Do you not see how the graves open their jaws for prey?

GERT [*whispers*]: Come, Olof. We have no time to waste here.

ABBESS: Give us back our shrine, that we may leave this
place of desolation.

MARTIN: Better that the Saint's bones should be scattered in
this holy soil than be exposed to the foul hands of heretics.

GERT *beckons to* OLOF *again. The* PROCESSION *has dispersed,
so that only a few remain.*

OLOF: Cowards! You run away because you fear this plague.
Was your faith in these holy bones so weak? Go, run to the
King – tell him the people are burying a silver casket and
he will come and claw it from the soil with his own nails.
Tell him that the moon has changed from silver to gold and
for once he will turn his eyes towards heaven. And tell him
that by your heathen folly you have provoked the anger of
an honest man.

The Nuns and MARTIN *have gone.*

GERT: That will do. [*To the Conspirators.*] Leave us.

They whisper among themselves and go.

GERT: Words are not enough, Olof. Have you forgotten what
we must do? It is too late to turn back now.

OLOF: Tell me what you want.

GERT: Do you confirm your oath against the King?

OLOF: Yes.

GERT: Swear on this book.

OLOF: I swear. [*Pause.*] This is not a Bible.

GERT: It is the fruit of my silent work. On every page you
will read a cry of complaint, the sighing of thousands blind
enough to believe it is God's will that they should endure
the tyranny of one man. They dare not believe in
liberation. They tell how from the broken fragments of the
Church the nobles are building new castles and new

prisons for the people. You will read how the King sells law and justice, allowing murderers to escape punishment – how he taxes vice by granting whores a licence to ply their trade. The very fish in the rivers, the very waters of the sea, he has made his. But now it is finished, the eyes of the people have been opened, they seethe and ferment. Soon the oppressor will be crushed and they will be free.

OLOF: Who wrote this book?

GERT: The people! These are folk songs, Olof, this is how people sing when they bend beneath the yoke. I have travelled in the cities and around the country, I have asked them: 'Are you happy?', and this is their reply. Do you think the will of millions will not prevail over one man? Do you believe God gave this land with its men and women and lakes and forests to one man for him to do as he pleases, or do you believe he should do as the people will? You do not answer. You tremble at the thought that all this might end. Now hear my confession, Olof. Tomorrow the tyrant shall die.

OLOF: What?

GERT: Have you not understood all I have said?

OLOF: You have deceived me.

GERT: I told you: 'One must die that all may live.' You chose not to believe me then. Now you know it is true. Once it is done you will be free.

OLOF: But the consequences?

GERT: Blind man! It is because of the consequences that I have done this.

Pause.

OLOF: If it should fail?

GERT: We must risk that. The whole of Europe is in revolt.

Our King has broken his promises, and when his subjects ask for justice he cries treachery and treason.

OLOF: So this was where you wanted to lead me, Gert. Murder.

GERT: The current has carried you here. You want the same as I do, but you shrink from it. Tomorrow in the Cathedral at a given signal the people will rise and choose their own leader.

OLOF: If it is the will of the people, no man can stop it. But, Gert, let me go to the King with this book, show him what his people want. He will give them justice.

GERT: Justice! He will be scared for a moment, return some silver chalice or other to some church – then he'll point to heaven and cry: 'It is not my will that I sit here and commit injustices, but God's!'

Pause.

OLOF: Then God's will be done.

GERT: How?

OLOF: 'One must die that all may live.' Men will call me murderer, regicide, traitor, no matter. I sacrificed everything – even honour and conscience and faith. Could I give more to these poor people who cry for freedom? Let us go before I repent.

GERT: Even if you did, it would be too late. Brother Martin now spies for the King. Sentence may already have been pronounced on you as a rebel.

OLOF: I have no need of repentance. Why should I repent of carrying out the sentence of God? Onward, in the Lord's name!

They go.

WINDRANK: A man can't even rest in peace among the corpses. Why did I have to hear what they said? Why drag me into such matters? If I tell, I'll get well paid and

become a rich man – but I don't want to, I don't want to! I
want to sleep at night and not be disturbed by ghosts. Shall
I go and tell about this? No, they'll arrest me.

The WHORE *enters.*

Who is this? One of the nuns come back to search for the
holy relics?

The WHORE *kneels on a grave mound, which she bestrews with
flowers.*

WHORE: Have You punished me enough, Lord? Will You
never forgive me?

KRISTINA [*runs in*]: Have you seen Master Olof?

WHORE: Are you his friend or his enemy?

KRISTINA: You insult me –

WHORE: Forgive me. I have seen him in my prayers.

KRISTINA: I recognize you. You are the woman Olof spoke
to in the Cathedral.

WHORE: You shouldn't let anyone see you talking to me. You
don't know who I am.

KRISTINA: Yes, I do.

WHORE: You know? Then someone has told you?

KRISTINA: Olof has told me.

WHORE: And you do not despise me?

KRISTINA: Olof says you are an unhappy and abused
woman. Why should I despise unhappiness?

WHORE: Then you are unhappy too?

KRISTINA: Yes. We have shared the same fate.

WHORE: Then I am not alone. Tell me, what unworthy man
did you love?

KRISTINA: Unworthy?

WHORE: To whom did you give your love?

KRISTINA: Master Olof.

WHORE: No! Tell me it is not true! Don't rob me of my faith in him. It's the last thing I have left since God took my child from me.

KRISTINA: You have had a child? Then you have been happy once.

WHORE: I thank God that He never let my son know how unworthy his mother was.

KRISTINA: You speak as if you have committed some sin. Why are you strewing flowers on this grave?

WHORE: My son, conceived in sin, my shame, lies buried here.

KRISTINA: Your child? What are you saying? I pray to God every day to give me one human creature, just one, for me to love.

WHORE: Unhappy creature. Pray God to protect you.

KRISTINA: I don't understand you, good woman.

WHORE: Don't call me that. You know what I am.

KRISTINA: Doesn't one pray in church for those who hope?

WHORE: Not for us.

KRISTINA: Us?

WHORE: They pray for the others but they curse us.

KRISTINA: What do you mean, the others? I don't understand –

Pause.

WHORE: Do you know Master Olof's wife?

KRISTINA: I am she.

WHORE: You? Yes, of course. How could I have doubted it
for a moment? Could evil dwell in him or you? Oh, no.
Leave me, you are a child who knows nothing of evil. You
mustn't talk with me any more. Goodbye. [*Turns to go.*]

KRISTINA: No, don't leave me. Whoever you are, stay. They
have smashed into our home, abused me – and my
husband has disappeared. Leave this place with me, let us
go to your home, anywhere. You are a good person, you
cannot be evil –

WHORE [*interrupts her*]: The mob's abuse cannot hurt you half
as much as being seen with me.

KRISTINA: Who are you?

WHORE: I am an outcast, upon whom the curse that God set
upon Eve has fallen in full measure. Ask me no more. Here
comes someone who may be kind enough to go with you.
Forgive me. I do not mean to be bitter.

WINDRANK [*approaching them, drunk*]: You must help me. You
are nuns and can help a soul in anguish.

KRISTINA: Tell us what you want.

WINDRANK: The day after tomorrow I'll tell you. But then
it'll be too late.

KRISTINA: If your conscience is troubled you can tell us now.

WINDRANK: Why should I be involved? Why me? It is
wrong. A crime –

KRISTINA: Are you thinking of committing – ?

WINDRANK: A murder! Who told you? Thank God you
know. Go and tell them – at once, or I'll have no peace. No
peace for eternity.

KRISTINA [*is amazed; collects herself*]: Why must you murder
this person?

WINDRANK: There's so much evil he's done. Look how he's pulled down your abbeys.

KRISTINA: The King!

WINDRANK: Yes, Gustav Vasa. The liberator and father of our country. He's bad all right, but that's no cause to murder him.

KRISTINA: When will it happen?

WINDRANK: Tomorrow in the Cathedral.

KRISTINA *gestures silently to the* WHORE, *who goes.*

KRISTINA: How did they choose you?

WINDRANK: I have a few acquaintances among the Cathedral staff. But why don't you go and tell someone about it?

KRISTINA: It has already been done.

WINDRANK: Thank God and praise Him!

KRISTINA: Tell me, who else is involved?

WINDRANK: I don't want to name them.

NILS, *Soldiers and People pass across the stage.*

KRISTINA: They're already looking for you.

WINDRANK: I wash my hands of it. I know nothing.

NILS [*goes to* WINDRANK *without seeing* KRISTINA]: You. Have you seen Master Olof?

WINDRANK: Why?

NILS: They're looking for him.

WINDRANK: No, I haven't seen him. Are they looking for anyone else?

NILS: Oh, yes. Quite a few people.

WINDRANK: I haven't seen anyone, anyone at all.

NILS: We'll be coming back soon to talk to you. [*They go.*]

WINDRANK: What a business. I'm off. Goodbye.

KRISTINA: Tell me before you go –

WINDRANK: I haven't time. They'll return soon.

KRISTINA: Is Master Olof one of them?

WINDRANK: Of course.

> KRISTINA *falls senseless on one of the graves.* WINDRANK *becomes sober and anxious. He goes to her.*

WINDRANK: God in heaven, it's his wife. Oh, Hans, Hans, what have you done? Why did you get mixed up in such great matters? Help!

> OLOF *is brought in by Soldiers with torches. He sees* KRISTINA, *wrenches himself loose and kneels beside her.*

OLOF [*cries out*]: Kristina!

KRISTINA: Olof! You're alive! Who are these men? Why are your hands bound? [*Screams.*] Olof!

Scene 3

In the Cathedral. OLOF *and* GERT *in prison clothes on pillories by the door. The organ is playing, the bells are ringing. Service is finished and* PEOPLE *are leaving. The* VERGER *and his* WIFE *stand apart downstage.*

VERGER: You can't help feeling sorry for them.

WIFE: Especially Master Olof. They should never have made such a young lad Rector.

VERGER: Mm, he was rather young – that's a bad fault. But youth passes with time.

WIFE: It will with him. He's to die today.

VERGER: Yes. Good God, I was forgetting. It don't seem
right.

WIFE: Do you know if he's repented?

VERGER: I doubt it, he's still too proud.

WIFE: Surely he'll melt when he sees his pupils. He should
have been confirming them this morning.

VERGER: The King's real mean once he starts. Making
Master Olof stand in the pillory on the very day when his
children are to be confirmed.

WIFE: And his own brother is to prepare him for death.

VERGER: Yes. Here they come. How sad they
look.

Confirmation Candidates, both Girls and Boys, file past OLOF *with
bunches of flowers in their hands. They are tearful and walk with
downcast eyes. Some point curiously at* OLOF, *others rebuke them.*
VILHELM *comes last. He stops shyly before* OLOF, *kneels,
and places his flowers at* OLOF's *feet.* OLOF *has drawn his hood
over his face and does not see this. Some of the People murmur
disapprovingly, others sympathetically.* MARTIN *goes forward to
remove the flowers but is pushed back by the People. Soldiers open a
path for* LARS PETRI, *who comes forward in full canonicals. The
People go.* LARS, OLOF *and* GERT *are left alone. The organ
falls silent. The bells go on ringing.*

LARS: Olof, the King has rejected the people's petition for
mercy. Are you prepared to die?

OLOF: Oh, Lars, I can't think that far ahead.

LARS: I have been sent to prepare you.

OLOF: You'd best be quick, then. The blood still surges in
my veins.

LARS: Have you repented?

OLOF: Lars, forget the formalities if you want me to listen to you. I don't think I can die now, I've too much life left in me.

LARS: I think so too, and it is for a new life in this world that I am to prepare you.

OLOF: In this world?

LARS: If you are willing to confess that what you did was wrong, and to renounce all you said against the King.

OLOF: How can I? That would be to die.

LARS: That is what I have to tell you. You must decide.

OLOF: One doesn't bargain about one's beliefs.

LARS: One can believe in what is wrong. I will leave you to think it over. [*Goes.*]

GERT: Our harvest was not ripe, Olof. Much snow must fall if the autumn seed is to flourish, centuries may pass before a single shoot is seen. They say 'The conspirators are taken', and offer thanks for it, but they are wrong. The conspirators are everywhere, in the King's rooms, in the churches, in the market-place. But they do not dare as we dared, though it will happen some time. Goodbye, Olof. You should live long, you are young. I shall die happy – every new martyr's name will be a battle-cry for a new army. Never believe that any lie ever kindled a mortal soul, never cease to believe in the passions that shook your heart when you saw someone spiritually or physically tortured. Even if the whole world says you are wrong, trust your heart and your courage. The day you deny this you are dead, and eternal damnation is a mercy to one who has sinned against the Holy Ghost.

OLOF: You talk as though my release was certain.

GERT: The citizens have offered five hundred ducats as ransom for you. It only cost two thousand to get Clara declared a saint, so five hundred should be enough to get you proclaimed innocent. The King dare not take your life.

The EARL MARSHAL *enters with the* HEADSMAN *and Soldiers.*

EARL MARSHAL: *Take Gert the Printer to the scaffold.*

GERT [*as he is led away*]: Goodbye, Olof. Take care of my daughter, and never forget our great day of Pentecost.

EARL MARSHAL: Master Olof. You are a young man who has been led astray. The King pardons you because of your youth, but demands that you publicly recant all that you have done over and against his orders.

OLOF [*cynically*]: Does the King still need me?

EARL MARSHAL: There are many who need you. But don't imagine you will be freed until you have fulfilled the conditions. Here is the King's pardon. In a moment your chains can be struck off. But in a moment, too, this paper can be torn up.

OLOF: A man who is content with a ransom of five hundred ducats will not bother about a recantation –

EARL MARSHAL: You are wrong. The headsman is still waiting for you too. But I beg you, listen to a few words from an old man. Once I was like you and went around proclaiming truths. I too wanted to build a small heaven here on earth, but I soon came to my senses and banished such hallucinations. You are an idealist but your idealism is dangerous. Your hot blood blinds you. By preaching freedom you would plunge thousands into slavery. Turn back, young man, mend what you have broken, restore what you have torn down, and the people will bless you.

OLOF: Can I have lived and fought only for a lie? Must I publicly declare my whole youth, the best years of my life, useless and wasted? Let me rather die with my illusions.

EARL MARSHAL: You should have stopped dreaming earlier. Life still awaits you. The priests of the new Church demand that you live to complete what you so splendidly began. The citizens demand to keep their Secretary in Council, the congregation demand their shepherd and the pupils their teacher. And there is another to whom you perhaps owe most, yet who demands nothing, your young wife. You took her from her father and then cast her into the storm, you destroyed her childhood faith, forced her into confusion. Your heresies incited a mob to drive her from her home. She does not even ask you for love, only to be allowed to live out her life suffering at your side. You see that we too care about others, though you call us selfish. Bow your heart, and thank God Who still offers you time to serve humanity.

OLOF [*weeps*]: I am lost.

The EARL MARSHAL *makes a sign to the* HEADSMAN, *who removes* OLOF's *chains and prison clothes. The* EARL MARSHAL *then opens the door to the sacristy. Representatives of the Council,* KRISTINA, LARS, *Priests and Citizens enter.*

EARL MARSHAL: Olaus Petri, sometime Rector of this Cathedral, do you hereby repent what you have done, recant what you have said over and against the King's commands, and declare yourself willing to keep your oath to His Majesty the King and serve him faithfully?

KRISTINA [*pleadingly*]: Olof!

PEOPLE [*softly*]: Master Olof! We need you. Return to us. We need you.

Pause.

OLOF: Very well.

EARL MARSHAL: In the King's name, you are free.

OLOF *and* KRISTINA *embrace. The* PEOPLE *shake* OLOF's *hand and congratulate him.*

OLOF [*coldly*]: Before I leave this place, let me be alone here for a moment with my God. Here I struck my first blow, and here –

LARS: Here today you have won your greatest victory.

All leave except OLOF, *who falls on his knees.* VILHELM *enters cautiously.*

VILHELM: I hid in the church so that I could speak to you alone. I have come to bid you farewell before you go to another life.

OLOF [*gets to his feet*]: Vilhelm! You did not abandon me. Let me weep for a moment with you and remember the happy hours of my youth.

VILHELM: Before you die, I wanted to thank you for all the good you did for us. It was I who laid these flowers at your feet, but you did not see them – now I see they have been trampled to pieces. I wanted to remind you of the time when we rehearsed our play beneath the lime-trees in the garden. I thought it would please you to know that we did not thank God that you did not return, as you said we would. We shall never forget you, for you saved us from those cruel punishments, it was you who gave us back freedom and the joy of life. Why you must die we don't know, but you could never do anything that is not right, and if, as is said, you are dying because you helped the poor and oppressed, then it should not make you sad, though it will grieve us. You told us once of a man condemned to die by burning because he had dared to speak the truth, and how he climbed on to the pyre and gave himself joyfully into God's hands, prophesying that a day would come when the bird of freedom would return with new songs of the promised liberty. That is how I know that you will go to meet your death, fearlessly, your eyes blazing with joy and fixed on God's grace, while the people cry: 'He gave witness to the truth!'

OLOF: No, Vilhelm, no.

   Pause.

VILHELM: Traitor!

   OLOF *weeps in agony and torment.*

Creditors

A Tragi-Comedy

(1888)

Introduction to

CREDITORS

Strindberg wrote *Creditors* at Holte in Denmark in
August–September 1888, immediately after completing *Miss
Julie*. It seems to have taken him barely a month, if that. On
29 September he wrote to Joseph Seligmann, the Swedish
publisher who had accepted *Miss Julie* after its rejection by
Strindberg's regular publisher, Albert Bonnier:

> 'The attached tragedy was written for the Théâtre Libre
> [an experimental theatre which Strindberg was planning to
> open in Denmark on the model of Antoine's Théâtre Libre
> in Paris] at the same time as my *Miss Julie*. I didn't want to
> publish it in Swedish because my enemies always write
> commentaries on my work designed to damage me. But
> now that I have seen from the attached advertisement [of a
> translation of Ernst Ahlgren's *roman à clef, Money*] how
> intimately one is allowed to write, I send for your perusal
> this play, which is finer than *Miss Julie* and in which I have
> more successfully achieved this new form, in the hope that
> you may be willing to print it with the other play in one
> volume. The plot is exciting, as spiritual murder must be;
> the analysis and the motivation are exhaustive, the
> viewpoint impartial; the author judges no one, he merely
> explains and forgives; and although he has made even the
> promiscuous woman sympathetic, this does not mean that
> he is advocating promiscuity. On the contrary, he says
> specifically that it is a bad thing, because of the
> disagreeable consequences which it brings.'

Seligmann, however, refused *Creditors* on the grounds not that
it was immoral but that it was too intimate and too obviously
descriptive of Strindberg's own marriage with Siri von Essen.
Strindberg replied that he had based Tekla on the authoress
Victoria Benedictsson ('Ernst Ahlgren'), who had committed

suicide a few months earlier – an explanation which is
difficult to accept, for *Creditors* paints a very accurate picture
of his own marital troubles, or at any rate his view of them.
The previous spring he had completed an autobiographical
novel in French (because he thought it too frank to appear in
Swedish) entitled *Le Plaidoyer d'un Fou (A Madman's Defence)*,
which deals in embarrassing detail with Strindberg's relations
with Siri and her former husband Baron Carl Gustav von
Wrangel. *Creditors* overlaps to a considerable degree with this
novel, in which Strindberg describes how his wife prepares to
free herself from 'her troublesome creditor', and refers to her
former husband as 'an idiot'. Strindberg still feared that
Wrangel (who, like the ex-husband in the play, was called
Gustav) might reappear and regain her affections, or take
some kind of revenge. At the same time, Strindberg put much
of himself into this character, as well as into Adolf; he was
already seeking a divorce from Siri, and this was how he
would like to behave towards any future husband whom she
might acquire.

Adolf was his present self; Gustav a kind of idealized future
self. This idea of the strong and ruthless man he had taken, at
any rate partly, from Nietzsche, whom he had begun to read
that spring and with whom he was about to enter into a brief
but eloquent correspondence. The power of 'suggestion' was
something that had interested Strindberg for a long time. In
1886–7, just before he began *The Father*, Strindberg had
written a series of essays entitled *Vivisections* on what we would
nowadays call psychological warfare between individuals.
Two important starting-points for these essays had been
Hippolyte Bernheim's book *De la suggestion* and Max Nordau's
Paradoxes. In one of them, Strindberg described how he had,
by means of his superior brain and stronger nerve-power,
been able to 'crush into powder' the brain of a man who he
believed was trying to do the same to him. This power of
suggestion he had of course used as thematic material in both
The Father and *Miss Julie*. But in the opening scene of *Creditors*
he shows it actually taking place on the stage. In an essay on
Ibsen's *Rosmersholm*, which Strindberg wrote after *The Father*,

he refers to Rebecca, whom he regarded as having driven
Rosmer's wife to her death by suggestion, as 'an unconscious
cannibal, who has devoured the dead wife's soul'. He was to
employ this image of the 'suggester' as a cannibal in *Creditors*,
as indeed he already had in *The Father*.

On 16 October 1888 he wrote again to Seligmann asking
him to reconsider his position regarding *Creditors*. 'It is a great
favourite with me, and I read it again and again, continually
discovering new subtleties. Everything is intimate nowadays
. . . [He lists several examples, including works by Zola,
Daudet and the Goncourts.] *Miss Julie* is still a compromise
with romanticism and *coulisses* [scenery flats] . . . but *Creditors*
is modern right through, humane, lovable, all three of its
characters sympathetic, interesting from start to finish.' He
did not receive a reply to this letter, and on 4 November he
informed Seligmann: 'Upon mature consideration I have now
decided not to publish *Creditors* in Swedish, and beg you to
return it.' Accordingly, *Creditors* was first published in Danish
in February 1889, and did not appear in Swedish until a year
later.

That winter Strindberg developed his plans for a
Scandinavian Théâtre Libre in Copenhagen. *Creditors* was to
form one of the first offerings, and astonishingly, except that
no action of Strindberg's is really astonishing, he offered the
part of Tekla to Siri. Even more astonishingly, considering
that the character was so plainly and spitefully based on her,
she accepted it. On 16 November he wrote to his French
translator, David Bergström, in a mixture of incredulity and
jubilation: 'Here's news for you! My wife has read *both* the
plays [*Miss Julie* and *Creditors*], is thrilled with the parts, and
is willing to play them. So there'll be no difficulty about
anything being too "intimate", for who is in a better position
to judge than she?' On 21 November he told Bergström that
his theatre was to open around 6 January with the two plays
in a double bill. '*Miss Julie* entirely in Swedish; *Creditors* in
Danish, acted by Danes. Two performances at the Dagmar
Theatre, and then out on the road!'

Various delays, however, postponed the opening, and when

it had been finally fixed for 2 March *Miss Julie* was banned by
the Danish censor. *Creditors* had therefore to wait until the
following week, 9 March 1889, before receiving its première at
the Dagmar Theatre in Copenhagen, where it shared a triple
bill with *Pariah* and *The Stronger*, both of which Strindberg had
written that January. Tekla was played, not by Siri but by a
young and inexperienced Danish actress named Nathalia
Larsen; Gustav by Hans Riber Hunderup, who had created
the role of the Captain in *The Father* sixteen months before;
and Adolf by Gustav Wied, a young man who was later to
make something of a name for himself as a comic writer.
Wied's performance as the weakling husband was apparently
most unfortunate. The correspondent of *Vort Land* wrote:
'People laughed till the tears sprang to their eyes as the tiny,
slender author writhed like a snake in a monster of an
armchair up there on the stage. There was no question of
hearing his lines; he practically whispered, partly from stage-
fright, partly through lack of voice.' Nathalia Larsen was
obviously too inexperienced for the difficult role of Tekla, and
the play, not surprisingly, created only a moderate
impression. A week later the company crossed the Sound and
repeated their performance in Malmö, where the critic of
Sydsvenska Dagbladet disliked the play and complained of 'the
acting style of these dilettantes, which is very different from
what we are accustomed to seeing and hearing. (Among other
things, we are used to hearing the actor speak louder than the
prompter, and not, as here, vice versa)'.

The following year, *Creditors* was acted in Stockholm in a
matinée double bill by a more experienced cast, and created
considerable interest. *Aftonbladet* found the play 'unreservedly
brilliant', *Dagens Nyheter* wrote 'No one can deny the genius of
this tragedy' and the newly founded *Stockholm-Tidningen* called
it 'a small dramatic masterpiece'. Yet public interest was not
reckoned sufficient to justify more than one further matinée,
whereas a revival of *Master Olof* the same month achieved
fourteen performances. This was to be the pattern:
Strindberg's historical plays, at any rate when they dealt with
Swedish history, were to succeed where his plays with a

modern setting would fail or at best have only a limited success.

Creditors soon came to be appreciated abroad. On 22 January 1893 it was performed at the Residenztheater in Berlin with Rosa Bertens as Tekla, and aroused much admiration; while on 21 June 1894, Aurélien Lugné-Poe produced it, in a somewhat cut version, at his newly-founded Théâtre de L'Oeuvre in Paris, himself taking the part of Adolf. The public received it with 'tumultuous applause'. In 1895 it was played at the Freie Bühne in Munich, in the corner of a room in a private apartment before an audience of fifty people; in 1898 it received a full-scale production in the same city at the new Schauspielhaus; and in 1899 it was staged in Vienna. But it was not until after the turn of the century that it was again performed in Sweden.

Creditors has gradually come to be regarded, both in Scandinavia and elsewhere, as one of Strindberg's most powerful plays. After small-scale productions in London in 1912, 1927 and 1952, it was presented on 3 March 1959 by the Fifty-Nine Theatre Company at the Lyric Opera House, Hammersmith, with Mai Zetterling, a memorable Tekla, Michael Gough and Lyndon Brook acting under the direction of the Finnish director Casper Wrede in one of the most effective performances of a Strindberg play that Britain has seen. T. C. Worsley, in the *Financial Times*, wrote of 'the richness and compression of this superbly taut, tense and terrible little play'; Milton Shulman in the *Evening Standard* observed: 'Strindberg's character delineation and barbed, incisive prose vibrate with a subtle intellectual power that has a fresh contemporary ring to it even after seventy years'; and Sir Gerald Barry, in the BBC Critics Programme, remarked upon 'the enormous and amazing psycho-analytical insight of a man writing before a word of Freud had ever been read'. Of the eight subsequent productions of the play in London (to 1990), the most notable were those at the Open Space Theatre on 22 March 1972, with Brian Cox as Gustav, Gemma Jones as Tekla and Sebastian Graham-Jones as Adolf, directed by Roger Swaine, and at the Almeida Theatre on 19 May 1986, with Ian MacDiarmid as Gustav, Suzanne Bertish as Tekla and Jonathan Kent as Adolf, directed by the cast. On 16 March 1988 this production was shown on Channel 4 television, directed by Geoffrey Sax.

On 26 June 1892 Strindberg recommended *Creditors* to a French admirer, Charles de Casanove, as 'my most mature work', adding: 'You will find the vampire wife charming, conceited, parasitical . . . loving (two men at once!), tender, falsely maternal, in a phrase, woman as I see her!' Tekla is one of Strindberg's subtlest creations: approaching middle-age and fearful of it, her vulgarity concealed by a veneer of gentility, readily responsive to sexual flattery. The precise ages of the three characters are not specified, but in practice it works well if Adolf is up to ten years her junior and Gustav up to twenty years her senior, so that Gustav is old enough to be Adolf's father. Above all, Tekla must be sensual; we need to feel that to her the sexual act is as natural as breathing, nor is she particular with whom it occurs.

Creditors

A Tragi-Comedy

(1888)

CHARACTERS

TEKLA
ADOLF, her husband, a painter
GUSTAV, her former husband, a teacher, travelling under an
    assumed name
TWO LADIES
A PORTER

This translation of *Creditors* was commissioned by the 59 Theatre Company, and was first performed on 3 March 1959 at the Lyric Opera House, Hammersmith. The cast was:

ADOLF	Lyndon Brook
GUSTAV	Michael Gough
TEKLA	Mai Zetterling
TWO LADIES	June Bailey, Helen Montague
A PORTER	Howard Baker

Designed by Malcolm Pride
Directed by Casper Wrede

A drawing room at a seaside resort. In the background, a door leading to a verandah with a view of the landscape. Right, a table with newspapers. A chair stands to the left of the table, and a sofa to the right. In the right-hand wall is a door to another room.

ADOLF *and* GUSTAV *are at the table, right.* ADOLF *is modelling a wax figure on a miniature stand. His two crutches are beside him.* GUSTAV *is smoking a cigar.*

ADOLF: . . . and for all this, I have to thank you, my dear Gustav.

GUSTAV: Oh, nonsense.

ADOLF: No, I mean it. The first few days my wife was away, I just lay on a sofa absolutely helpless, couldn't do anything, I just lay there longing for her to come back. It was as if she'd gone off with my crutches. I couldn't move. Then, when I had slept for a few days, I began to come alive again and collect my thoughts. My brain, which had been in a fever, gradually cooled, my old ideas came back to me, my passion for work, my urge to create, returned, my eye re-discovered its old sureness, its daring. And then you came.

GUSTAV: You were in a miserable state when I met you, I admit, hobbling around on those crutches. But I don't think you should assume that I'm responsible for your recovery. You just needed rest, and a man to talk to.

ADOLF: Yes, I suppose that's true, like everything you say. I used to have a lot of friends, but when I married I didn't think I needed them any more. I was content with the woman of my choice. Then I began to mix in new circles and made new friends. But my wife grew jealous of them. She wanted to have me to herself, and, what was worse, she wanted to have my friends to herself, too. And I was left alone with my jealousy.

GUSTAV: You are prone to that disease, aren't you?

ADOLF: [I was afraid of losing her – and wanted to make sure I wouldn't. Was that so strange?]* Mind you, I was never afraid of her being unfaithful to me –

GUSTAV: Oh no, husbands never fear that.

ADOLF: Yes, isn't that strange? What I was afraid of was that her friends might gain influence over her, and so come indirectly to have power over me. And I couldn't bear that.

GUSTAV: You and your wife didn't always agree, then?

ADOLF: My wife's a very independent woman – why are you smiling?

GUSTAV: Go on. A very independent woman.

ADOLF: – who doesn't want to take anything from me.

GUSTAV: But will take anything from anyone else?

ADOLF [pauses]: Yes. She seems to hate everything I say simply because I say it, not because it's unreasonable. In fact, she often repeats my ideas as though she'd thought of them herself. It's even happened that a friend of mine has repeated something to her which I'd said to him, and she's thought it splendid. Anything's splendid as long as it doesn't come from me.

GUSTAV: In other words, you're not really happy?

ADOLF: No, I'm very happy. I've got the woman I wanted, and I've never wanted anyone else.

GUSTAV: And you've never wanted to be free?

ADOLF: No, I don't think so. Sometimes I've thought I might find a kind of peace if I was free, but every time she goes away I long for her as I long for the use of my legs. It's

* Square brackets indicate suggested cuts made for performance.

funny, but sometimes I feel she doesn't really exist except as a part of me, an intestine which has been taken out and has carried my will and my appetite for life with it. [As though my spirit had passed from me into her.]

GUSTAV: Perhaps you're right. Perhaps she has.

ADOLF: Oh, no, she wouldn't. She's a very independent woman, with lots of ideas of her own. When I first met her, I was nothing. A would-be artist, a child, whom she decided to bring up and educate.

GUSTAV: But later you developed her mind and educated her?

ADOLF: No. She stopped developing. I went on.

GUSTAV: Yes, it's odd the way her writing deteriorated after that first book, or at any rate got no better. But of course she had a rewarding subject. Her first husband, they say. You never met him, did you? He's said to have been an idiot.

ADOLF: No, I never met him. He'd gone abroad for six months. But, judging by the picture she drew of him, he must have been a prize idiot. [*Pause.*] And her picture was a true one, you can be sure of that.

GUSTAV: Mm. Then why do you suppose she married him?

ADOLF: Because she didn't know him. You can't really know a person until you've – er –

GUSTAV: Exactly. Which is why people should not marry until they've – er – ! Well, he was a tyrant, of course.

ADOLF: Of course?

GUSTAV: Aren't all husbands? [*Chancing his arm.*] You, for instance?

ADOLF: I? I let my wife come and go exactly as she pleases.

GUSTAV: What else could you do, lock her up? But, tell me, do you like her being away for the night?

ADOLF: No, I do not!

GUSTAV: You see! [*Changes his tone.*] Between us, it might make you look a bit ridiculous.

ADOLF: Ridiculous? Can a man become ridiculous simply because he shows he trusts his wife?

GUSTAV: Certainly he can. And you are. Utterly ridiculous.

ADOLF [*violently*]: Am I? We'll soon change that.

GUSTAV: Now don't get so excited. You'll have a fit.

ADOLF: But why doesn't it make her look ridiculous if I'm away for the night?

GUSTAV: That's the way things are. And while you sit here working out the whys and wherefores, the damage is done.

ADOLF: What damage?

GUSTAV: However, that first husband of hers was a tyrant, and she married him to make herself independent. A girl can only become independent by acquiring a *chaperon*, the so-called husband.

ADOLF: I see what you mean.

GUSTAV: And you're the *chaperon*.

ADOLF: I?

GUSTAV: Well, you're her husband, aren't you? [ADOLF *is speechless.*] Aren't I right?

ADOLF [*uneasily*]: I don't know. You live with a woman for years, without ever really thinking about your relationship with her, then one day you ask yourself a question about it, and then there's no end to it. Gustav, you are my friend! You are the only real friend I have ever had. These last eight days, since you came to this hotel, you have given me

courage to face life again. Your magnetism has infected me,
you've been like a watchmaker, mending the works inside
my head and winding up the mainspring. You can hear for
yourself how much more clearly I think, how much more
freely I talk. My voice has got back its old resonance – I
think, anyway.

GUSTAV: Yes, why is that?

ADOLF: I don't know, perhaps it becomes a habit to lower
one's voice when one speaks to a woman. Tekla is always
telling me that I shout.

GUSTAV: So you drop your voice to a whisper and creep back
under the doormat?

ADOLF: Don't say that! [*Reflects.*] Perhaps it's even worse –
but don't let's talk about it now. Where was I? Ah, yes.
You came here, and opened my eyes to the secrets of my
art. Mind you, I'd been conscious for some time of a
waning interest in painting, because it didn't afford me an
adequate means of expressing what I wanted to say, and
when you rationalised it for me, when you explained why
painting is not contemporary enough to be a satisfactory
medium for the creative artist today, then it all suddenly
became clear, and I realised I could never work in colour
again.

GUSTAV: Are you quite sure you'll never be able to paint
again? You don't think there's any danger of your having a
relapse?

ADOLF: Absolutely none! I've proved it! When I went to bed
the evening after our conversation, I went through your
line of reasoning point by point, and I was convinced you
were right. But when I woke, after a good night's sleep
which had cleared my head, it suddenly hit me that you
might have been wrong; so I jumped out of bed, picked up
my brushes to start painting – but I couldn't! The illusion
was gone – the canvas was just a daub of colours – it
seemed incredible that anything I'd ever done had ever

been more than a square of canvas smudged with paint.
The veil had fallen from my eyes, and I could no more have
started to paint again than I could have become a child
again.

GUSTAV: You realised that the fundamental yearning of our
age for reality, its craving for the concrete and tangible,
could only find expression through sculpture – wrestling
with the third dimension?

ADOLF [*uncertainly*]: The third dimension – yes.

GUSTAV: So you became a sculptor. Or rather, you were a
sculptor already, but had lost your way and needed a guide
to put you back on the right road again. [Tell me, do you
feel the true creative urge when you work now?

ADOLF: Now I am alive!]

GUSTAV: May I see what you are doing?

ADOLF: A female figure.

GUSTAV: No model! And so full of life!

ADOLF [*dully*]: Yes, but it does resemble someone. It's
strange; she's got into my blood, as I have into hers.

GUSTAV: There's nothing strange about that. You know what
transfusion is?

ADOLF: Blood transfusion? Yes.

GUSTAV: You have bled yourself too much. Looking at this
figure, I understand a thing or two I had only guessed at
before. You have loved her tremendously.

ADOLF: Yes. So much so that I couldn't tell whether she is I
or I am she. When she smiles, I smile. When she cries, I
cry. And, imagine it, when she bore our child, I distinctly
felt the labour pains.

GUSTAV: My dear friend, it hurts me to say this, but you are
already displaying the first symptoms of epilepsy.

ADOLF [*shaken*]: I? How can you say that?

GUSTAV: I've seen the same symptoms in a younger brother I once had who indulged in carnal excess.

ADOLF: How – what were the symptoms?

GUSTAV *demonstrates vividly.* ADOLF *listens attentively, unconsciously imitating him.*

GUSTAV: It was a horrible sight, and if you're not feeling well I shan't torture you with a description of it.

ADOLF [*in agony*]: No, no, go on, go on.

GUSTAV: Well, the poor boy had gone and married an innocent young girl – you know, pretty curls, doe eyes, a baby face, and a mind as pure as an angel's. But none the less, she managed to usurp the male prerogative –

ADOLF: What's that?

GUSTAV: The initiative, of course; and the result was that his angel very nearly wafted him up to Heaven. But first he had to hang upon his cross and feel the nails in his flesh. It was horrifying.

ADOLF [*breathlessly*]: How do you mean?

GUSTAV [*slowly*]: We'd be sitting, he and I – and after a while, his face would go as white as chalk. His arms and legs went stiff, and his thumbs twisted round inside his hands, like this. [*Makes a gesture, which* ADOLF *imitates.*] Then his eyes became bloodshot, and he began to chew like this. [*Chews.* ADOLF *copies him.*] The saliva rattled in his throat, his chest contracted as though it was being crushed in a vice, the pupils of his eyes flickered like gas-jets, his tongue whipped the saliva into a froth, and he sank – slowly – back – and – down – in his chair, as though he was drowning. Then –

ADOLF [*whispers*]: Stop.

GUSTAV: Aren't you feeling well?

ADOLF: No.

GUSTAV [*gets up and fetches a glass of water*]: Drink this, and
we'll talk about something else.

ADOLF [*feebly*]: Thank you. But – go on.

GUSTAV: Oh, yes. Well, when he came to he couldn't
remember anything that had happened. He'd been quite
unconscious. Has that happened to you?

ADOLF: Yes, I've had fainting fits once or twice, but the
doctor says it's due to anaemia.

GUSTAV: That's the way it begins, but, believe me, it'll
develop into epilepsy if you don't take care of yourself.

ADOLF: What shall I do?

GUSTAV: Well, to begin with you must abstain entirely from
intercourse.

ADOLF: How long for?

GUSTAV: Six months, at least.

ADOLF: I can't. It'd upset our marriage.

GUSTAV: Goodbye to you, then.

ADOLF [*drapes a cloth over the wax figure*]: I can't.

GUSTAV: You can't save your life? But, tell me, since you've
already taken me so deeply into your confidence, is there
nothing else, [no little secret that torments you? It's rare to
find only one cause of discord – life is so varied and full of
occasions for conflict. Have you] no skeleton you're hiding
away? [You said just now that you had a child whom you –
gave away. Why didn't you keep it?

ADOLF: My wife wanted it that way.

GUSTAV: Why? You can tell me.

ADOLF: At the age of three it began to look like him. Her
former husband.

GUSTAV: Ah!!] Have you seen this former husband?

ADOLF: No, never. [I caught a glimpse of a bad portrait of him once, but I couldn't see any likeness.

GUSTAV: Well, you can never trust portraits. Anyway, he might have become quite a different person since. But, tell me, didn't this arouse your suspicions at all?

ADOLF: Not at all. The child was born a year after our marriage, and anyway her husband was abroad when I met Tekla – here, in this very house, as a matter of fact. That's why we come here every summer.]

GUSTAV: [Well then, you've no possible ground for suspicion. And why should you have any? It often happens when a widow remarries that her new child resembles the dead husband. Tiresome business – that's why they used to burn widows in India, as you know.] But have you never been jealous of him? Of his memory? Wouldn't it sicken you if you met him when you were out for a walk, and with his eyes on your Tekla he said 'we' instead of 'I'? 'We'!

ADOLF: I won't deny that idea has haunted me.

GUSTAV: There you are! And you'll never be rid of it. Don't you realise there are false notes in life which can never be tuned? The only thing to do is to stop your ears with wax and work. Work, grow old, pile as many new impressions as you can into the cupboard to keep the skeleton from rattling.

ADOLF: Sorry to interrupt you, but it's extraordinary how much you resemble Tekla sometimes when you talk. You've a habit of half-closing your left eye as though you were squinting down a rifle. And your eyes – almost seem to hypnotise me, the way hers sometimes do.

GUSTAV: In-deed?

ADOLF: There! You said: 'In-deed?' in just the same casual way that she does.

GUSTAV: Perhaps we're distantly related – since all human beings are related. Still, it is curious, and it'll be most interesting to meet your wife and see these things for myself.

ADOLF: Mind you, she never borrows any of my expressions. Indeed, she seems to avoid using phrases which I use. And I've never seen her imitate my mannerisms, the way married people usually do.

GUSTAV: This woman has never loved you.

ADOLF: What!

GUSTAV: Forgive me, but – for a woman loving means taking, taking, and if she doesn't take anything from a man it means she doesn't love him. She has never loved you.

ADOLF: Do you think it's impossible for her to love more than once?

GUSTAV: Yes. One only gets fooled once; after that, one goes round with one's eyes open. You've never been deceived – beware of those who have. They're dangerous.

ADOLF: Your words are like knives – I can feel them cutting something to pieces inside me – but I can't prevent it, and it's good, because I know these are boils that are being lanced. She has never loved me! Why did she take me, then?

GUSTAV: Tell me first how she came to take you. [And whether it was you who took her or she who took you.]

ADOLF: God knows if I can do that. [Or how it came about. It didn't happen in a day.]

GUSTAV: Shall I try to guess how it happened?

ADOLF: You can't!

GUSTAV: Oh, from what you've told me about yourself and your wife, I think I can work it out. [Listen, and I'll tell you.] [*Nonchalantly, almost jokingly.*] Her husband is away on

a study trip, and she is alone. First, she is aware of the
pleasure of being free; then of a feeling of emptiness – she
must have felt a bit empty after living alone for a fortnight.
Then he turns up, and gradually the emptiness is filled. She
begins to compare the two men, and the memory of her
husband begins to pale – well, he's a long way away – the
square of the distance, etcetera. But when they find their
passions awakening, they become uneasy, their consciences
prick them, they remember him. They look for some kind of
protection, cover their shame with fig-leaves, and play at
being brother and sister – and the more their bodies want
each other, the more desperately they try to persuade
themselves that their relationship is spiritual.

ADOLF: Brother and sister? How do you know that?

GUSTAV: I guessed. Children play mummy and daddy, but
when they're grown up they play brother and sister. To
hide what must be hidden. They take a vow of chastity,
and begin a little game of hide-and-seek, until, one day,
their hands touch in a dark corner where they are sure no
one can see them. [*With assumed severity.*] But in their hearts
they know that there is someone who can see them through
the darkness, and they become frightened, and then, once
they are frightened, the absent one begins to haunt them –
he looms larger, is transformed, and becomes a nightmare
which disturbs their blissful slumbers, a creditor knocking
on the door. They see his black hand between theirs as they
eat at table, they hear his harsh breathing in the stillness of
the night, which no sound should disturb but the thumping
of their pulses. He cannot stop them from having each
other, but he can disturb their happiness. And then they
sense his invisible power, they try, vainly, to flee from the
memory which dogs them, from the debt they have left
unpaid, [from the reproach of public opinion] and because
they lack the strength to carry the burden of their guilt, a
scapegoat must be found and sacrificed. They were
freethinkers, but dared not go to him and tell him to his

face: 'We love each other!' Well, they were cowards, and so they had to lay his ghost. Am I right?

ADOLF: Yes. But you forget that she educated me and gave me new ideas —

GUSTAV: No, I hadn't forgotten. But, tell me, why didn't she succeed in educating the other fellow too, and turn him into a freethinker?

ADOLF: Oh, he was an idiot.

GUSTAV: True, he was an idiot. But that's a very vague word, and in her novel the main proof of his idiocy seems to have been that he didn't understand her. Forgive me, but is your wife such a profound person? I have found no evidence of it in her writing.

ADOLF: Neither have I. But I confess that I, too, have some difficulty in understanding her. Our minds don't work the same way. Every time I try to understand her, something seems to break inside my head.

GUSTAV: Perhaps you're an idiot, too.

ADOLF: No, I don't think so. I almost invariably think she's wrong. For example, read this letter that I received from her today. [*Takes a letter from his pocket-book.*]

GUSTAV [*glances through it*]: Hm. This handwriting seems familiar.

ADOLF: Almost like a man's, isn't it?

GUSTAV: Yes, I know at least one man whose handwriting it resembles. She calls you 'brother'. Do you still act that little comedy? The fig-leaf stays in position, if somewhat withered.

ADOLF: I like to show respect for her.

GUSTAV: I see, it's to make you respect her that she calls herself 'sister'?

ADOLF: I want to respect her more than myself. [I want her to be my better self.

GUSTAV: Be that yourself! It's more uncomfortable, but do you want to be subservient to your wife?

ADOLF: Yes, I do.] I like being a little worse than she is. For example, I've taught her to swim, and now I like to hear her boast that she's a stronger and bolder swimmer than I am. At first I pretend to be slow and timid to encourage her, and then one fine day I found I was in fact slower and more timid than she. It was as if she'd really taken my courage from me.

GUSTAV: Have you taught her anything else?

ADOLF: Yes – between ourselves. I've taught her to spell. She couldn't before. But when she took over the household correspondence, I stopped writing, and – would you believe it? – I'm so out of practice that I now sometimes make mistakes. But do you think she remembers it was I who taught her to spell in the first place? Oh, no. I'm the idiot now.

GUSTAV: So you're the idiot already?

ADOLF: Only jokingly, of course.

GUSTAV: Of course! But this is cannibalism! [You know what cannibalism is? Savages eat their enemies to gain possession of their most enviable qualities.] The woman has eaten your soul, your courage, your learning –

ADOLF: And my faith in myself! It was I who encouraged her to write her first book –

GUSTAV [pulls a face]: Really?

ADOLF: I praised her, even when I thought it was rather cheap. It was I who introduced her into literary circles, where she was able to feed on the best minds. It was I who, through my personal intervention, protected her from criticism. It was I who fanned her belief in herself and kept

it alive, fanned so hard that I had no energy left for my
own work. I gave and gave and gave, till I had nothing left
for myself. Do you know, when my success as a painter
seemed to be overshadowing her and her reputation, I tried
to sustain her belief in herself by belittling myself and my
work. I talked so much about the unimportance of painting
as an art, and found so many arguments to support my
thesis, that in the end I found I believed it myself. So it was
only a house of cards that you blew down.

GUSTAV: Forgive me for reminding you of this, but when we
started this conversation you said she never took anything
from you.

ADOLF: Not now. There isn't anything left to take.

GUSTAV: The snake is full. Now she vomits up her victim.

ADOLF: Perhaps she took more than I realise. [Things I
wasn't aware of.]

GUSTAV: You can be sure she did. And she took without your
noticing it. That's called stealing.

ADOLF: Perhaps she never educated me after all.

GUSTAV: No. You educated her. But she was clever enough
to make you think that it was the other way round. How
did she educate you, if I may ask?

ADOLF: Well, first of all – er –

GUSTAV: Yes?

ADOLF: Well, I –

GUSTAV: Never mind about yourself. What did she do?

ADOLF: I don't know.

GUSTAV: You see!

ADOLF: Anyway, she'd destroyed my faith, too, and I began
to go further and further downhill until you came and gave
me a new belief.

GUSTAV [*smiles*]: In sculpture?

ADOLF [*uncertainly*]: Yes.

GUSTAV: And you believe in it? That *passé*, abstract survival from man's infancy? You really believe that you can [work with pure form – the third dimension – that you can] satisfy the craving of our age for reality – that you can create illusion without the aid of colour? You really believe that?

ADOLF [*crushed*]: No.

GUSTAV: Neither do I.

ADOLF: Why did you say you did, then?

GUSTAV: I felt sorry for you.

ADOLF: Yes. I am to be pitied. For now I am bankrupt. I haven't even got her.

GUSTAV: What do you need her for?

ADOLF: What I needed God for, before I became an atheist. Something to worship –

GUSTAV: Bury your need to worship, and let some healthier plant grow on its grave. A little honest contempt, for example –

ADOLF: I can't live without something to worship –

[GUSTAV: Slave!

ADOLF: Without a woman to worship.]

GUSTAV: Oh, for Christ's sake, go back to your God, then, if you must have something to abase yourself before. [An atheist who worships women! A freethinker who can't think freely!] Don't you realise what this profound, mystical, sphinx-like quality in your wife really is? It's just stupidity. Look at this! She doesn't know when to use 'ph' and when to use 'f'. Skirts, that's all. Dress her in trousers, draw a charcoal moustache under her nose, sit down and listen to

her coldly and soberly, then you'll hear the difference. She's
just a phonograph which plays back your words and other
people's with most of the quality gone. Have you ever seen
a naked woman? Yes, of course. A half-developed man, a
child stunted in mid-growth, a youth with udders on his
chest, a case of chronic anaemia who has regular
haemhorrages thirteen times a year. What can become of
that?

ADOLF: Assuming that everything you say is right, why do I
still feel that she and I are one?

GUSTAV: A hallucination – the fascination of a skirt. Or –
perhaps you have in fact become alike. [There has been a
levelling. Her capillary power has sucked her up to your
level.] [*Takes out his watch.*] We have been talking for six
hours and your wife will be here soon. Shall we stop now so
that you can get some rest?

ADOLF: No, don't leave me. I daren't be alone.

GUSTAV: It's only for a moment, then your wife'll be here.

ADOLF: Yes, she'll be here. It's strange – I long for her, but
I'm afraid of her; [she caresses me, she's tender, but] her
kisses stifle me, drain something from me, anaesthetise me.
I feel like the child in a circus whom the clown pinches
backstage so that it'll look rosy-cheeked before the public.

GUSTAV: My friend, your condition alarms me. Without
being a doctor, I can tell you that you are a dying man.
One only has to look at your latest paintings to know that.

ADOLF: Really? How?

GUSTAV: Your colour is so watery and pale and thin that the
canvas stares through it like a yellow corpse. I seem to see
your sunken, putty-coloured cheeks –

ADOLF: Stop, stop.

GUSTAV: But it's not just my personal opinion. Haven't you
read today's paper?

ADOLF [*starts up*]: No.

GUSTAV: Here it is, on the table.

ADOLF [*gropes towards the paper, but lacks the courage to take hold of it*]: Is there something about it here?

GUSTAV: Read it. Or would you like me to read it to you?

ADOLF: No.

GUSTAV: I'll go if you'd rather.

ADOLF: No, no, no! I don't know – I think I'm beginning to hate you – and yet I can't let you go. You haul me up out of the ice-cold water, but as soon as I'm out you hit me on the head and push me under again. As long as I kept my secrets to myself, I still had some entrails left inside me, but now I'm empty. There's a painting by one of the Italian masters which shows a torture scene. They are winding the entrails out of a saint on a winch. The martyr lies there and sees himself growing thinner and thinner while the roll on the winch grows thicker and thicker. It seems to me that you have been growing all the while you have been digging into me so that when you go you'll take all my entrails with you and leave only a shell behind.

GUSTAV: What an imagination you've got! Still, your wife will be bringing home your heart soon.

ADOLF: No. Not now. You've burned her. You've laid everything in ashes. My art, my love, my hope, my faith.

GUSTAV: That had been done already.

ADOLF: At least there was something that could have been salvaged. Now it's too late. Murderer!

GUSTAV: We've only burned the rubbish. Now we can sow in the ashes.

ADOLF: I hate you. Curse you!

GUSTAV: That's a good sign. You've still some spirit left. Now I shall haul you up again. Adolf! Will you obey me?

ADOLF: Do what you want with me. I'll obey.

GUSTAV [*gets up*]: Look at me.

ADOLF [*looks at him*]: Now you're looking at me with those other eyes – that seem to attract me.

[GUSTAV: Now listen carefully.

ADOLF: Yes, but talk about yourself. Don't talk about me any more. I'm like an open wound, I can't bear to be touched.]

GUSTAV: [There's nothing to say about me. I'm a teacher of dead languages and a widower. That's all.] Take my hand.

ADOLF: How terribly powerful you are! It's like gripping an electrical machine.

GUSTAV: And I was once as weak as you. Get up!

ADOLF [*gets up, and falls around* GUSTAV's *neck*]: I am like a legless child, and my brain lies open.

GUSTAV: Walk across the floor.

ADOLF: I can't.

GUSTAV: Walk across the floor, or I'll hit you.

ADOLF [*straightens up*]: What did you say?

GUSTAV: I shall hit you, I said.

ADOLF [*takes a jump backwards, furious*]: You?

GUSTAV: There, you see! The blood went to your head, and your self-esteem was aroused. Now I shall pass some electricity into you. Where is your wife?

ADOLF: Where is she?

GUSTAV: Yes.

ADOLF: She is – at – a meeting.

GUSTAV: Are you sure?

ADOLF: Quite sure.

GUSTAV: What kind of a meeting?

ADOLF: To discuss a children's home.

GUSTAV: Did you part friends?

ADOLF [*hesitates*]: Not friends.

GUSTAV: Enemies, then. What did you say to annoy her?

ADOLF: I'm frightened of you. How can you know this?

GUSTAV: It's simple. I have three known factors, and from them I work out the unknown. What did you say to her?

ADOLF: I said – I only said three words, but they were dreadful and I regret them.

GUSTAV: Don't regret. What were they?

ADOLF: I said: 'You old flirt!'

GUSTAV: And then?

ADOLF: That was all.

GUSTAV: No. You said something else, but you've forgotten it, perhaps because you dare not remember it. You've hidden it away in a secret drawer. Now you must open it.

ADOLF: I don't remember!

GUSTAV: But I know what it was. You said: 'You ought to be ashamed of yourself. You're too old to get another lover.'

ADOLF: Did I say that? I must have said it. But how do you know?

GUSTAV: I heard her telling the story on the steamer while I was on my way here.

ADOLF: To whom?

GUSTAV: To four young men she had with her. She has a
weakness for clean young men already –

ADOLF: Oh, that doesn't mean anything.

GUSTAV: Like playing brother and sister when in fact you're
playing mummy and daddy.

ADOLF: You've seen her, then?

GUSTAV: Yes, I have. But you've never seen her as she is
when you're not there. That, my dear friend, is why a man
can never know his wife. Have you a photograph of her?

ADOLF *takes a photograph out of his pocket-book, curious.*

GUSTAV: Were you there when this was taken?

ADOLF: No.

GUSTAV: Look at it. Is it like the picture you painted of her?
No. The features are the same, but the expression is quite
different. But you can't see that, because you project your
own image of her in front of it. Look at this now, look at it
as a painter, forget the original. What does it show? I can
see nothing but an affected coquette, inviting me to flirt
with her. Can't you see that cynical expression round her
mouth, which she always hides from you? Can't you see
that her eyes are looking for a man, someone else, not you?
Can't you see that her neckline is too low, that she's
prinked up her hair, that her sleeve has ridden up? Can't
you see it all?

ADOLF: Yes, I can see it now.

GUSTAV: Beware, my friend.

ADOLF: Of what?

GUSTAV: Of her revenge. Remember you wounded her where
it hurts most, when you told her she can no longer attract
another lover. If you had told her that her writing was
rubbish, she would simply have laughed at your bad taste,

but now – believe me, if she has not avenged herself on you already, it won't be her fault.

ADOLF: I must know the truth.

GUSTAV: Find out.

ADOLF: Find out?

GUSTAV: I'll help you if you like. [*Steamer hoots in distance.*] There's the steamer. She'll be here soon.

ADOLF: I must go down to meet her.

GUSTAV: No. You must stay here. Be off-hand with her. If her conscience is clear, she'll give you a dressing-down, if she's guilty she'll cuddle up to you and kiss you.

[ADOLF: Are you absolutely sure about that?

GUSTAV: Not absolutely. The hare sometimes turns on its track and throws a false scent, but I'll ferret out the truth.] [*Points to the door behind the chair.*] I shall take up my post over there in my room, and keep a watch, while you act in here. Then, when the performance is over, we will change parts; I shall come in and charm the snake while you go into my room through the other door. Then we will meet and compare notes. But stick to your guns! If you start to falter, I shall bang twice on the floor with a chair.

ADOLF: All right, but don't go away. I must be sure you're in the next room.

GUSTAV: Don't worry, I shall be there. [But don't be afraid later, when you see me at work dissecting a human soul and laying out the bits and pieces here on the table. It sounds nasty if you're a beginner, but once you've seen it you won't regret the experience.] Remember one thing. Not a word about your having met me, or anyone, while she's been away. Not a word. [I'll ferret out her weakness myself.] Ssh, she's here already, up in her room. Singing to herself – that means she's furious. Shoulders back, now, and sit there; then she'll have to sit here, and I can watch you both.

[ADOLF: We've an hour left before dinner. There aren't any other guests, or we'd have heard the bell, so that means we'll be alone, I'm afraid.

GUSTAV: Are you feeling faint?

ADOLF: I don't feel anything. Yes, I feel afraid of what's coming. But I can't stop it. The stone's begun to roll downhill, but it wasn't the last raindrop that started it off, nor the first one, but the sum of them all put together.

GUSTAV: Let it roll. You'll have no peace till it's started. *Au revoir!*]

GUSTAV *goes.* ADOLF *nods goodbye; stands looking at the photograph, tears it up, and throws the bits under the table. Then he sits down in his chair, fingers his cravat nervously, runs his hand through his hair, plays with his coat lapel, etc.* TEKLA *enters, walks straight towards him, and kisses him – friendly, open, gay and charming.*

TEKLA: Good afternoon, Little Brother. How are you today?

ADOLF [*half conquered, tries to resist her, says jokingly*]: What have you been up, kissing me like that?

TEKLA: All right, I'll tell you. I've been wickedly extravagant.

ADOLF: Have you been enjoying yourself?

TEKLA: Very much! Not at that ghastly meeting, though. That was what the French call *merde.* But, tell me, what has Little Brother been doing while Squirrel was away? [*Looks around the room as though she was looking for someone or trying to sniff out something.*]

ADOLF: Just sitting here, being bored.

TEKLA: No one to keep you company?

ADOLF: No, all alone.

TEKLA [*looks at him, then sits on the sofa*]: Who's been sitting here, then?

ADOLF: There? Nobody.

TEKLA: That's very strange. The sofa's still warm, and this cushion's rumpled. Have you had a woman here?

ADOLF: I? You don't mean it.

TEKLA: You're blushing! I think Little Brother's been telling fibs. Come over here. Tell Squirrel what you have on your conscience. [*Pulls him over to her. He sinks down with his head on her knees.*]

ADOLF [*smiles*]: You're a little devil. Do you know that?

TEKLA: No, I'm terribly ignorant about myself.

ADOLF: You never think about yourself.

TEKLA [*sniffs and glances around*]: I only think of myself – I'm a dreadful egotist. But why so philosophical?

ADOLF: Put your hand on my forehead.

TEKLA [*flippantly*]: Is he tied up in knots? Shall I make it better: [*Kisses his forehead.*] There! Is that better?

ADOLF: Now it's better.

Pause.

TEKLA: Well, what have you been amusing yourself with? Have you been painting something?

ADOLF: No, I've given up painting.

TEKLA: What? You've given up painting?

ADOLF: Yes. Don't scold me. I can't help it, but I just cannot paint any more.

TEKLA: What are you going to do now?

ADOLF: I'm going to be a sculptor.

TEKLA: More new ideas!

ADOLF: Yes, now don't make a scene. Look at that figure.

TEKLA [*takes the cloth off the wax figure*]: Well, look at this! Who's it meant to be?

ADOLF: Guess!

TEKLA [*softly*]: Is it little Squirrel? Shame on you!

ADOLF: Don't you think it's a good likeness?

TEKLA: How should I know, when it hasn't got any face?

ADOLF: Yes, but – there's so much else that's beautiful –

TEKLA [*slaps his cheek provokingly*]: Be quiet, now, or I'll kiss you.

ADOLF [*protecting himself*]: Take care! Someone might come.

TEKLA: What do I care? Can't I kiss my own husband? I've got my legal rights.

ADOLF: Yes but, you know, the people here don't believe we're really married, because we kiss so much. The fact that we quarrel now and then doesn't convince them because lovers do that too.

TEKLA: Why do we need to quarrel? Why can't you always be nice like you are now? Tell me. Don't you want to be nice? Don't you want us to be happy?

ADOLF: Of course I do, but –

TEKLA: What's wrong now? Who's given you the idea that you mustn't paint any more?

ADOLF: You always suspect there's someone else behind everything I think. You're jealous.

TEKLA: Yes, I am. I'm afraid someone might take you away from me.

ADOLF: *You're* afraid? You know I could never love any woman but you. Without you I couldn't live.

TEKLA: It's not women I'm afraid of. No, it's the friends who put ideas into your head.

ADOLF [*probing*]: You are afraid, then. What are you afraid of?

TEKLA [*gets up*]: There has been someone here! Who was it?

ADOLF: Can't you bear me looking at you?

TEKLA: Not like that. That's not the way you usually look at me.

ADOLF: How am I looking at you now?

TEKLA: Lowering your eyelid, and squinting –

ADOLF: Yes! I want to see what you look like behind that pretty face!

TEKLA: Well, stare away! I've got nothing to hide! But – you're talking differently, too – you're using expressions – [*Probing.*] – you're philosophising. [*Goes threateningly towards him.*] Who has been here?

ADOLF: Only my doctor.

TEKLA: Your doctor? What doctor?

ADOLF: The doctor from Strömstad.

TEKLA: What's his name?

ADOLF: Svensson.

TEKLA: What did he say?

ADOLF: He said – yes – he said among other things that I was in danger of becoming an epileptic –

TEKLA: Among other things? What other things?

ADOLF: Something very distressing.

TEKLA: What? Tell me.

ADOLF: He forbade us to live like married people for a while.

TEKLA: I knew it. They want to part us. I've noticed it for some time.

ADOLF: You couldn't have noticed it, because it isn't true.

TEKLA: Couldn't I?

ADOLF: How could you notice something which isn't there unless fear had so over-excited your imagination as to make you see things which don't exist? What are you afraid of? That I might see you through someone else's eyes for what you really are, instead of what I've always thought you were?

TEKLA: Kindly control your imagination, Adolf. That is what makes men beasts.

ADOLF: Where did you learn that? From the clean young men on the boat?

TEKLA [*without losing her composure*]: Yes; there are things to be learned from young people, too.

ADOLF: I believe you're already beginning to fall in love with youth.

TEKLA: I always have done; that is why I have loved you. Do you object?

ADOLF: No. But I'd prefer to feel I was the only one.

TEKLA [*banteringly*]: My heart is so big, Little Brother, that there is room in it for many others besides you.

ADOLF: But Little Brother does not want to have any other little brothers.

TEKLA: Come to Squirrel now and have your hair pulled for being jealous. No, that's not the word. I think you're envious! Come!

GUSTAV *strikes twice with his chair from the next room.*

ADOLF: No, I don't want to play. I want to talk seriously.

TEKLA [*banteringly*]: Dear God, he wants to talk seriously!
You have become horribly serious, haven't you? [*Takes his
head and kisses him.*] Laugh a little now. That's better.

ADOLF [*smiles unwilling*]: Damn you, I really believe you're a
witch.

TEKLA: Indeed I am, so don't you start being quarrelsome,
or I shall witch away your life.

ADOLF [*gets up*]: Tekla! Sit over there and give me your
profile, so that I can put the face on your figure.

TEKLA: Like this? [*Turns her profile towards him.*]

ADOLF [*stares at her, pretends to start modelling*]: Don't think
about me, now, think about someone else.

TEKLA: I shall think about my latest conquest.

ADOLF: The clean young man?

TEKLA: Yes, him. He had such a tiny little moustache, and
cheeks like a juicy peach, so soft and pink I wanted to bite
them.

ADOLF [*his expression darkens*]: Keep that expression round
your mouth.

TEKLA: What expression?

ADOLF: That cynical, wanton expression – I've never noticed
it before.

TEKLA [*grimaces*]: Like this?

ADOLF: Just like that. [*Gets up.*] Do you know how Bret
Harte describes an adulterous wife?

TEKLA [*smiles*]: No, I have never read Bret – er –

ADOLF: As a pale creature who cannot blush.

TEKLA: Oh? But surely when she meets her lover she
blushes, even though her husband and Mr Bret may not be
there to see her do it?

ADOLF: You know that?

TEKLA [*in the same tone of voice*]: Yes. Since her husband
cannot bring the blood to her head, he never sees this
charming spectacle.

ADOLF [*furious*]: Tekla!

TEKLA: Little silly!

ADOLF: Tekla!

TEKLA: Say 'Squirrel' and I shall blush prettily for you.
Would you like me to? Shall I?

ADOLF [*disarmed*]: I'm so angry with you, you little monster,
I've a good mind to bite you.

TEKLA [*playfully*]: Come and bite me, then. Come. [*Stretches
out her arms towards him.*]

ADOLF [*puts his arms round her neck and kisses her*]: Yes, I'll bite
you to death.

TEKLA [*jokingly*]: Take care. Someone might come.

ADOLF: What do I care? I don't care about anything in the
world as long as I have you.

TEKLA: And – when you no longer have me?

ADOLF: Then I shall die.

TEKLA: But you don't have to worry about that, because I'm
so old that no one else wants me.

ADOLF: Tekla, you haven't forgotten what I said that
morning. I take it back.

TEKLA: Can you explain to me why you are so jealous and at
the same time so sure of yourself?

ADOLF: No, I can't explain anything. Perhaps the knowledge that someone else once owned you still rankles inside me. Sometimes I feel our love is a fiction, a defence pact, a passion elevated into an affair of honour, and I dread nothing so much as that he should know I was unhappy. Ah! I have never seen him, but the mere thought that somewhere a man is waiting for our marriage to break up, a man who curses me every day and will howl with joy when he hears I have failed, the mere thought of it drives me mad, drives me into your arms [– fascinates me, paralyses me].

TEKLA: Do you think I would ever allow him that pleasure? Do you think I want to prove him a true prophet?

ADOLF: No, I can't believe you would.

TEKLA: Keep calm, then.

ADOLF: I can't. Your incessant flirting drives me crazy. Why do you have to play this game?

TEKLA: It isn't a game. I want to be liked. That's all.

ADOLF: Yes, but only by men.

TEKLA: Of course. Don't you know that a woman is never liked by other women?

ADOLF: Have you heard from – him – lately?

TEKLA: Not for six months.

ADOLF: Do you never think about him?

TEKLA: No. [We've had no communication with each other since the child died.]

ADOLF: And you haven't seen him?

TEKLA: No. I have heard he lives somewhere here on the west coast. But what makes you worry your head about him?

ADOLF: I don't know. These last few days, when I've been

alone, I've sometimes thought how he must have felt when he suddenly found himself alone.

TEKLA: I believe your conscience is beginning to prick you.

ADOLF: Yes.

TEKLA: You feel like a thief, don't you?

ADOLF: Almost.

TEKLA: Charming! One steals a woman as one steals a child or a chicken. So you regard me as his private property. Thank you.

ADOLF: No, I regard you as his wife. That's much more than a property. That can never be replaced.

TEKLA: Don't be silly. As soon as you hear that he has remarried, these stupid ideas will vanish. You have replaced him for me.

ADOLF: Have I? Did you ever love him?

TEKLA: Certainly I did.

ADOLF: But then – ?

TEKLA: I grew tired of him.

ADOLF: What if you should tire of me, too?

TEKLA: I won't.

ADOLF: Suppose another man should turn up with just those qualities which you now look for in a man? Just suppose he did. You would leave me.

TEKLA: No.

ADOLF: If you were so attracted to him that you couldn't give him up? You'd give me up, it stands to reason.

TEKLA: No, not necessarily.

ADOLF: You couldn't love two men at the same time?

TEKLA: Yes. Why not?

ADOLF: I can't see that.

TEKLA: It's possible, even if you can't see it. All people weren't created alike.

ADOLF: Now I am beginning to understand.

TEKLA: In-deed?

ADOLF: Indeed.

Pause. ADOLF *is trying hard to remember something that eludes him.*

ADOLF: Tekla! Do you know I am beginning to find your outspokenness rather painful?

TEKLA: You always used to regard it as my supreme virtue. You taught it to me.

ADOLF: Yes, but now it seems to me you're using it as a mask to hide behind.

TEKLA: It's my new strategy, you see.

ADOLF: I'm beginning to dislike this place. Let's go home tonight.

TEKLA: What a silly idea! I've only just come, and I don't want to go back again.

ADOLF: No, but I want to.

TEKLA: What do I care what you want? Go.

ADOLF: I order you to follow me by the next boat.

TEKLA: You order me? What kind of talk is that?

ADOLF: Do you realise that you are my wife?

TEKLA: Do you realise that you are my husband?

ADOLF: Yes, and there's a difference between the two.

TEKLA: So that's the tone you're taking. You've never loved me.

ADOLF: Haven't I?

TEKLA: No. Loving means giving.

ADOLF: Loving means giving if one is a man. If one is a woman, it means taking. And I've always been the one who has given, given, given!

TEKLA: What have you given?

ADOLF: Everything!

TEKLA: A great deal that was. Well, suppose you have. I have accepted, haven't I? Are you now going to show me the bill for all the presents you have given me? And if I have accepted, that only goes to prove that I have loved you. A woman only takes presents from her lover.

ADOLF: Lover, yes! You never said a truer word. I have been your lover, but never your husband.

TEKLA: How much more pleasant for you, not having to be my *chaperon*. But if you're not happy with your position, you'll have to go, for a husband is the last thing I want.

ADOLF: Yes, I've noticed that. These last months, when I saw you itching to sneak away like a thief, to find your own circle of friends where you could shine in my feathers, glitter with my jewels, I wanted to remind you of the debt you owed me. And then I was transformed into the unpleasant creditor, whom one doesn't want to have about the place; then you wanted to cancel the debt you owed me, and stopped drawing from my account and turned to other lenders. Then I became your husband, in spite of myself, and then you began to hate me. Well, now I shall be your husband whether you like it or not, since I may not be your lover.

TEKLA [*playfully*]: Don't talk such nonsense, you little idiot.

ADOLF: Look, it's dangerous to go round thinking everyone is an idiot except yourself.

TEKLA: Doesn't everyone think that?

ADOLF: And I'm beginning to suspect that he – your first husband – may not have been such an idiot after all.

TEKLA: Oh, God, I believe you're beginning to feel sorry for him.

ADOLF: Yes, almost.

TEKLA: Well, well, Perhaps you'd like to meet him, and pour out your heart to him? What a charming picture! But I too am beginning to feel a certain nostalgia for him. I'm getting tired of being a nanny. At least he was a man! Though he had the disadvantage of being my husband.

ADOLF: Oh, indeed? But you mustn't talk so loud, people can hear us.

TEKLA: What does that matter? They know we're married.

ADOLF: I see, you're beginning to go for strong men too, as well as clean young men.

TEKLA: I don't limit myself to one type. My heart is open to everyone, big and small, beautiful and ugly, young and old. I love the whole world.

ADOLF: Do you know what that means?

TEKLA: No, I don't know anything. I only *feel*.

ADOLF: It means age is beginning to tell.

TEKLA: Are you on to that again? You be careful.

ADOLF: You be careful, too.

TEKLA: Of what?

ADOLF [*holds up the paper-knife*]: This!

TEKLA [*teasingly*]: Little Brother mustn't play with such dangerous toys.

ADOLF: I'm not playing any longer.

TEKLA: Oh, I see, you're in earnest. Then I shall show you that you are wrong. But *you* will never see it, or know it, but everyone else will know it except you. But you'll suspect, you'll wonder, and you'll never have another peaceful minute. You'll feel you're looking ridiculous, you're being cuckolded, but you'll never have proof; because husbands never do have proof. You'll learn what it's like.

ADOLF: You hate me?

TEKLA: No, I don't hate you. I don't think I shall ever be able to hate you. But that's probably because you're a child.

ADOLF: Now, yes. But do you remember that time when the world was against us? You lay there screaming like a baby; then you sat on my knee, and I had to kiss you and lull you to sleep. In those days, *I* was your nurse. I had to see to it that you remembered to brush your hair before you went out, I had to take your boots to be mended, I had to see that there was food in the house. I had to sit by your side hour after hour, holding your hand, because you were afraid, afraid of the whole world, because you hadn't a single friend left, and the scandal had crushed you. I had to force courage into you until my mouth was dry and my head splitting. I had to make myself imagine that I was strong, make myself believe in the future, until I finally managed to bring you back to life as you lay there dead. Then you admired me; then *I* was the man, not the athlete you had left, I was the strong-willed magnetiser who massaged your slack muscles with my own nervous energy, charged your empty brain with new electricity. I put you back on your feet again, found you friends, built a little court for you for people who, for the sake of my friendship, were fooled into admiring you. I gave you control of me

and my house. I painted you in my best pictures, [in rose
and azure on a gold background,] and there wasn't an
exhibition where you didn't hold pride of place.
[Sometimes you were St Cecilia, sometimes Mary Stuart,
sometimes Joan of Arc.] I awoke people's interest in you, I
compelled the public to look at you through my infatuated
eyes, I forced your personality on them, pushed you down
their throats, till you had gained their sympathy and could
go ahead on your own. By then I was exhausted and I
collapsed. The effort of lifting you into the limelight had
overtaxed my strength, and I became ill. My illness
embarrassed you, for now at last life was beginning to smile
for you. I began to feel that you were driven by a secret
longing to be rid of your creditor, the only witness of your
degradation. Your love becomes like that of an elder sister,
and I have to accept the role of Little Brother. Your
tenderness remains, it even grows, but it is lined with a
measure of pity, and that's largely made up of disdain,
increasing to contempt as my sun sinks and yours rises. But
somehow or other your inspiration seems to have dried up
too, now that I can no longer replenish it, or rather now
that you want to show that you no longer need to draw on
me. And so we both sink. And now you must have someone
to blame, someone new. Because you are weak and can
never shoulder a debt yourself. So I became the scapegoat
who had to be slaughtered. But when you cut my sinews,
you didn't realise that you would hamstring yourself,
because the years we have spent together have made us like
twins. You were an offshoot of my stock, but you wanted to
make yourself independent before you had taken fresh root,
and you couldn't grow by yourself. The offshoot couldn't
live without its stock; so they both died.

TEKLA: What you're really trying to say is that you have
written my books?

ADOLF: No, you're saying that to make me out a liar. I
haven't your talent for expressing myself bluntly, I've been
talking for five minutes to give you all the nuances, all the

undertones and overtones, but you're like a penny whistle, you can only play one note.

TEKLA: Yes, yes, yes, but the *resumé* of it all was that you have written my books.

ADOLF: No, there isn't any *resumé*. You cannot resolve a chord into one note. You cannot resolve a complex life to a single figure. I haven't said anything so insane as that I've written your books.

TEKLA: But you implied it?

ADOLF [*furious*]: I did not imply anything.

TEKLA: But the sum total of it all –

ADOLF [*demented*]: There is no sum total unless one adds, and I have not added, but when you divide there is a quotient, a long unending decimal quotient which won't go out. I have not added.

TEKLA: You may not be able to add, but I can.

ADOLF: I am sure you can, but I have not added.

TEKLA: But that's what you meant.

ADOLF [*impotently, closing his eyes*]: No, no, no – don't speak to me. I shall have a fit. Shut up. Leave me. You are clawing my brain apart with your rough pincers. You are tearing my thoughts to pieces. [*He becomes unconscious; stares vacantly and twiddles his thumbs.*]

TEKLA [*gently*]: How are you feeling? Are you ill? Adolf?

ADOLF *waves her away.*

TEKLA: Adolf!

ADOLF *shakes his head.*

TEKLA: Adolf!

ADOLF: Yes.

TEKLA: Admit that you were unfair to me just now.

ADOLF: Yes, yes, yes, yes, I admit.

TEKLA: And you ask my forgiveness.

ADOLF: Yes, yes, yes, yes, I ask your forgiveness. Just don't talk to me.

TEKLA: Kiss my hand.

ADOLF [*kisses her hand*]: I kiss your hand. Anything, only don't talk to me.

TEKLA: And now go out and get some fresh air before dinner.

ADOLF: Yes, I need it. And then we can pack and leave.

TEKLA: No.

ADOLF [*starts up*]: Why not? There must be some reason.

TEKLA: The reason is that I have promised to attend a *soirée* this evening.

ADOLF: Oh, so that's it.

TEKLA: Yes, that's it. And I have promised to take part.

ADOLF: Promised? You may have said that you were thinking of going, but that needn't stop you now from saying that you do not intend to go.

TEKLA: No, I'm not like you, I stand by my word.

ADOLF: Of course one should stand by one's word, but that doesn't mean one has to stand by every little thing one says. Or perhaps you have promised someone you'll go?

TEKLA: Yes.

ADOLF: Then you can ask to be freed from your promise, because your husband is ill.

TEKLA: I don't want to, and you're not so ill that you can't come with me.

ADOLF: Why do you always want to have me with you? Does it make you feel more safe?

TEKLA: I don't understand what you mean.

ADOLF: You always say that when you know I mean something you don't like.

TEKLA: Really? What is it that I don't like now?

ADOLF: No, no, no. Don't begin again. *Au revoir.* And be careful what you do.

He goes through the door upstage and exits right. TEKLA *is left alone. A few moments later,* GUSTAV *enters. He goes straight towards the table to get a newspaper, pretending not to see* TEKLA.

TEKLA [*starts, but controls herself*]: Is it you?

GUSTAV: It is I. Forgive me –

TEKLA: How did you get here?

GUSTAV: I came by road, but – I shan't stay, since you –

TEKLA: No, please stay. It's been a long time.

GUSTAV: It's been a long time.

TEKLA: You've changed a good deal.

GUSTAV: And you are as charming as ever. Almost – younger. But forgive me, I shan't sour your happiness with my presence. If I'd known you were here, I'd never have –

TEKLA: I beg you – if you do not think it indelicate of me – stay!

GUSTAV: I have no objection, but I thought – ah, whatever I say it will hurt you.

TEKLA: Sit down for a minute. You won't hurt me, because you have, and always had, an unusual gift for tact and delicacy.

GUSTAV: You are too kind. But I am not sure that your husband would view my character in such a flattering light.

TEKLA: On the contrary, he has just been speaking most sympathetically of you.

GUSTAV: Ah? Well, time erases all things. It is like carving one's name on a living tree. Not even animosity can keep a permanent place in our natures.

TEKLA: Oh, but he's never felt any animosity towards you, because he's never seen you. I myself have always cherished a secret longing to see you and him friends for a moment; or at least to let you meet once in my presence, shake hands, and part.

GUSTAV: I too have cherished a secret longing, to see the person I love more dearly than my life safe in really good hands. I have, of course, heard many good opinions of him, I know and admire all his work, but none the less I should like, before I grow old, to press his hand, look him in the eyes, and beg him to take good care of the precious jewel which Providence has entrusted to his keeping. At the same time I should like to quench this involuntary hatred which lies, alas, within my heart, and find peace and humility of spirit to solace me for the remainder of my melancholy days.

TEKLA: You have spoken my own thoughts exactly; you have understood my feelings. Thank you.

GUSTAV: [I am of small account, and I was too insignificant to be able to overshadow you.] My dull life, my dreary work, my narrow circle of friends, were not for your aspiring soul. I admit it. But you, who have studied the human soul, understand what it costs me to have to say this.

[TEKLA: It is noble, it is great, to be able to admit one's shortcomings; and not everybody can do it. [*Sighs*.] But you were always honest, loyal and reliable – I respect you – but –

GUSTAV: I wasn't – not then – but suffering purifies, grief
ennobles, and – I have suffered –]

TEKLA: Poor Gustav. Can you forgive me? Can you?

GUSTAV: Forgive? Forgive what? It is I who must beg your
forgiveness.

TEKLA [*turns away*]: Oh, dear. We are both crying. At our
age.

GUSTAV [*turns gently*]: At our age? Yes. I am old. But you!
You grow younger and younger.

He seats himself on the chair, left. TEKLA, *not noticing, sits on the
sofa.*

TEKLA: Oh, no, do you really think so?

GUSTAV: And you dress so well.

TEKLA: Oh, you taught me to do that. Don't you remember
that you discovered the colours that suited me best?

GUSTAV: No.

TEKLA: Yes, you did. Don't you remember? [*Laughs.*] I
remember that you were even angry with me whenever I
didn't wear a touch of poppy red.

GUSTAV: Angry? No! I was never angry with you.

TEKLA: Oh, yes. And when you were trying to teach me how
to think. Remember that? I couldn't think at all in those
days.

GUSTAV: Certainly you could. Everyone can think. And now
you're really sharp, at least when you write.

TEKLA [*annoyed, says quickly*]: Well, as I was saying, it was
lovely to see you again and in such a calm atmosphere.

GUSTAV: Well, I was never a trouble-maker, was I? Life with
me was always peaceful.

TEKLA: Yes. Indeed it was.

GUSTAV: Oh? But I thought that was the way you wanted me. So you led me to believe when we were engaged.

TEKLA: In those days one didn't know what one wanted. And then one's mother had taught one that one ought not to contradict a gentleman.

GUSTAV: Well, now you've plenty of excitement. An artist's life is always eventful, and your husband does not seem to be a sluggard.

TEKLA: One can have too much of a good thing.

GUSTAV [*changing the subject*]: What! Do you still wear those ear-rings I gave you?

TEKLA [*embarrassed*]: Yes, why shouldn't I? We've never been enemies, and I thought I'd wear them as a sign, a reminder that we weren't bad friends. Anyway, one can't buy ear-rings like this any more. [*Takes one off.*]

GUSTAV: That's all very well, but what does your husband say about it?

TEKLA: What do I care what he says?

GUSTAV: You don't care? But isn't it rather an insult to him? I mean, doesn't it make him seem a bit ridiculous?

TEKLA [*briefly, as though to herself*]: He's that already.

GUSTAV [*notices that she is having difficulty in fixing her ear-ring into place*]: Will you allow me to help you?

TEKLA: Oh, yes, thank you.

GUSTAV [*fixes it in her ear*]: That little ear. What if your husband were to see us now?

TEKLA: Yes, then there'd be tears.

GUSTAV: Is he jealous?

TEKLA: Is he jealous? I should say he is.

Noise in room to right.

GUSTAV: Who lives in there?

TEKLA: I don't know. Well, tell me how things are with you, and what you're doing.

GUSTAV: Tell me how things are with you –

TEKLA *pensively and abstractedly removes the cloth from the wax figure.*

GUSTAV: What! Who's that? No! It's you!

TEKLA: Oh, no, I don't think so.

GUSTAV: But it's exactly like you.

TEKLA: Do you really think so?

GUSTAV: It reminds me of the old story: 'But how did you know, Your Majesty?'

TEKLA [*shrieks with laughter*]: You're mad. Do you know any new stories?

GUSTAV: No; but you ought to know some.

TEKLA: No, I don't hear any these days.

GUSTAV: Is he shy?

TEKLA: As far as talking goes.

GUSTAV: Not otherwise?

TEKLA: He's so ill now.

GUSTAV: Poor girl. Well, serve Little Brother right for sticking his fingers into other people's stews.

TEKLA [*laughs*]: Oh, you're really mad.

GUSTAV: Do you remember, when we were newly married, we stayed in this room? Eh? It was furnished differently then. There used to be a chest of drawers over there, between the windows. And the bed stood there.

TEKLA: Be quiet!

GUSTAV: Look at me.

TEKLA: Yes, if you like.

They look at each other.

GUSTAV: Do you think one can forget what made so strong an impression?

TEKLA: No. One can't escape one's memories. Least of all the memories of youth.

GUSTAV: Do you remember when I first met you? You were a lovely child; a little slate on which your parents and governess had scrawled crows'-feet which I had to scratch out. Then I wrote new texts on you, texts of my own choosing, till you thought there was no room for more. That's the reason why I am glad I am not in your husband's shoes – ah, well, that's his business. But that's also why it is rather pleasant to meet you. Our minds think alike. Sitting here and talking to you is like decanting an old wine that I had bottled myself. I get my wine back again, but it has matured. And now that I am going to marry again, I have deliberately chosen a young girl whom I can educate according to my wish. For, my dear Tekla, a woman is a man's child, and if she isn't that, he will become her child, and then the world's upside down.

TEKLA: Are you going to get married again?

GUSTAV: Yes. I shall tempt Fortune once more, but this time I shall put a tight rein on her, so that she won't bolt.

TEKLA: Is she beautiful?

GUSTAV: Yes, to me she is. But perhaps I'm too old. It's strange, but now that fate has brought us together again, I'm beginning to doubt if I can play that game twice.

TEKLA: How do you mean?

GUSTAV: My roots are still in you. The old wounds bleed again. You are a dangerous woman, Tekla.

TEKLA: Really? And my husband says I shall never make another conquest.

GUSTAV: In other words, he has stopped loving you.

TEKLA: I don't know what he means by love.

GUSTAV: [You and he have played hide-and-seek for so long that you can no longer catch each other. It happens, you know. You've played the innocent so cleverly, you've quite sapped his courage.] Changing one's man has its dangers, you know. It has its dangers.

TEKLA: You are reproaching me?

GUSTAV: Not at all. What happens, happens with a kind of inevitability. If it had not happened, something else would have happened. But now it has happened, and it happened like that.

TEKLA: You understand so many things. I've never met anyone with whom it gives me so much pleasure to exchange ideas. You don't preach or moralise, you make so few demands upon people, one feels free when one's with you. Do you know, I'm jealous of your future wife?

GUSTAV: Do you know that I am jealous of your husband?

TEKLA [gets up]: And now we must part. For ever.

GUSTAV: Yes, now we must part. But not without a goodbye. Mm?

TEKLA [uneasily]: No.

GUSTAV [follows her across the room]: Yes. We shall say goodbye. We shall drown our memories in a drunkenness so deep that when we wake from it we shall have lost our memories. One can drink as deeply as that, you know. [Puts his arm round her waist.] His sick spirit drags you down, infects you with melancholy. I shall fill you with new life, I shall make your talent bloom again in its autumn like a September rose. I shall –

Two Ladies in travelling clothes appear at the verandah door, look surprised, point, laugh, and go on their way.

TEKLA [*tears herself loose*]: Who was that?

GUSTAV [*indifferently*]: Tourists.

TEKLA: Leave me. I'm afraid of you.

GUSTAV: Why?

TEKLA: You take my soul from me.

GUSTAV: And give you mine instead. Anyway, you have no soul, it's only an illusion.

TEKLA: You have a way of saying rude things that makes it impossible for one to be angry with you.

GUSTAV: That's because I have the first claim on you, and you know it. When? And where?

TEKLA: No. I feel sorry for him. I think he still loves me, and I don't want to hurt him.

GUSTAV: He doesn't love you. Do you want me to prove it?

TEKLA: Well, how can you prove it?

GUSTAV [*picks up the fragments of the torn photograph from beneath the table*]: There. See for yourself.

TEKLA: Oh! How beastly of him!

GUSTAV: You see! Well. When? And where?

TEKLA: The little hypocrite.

GUSTAV: When?

TEKLA: He's catching the boat at eight o'clock tonight.

GUSTAV: Then – ?

TEKLA: Nine o'clock. [*Noise from room to right.*] Who's making that noise in there?

GUSTAV [*goes to the keyhole*]: Let's see. No, there's a table lying

on its side and a broken water carafe. Nothing else.
Perhaps someone has locked a dog in there. Nine o'clock,
then.

TEKLA: Right. He's only got himself to blame. The little
hypocrite, preaching to me about truthfulness, and how
he'd taught me to be truthful. But – wait a minute, wait a
minute. He was very unfriendly when I got back this
afternoon. He didn't come down to the jetty to meet me –
and then – then he said something about the young men on
the boat, which I pretended not to understand. But how
could he have known about it? Wait – and then he went on
about women, and said how you haunted him – and then
he talked about becoming a sculptor, because that was the
art of our time – just the way you used to talk in the old
days.

GUSTAV: In-deed?

TEKLA: In-deed. Ah, now I understand. Now I begin to see
what a vindictive bastard you are. You've been here,
tearing him apart. It was you who sat on the sofa, it was
you who put it into his head that he had epilepsy and that
he ought to give up making love and prove himself a man
by rebelling against his wife. It was you. How long have
you been here?

GUSTAV: I have been here for eight days.

TEKLA: Then it was you I saw on the steamer?

GUSTAV: It was I.

TEKLA: And now you thought you would trap me.

GUSTAV: I have already done so.

TEKLA: Not yet.

GUSTAV: Oh, yes.

TEKLA: You sneaked up on my lamb like a wolf. You came
with your vile plan to destroy my happiness, and you went

ahead with it until I spotted what you were up to and
stopped you.

GUSTAV: No, it didn't happen quite like that. In fact, it was
like this. I wanted things to go badly for you, of course. But
I was almost sure that this would happen without my
interfering. Anyway, I've had no time for intriguing. But
when I was out for a stroll and saw you on the steamer
with your young gentlemen, I thought it was time I paid
you a visit. I came here and at once your little lamb threw
himself into the arms of the wolf. He took a liking to me as
the result of a reflex action which I shall not be so impolite
as to try to interpret. At first I felt sorry for him, because he
was in the same predicament as I once found myself in. But
then he began to rub up my old wounds – you know, the
book, and the idiot – and then I felt a desire to take him to
pieces and jumble them up so that he couldn't put them
together again – and I succeeded, thanks to the work you
had already put in on him. Then there was you. You were
the mainspring in the watch, and you had to be wound up
till you broke. And then – ! [*Makes a noise like a spring
breaking.*] When I came in just now, I wasn't quite sure
what I was going to say. As a chess player I had various
possible gambits ready, but which one I should use
depended on how you would open the game. One thing led
to another, luck played its part, and finally I mated you.
Now I have you where I want you.

TEKLA: No, you haven't.

GUSTAV: Yes, I have. What you least wanted to happen has
happened. The world – represented by two lady tourists,
whose appearance was not contrived by me – for I am no
Machiavelli – the world has seen how you became
reconciled with your former husband and crept back
remorsefully into his loyal embrace. Is that enough?

TEKLA: It should be enough for you to feel revenged. But,
tell me, you who are so enlightened and so righteous, if we

cannot act freely, since everything that happens is
predetermined –

GUSTAV [*corrects her*]: Only up to a point.

TEKLA: It's the same thing.

GUSTAV: No, it's not.

TEKLA: How can you, who must regard me as innocent
because my heredity and my environment drove me to act
as I did, how can you think yourself entitled to take
revenge on me?

GUSTAV: For the same reason. Because heredity and
environment drove me to take my revenge. Fair play, don't
you think? But do you know why you two drew the short
straws in this contest? [TEKLA *gives him a contemptuous look.*]
Why you were fooled by me? Because I am stronger than
you, and cleverer. You and he were the idiots, not I. That
shows you that a man isn't necessarily an idiot because he
can't paint pictures and write novels. Remember that.

TEKLA: You are utterly without feeling?

GUSTAV: Utterly. But that, my dear, is why I am able to
think – as you know from experience – and act, as you now
also know from experience.

TEKLA: And all this just because I wounded your self-esteem.

GUSTAV: What do you mean, 'just'? Don't go round
wounding people's self-esteem. That is where people are
most vulnerable.

TEKLA: You're a vindictive beast. I despise you.

GUSTAV: You're a wanton beast. I despise you.

TEKLA: Well, that's my nature, eh?

GUSTAV: 'Well, that's my nature'! You should find out a
little about other people's feelings before you abandon
yourself to your own, or it will end in tears.

TEKLA: You can never forgive me for –

GUSTAV: I have forgiven you.

TEKLA: Have you?

GUSTAV: Certainly. Have I ever raised my hand against you in all these years? No. But now I no sooner come here than you collapse. Have I reproached you, moralised, preached at you? No. I exchanged a few jokes with your husband, and that was enough to disintegrate him. But why should I, who am the plaintiff, defend myself? Tekla! Have you nothing to reproach yourself with?

TEKLA: No, nothing at all. The Christians say that it is Providence which governs our actions, others call it fate. Whichever it is, we cannot be blamed.

GUSTAV: To a certain degree we cannot be blamed. But there is a margin of choice, and if we offend there, we are guilty and, sooner or later, the creditors will knock on the door. We are innocent, but responsible; innocent in the eyes of God – but He no longer exists – yet responsible to ourselves and our fellow-beings.

TEKLA: You have come to sue for payment, then.

GUSTAV: I have come to take back what you have stolen from me, not what I gave you freely. You stole my honour, and the only way I could get it back was by robbing you of yours.

TEKLA: Honour? Hm. And now you are satisfied.

GUSTAV: Now I am satisfied.

He rings for the PORTER.

TEKLA: And now you are going to meet your *fiancée*?

GUSTAV: I haven't got one, and I don't want one. And I am not going home, because I haven't got a home, nor do I want any.

The PORTER *enters.*

GUSTAV: Get my bill ready. I shall be leaving by the eight
o'clock boat.

The PORTER *bows and exits.*

TEKLA: Can't we part friends?

GUSTAV: Friends? You use so many words which no longer
have any meaning. Friends? What do you expect us to do,
set up house together, all three of us? [You should bury our
hatred by indemnifying me for my loss, but you can't. You
have taken from me, and what you have taken you have
consumed so that you cannot give it back to me.] Will it
make you any happier if I were to say to you: 'Forgive me
for letting you claw my heart, forgive me for letting you rob
me of my honour, forgive me for being a laughing-stock to
my pupils every day for seven years, forgive me for [helping
you to escape from your parents, for freeing you from the
tyranny of your ignorance and superstitions, for] making
you mistress of my house, [for giving you a position and
friends,] for transforming you from a child into a woman?'
Forgive me, as I have forgiven you. Now I cancel the debt
you owe me. Go now, and settle your account with your
other creditor.

TEKLA: Where is he? What have you done to him?

GUSTAV: Done to him? Do you still love him?

TEKLA: Yes.

GUSTAV: And just now? Was that true?

TEKLA: Yes.

GUSTAV: Do you know what you are?

TEKLA: You despise me?

GUSTAV: I pity you. [It is part of your character. I won't say
it's a fault, but it is unfortunate because of the
consequences it brings in its wake.] Poor Tekla! I almost

begin to regret what I have done, although I am innocent, as you are. Still, it may be a useful experience for you to feel as you once made me feel. Do you know where your husband is?

TEKLA: Now I think I know. He's in there. And he has heard everything. And seen everything. And he who sees his own ghost dies.

ADOLF *enters. He is deathly pale, and has a bloodstain on one of his cheeks. His eyes are quite still and staring, and there is white froth around his mouth.*

GUSTAV [*recoils*]: No, there he is. Settle your account with him, now, and see if he'll be as generous as I have been. Goodbye.

He goes left, but stops.

TEKLA [*goes towards* ADOLF *with outstretched arms*]: Adolf!

ADOLF *sinks down on the floor.*

TEKLA [*throws herself on to* ADOLF's *body and caresses him*]: Adolf! My beloved child! Are you alive? Speak, speak. Forgive your cruel Tekla. Forgive me, forgive me, forgive me! Little Brother, answer me, do you hear? No, oh God, he doesn't hear me. He's dead. Oh, God in Heaven, oh my God, help us, help us!

GUSTAV: It's the truth. She loves him too, Poor woman!

To Damascus (Part I)

(1898)

Introduction to

TO DAMASCUS (PART I)

To Damascus, Part I, is one of Strindberg's finest plays, and
only the fact of its being the first part of a trilogy has
prevented it being staged more often in Britain. He wrote it,
as he was to write *The Dance of Death*, with no thought of a
sequel, let alone two; and, like *The Dance of Death, Part I*, or,
for that matter, Shakespeare's *Henry IV, Part I*, it should be
regarded as a play in itself (it is usually performed alone in
Sweden, though Parts I and II are sometimes staged together
with cuts). Part III is seldom acted, with or without the
preceding parts; by the time he began it he had married, and
by the time he completed it had parted from Harriet Bosse,
his first wife, and he confusingly changed the important
character of the Lady, originally based on his second wife,
Frida, so as to incorporate certain of Harriet's traits.

He began to plan Part I in Paris on 19 January 1898, three
days before his forty-ninth birthday. It was his first play for
nearly six years. In 1892, traumatically divorced from his first
wife Siri, still unrecognized as a dramatist although he had by
then written twenty-five plays including *The Father, Miss Julie*
and *Creditors*, impoverished, denounced as a blasphemer and
corruptor of the young, he had left Sweden for Berlin, to
dilute his sorrows in a Bohemian circle of writers and painters
which included Edvard Munch, Knut Hamsun and the Pole,
Stanislaw Przybyszewski, all of whom were to become friends
and, in due course, enemies. In May 1893 Strindberg married
a young Austrian journalist aged twenty-one, Frida Uhl; but
after a stormy eighteen months she left him, and he spent the
next two years in Paris, living in a succession of cheap hotels
and immersing himself in scientific experiments, trying to
discover the origin of all matter and, especially, to make gold.
At times during these years he walked the brink of insanity;
then he found solace in the works of his countryman

Emmanuel Swedenborg, that Blake-like visionary whom
Blake himself admired. Swedenborg taught Strindberg to
believe that some mortals are chosen to suffer, like Christ, for
the sins of others, and that all things are planned in detail by
a wise and merciful Providence. Punishment and suffering he
now accepted as a sign of grace, and each new agony as
evidence that a further sin had been erased from his book.
Through Swedenborg, too, he came to believe in the existence
of 'Powers', disciplinary spirits acting for the Almighty whose
principal task was to destroy the sin of pride.

   Shortly before he left Paris for Sweden, in the autumn of
1896, Strindberg's plays began to be performed again in his
homeland, which eased his financial worries. This, together
with his new-found peace of mind, enabled him to turn again
to creative writing. In May and June of 1897 he wrote (in
French, because he believed that no one would publish it in
Sweden) *Inferno*, an account in diary form of the Purgatory
through which he had just passed. That autumn and winter
he followed it with two sequels, entitled *Legends* and *Jacob
Wrestles*; then, after the turn of the year, he began *To
Damascus*.

   Part I of *To Damascus* was an attempt to state in dramatic
form what, in Strindberg's opinion, he had failed adequately
to describe in *Jacob Wrestles*: his strife with God and his
eventual, grudging acceptance of God's existence. A famous
writer in a strange city feels damned and persecuted. He
meets an unhappily married woman and takes her away from
her husband, but lacks the money to support her and is
humiliated by having to seek help from her relatives. He has
an accident and wakes in a monastery which is also a
madhouse; here his feelings of guilt become living figures,
people whom he has injured in the past. His mother-in-law, a
pious Catholic, explains that these torments are a necessary
part of the process of salvation; he must be humbled, like Saul
on the road to Damascus. Gradually and unwillingly he
comes to accept that his fate is directed by a benevolent, if
stern, power.

   During the previous decade or so Strindberg might have

been, and often was, described as a confirmed atheist; but he
had not always been one, if he was then (which is much
debated), and his atheism such as it was had been the defiant
and aggressive atheism of a man who is not completely sure of
his position. Like Ibsen, Strindberg was never fully able to
escape from his religious upbringing; unlike Ibsen, he
confessedly returned to a belief in God. But Strindberg's new-
found religion was not orthodox Christianity; it was no less
defiant and aggressive than his atheism. 'The fact was', he
wrote in *Inferno*, 'that a kind of religion had developed in me,
though I was quite unable to formulate it. It was a spiritual
state rather than an opinion founded upon theories, a hotch-
potch of impressions that were far from being condensed into
thoughts . . . In my boyhood I had borne the Cross of Jesus
Christ, but I had repudiated a God Who was content to rule
over slaves cringing before their tormentors.'* As an adult
Strindberg had always despised the meekness demanded and
demonstrated by Christ, and the idea of having someone else
to suffer on one's behalf. He wanted to settle his accounts
directly with God, and not through some intermediary to
whom he would have to feel a debt of gratitude.

At the same time, Parts I and II of *To Damascus* are (as
which of Strindberg's mature plays is not?) a survey of his
own married life, in this case his second marriage. When he
married Frida, and indeed throughout their brief time
together, he was poor and they were supported by her
parents; hence the haunting figure of the Beggar whom the
Stranger unwillingly recognizes as a mirror of himself, an
image which he would like to reject but cannot. The book
which the Lady reads against the Stranger's wishes and which
turns her against him is *A Madman's Defence*, Strindberg's
bitter account of his first marriage with Siri which, like *Inferno*
and for the same reason, he had written in French, and which
had been savagely attacked on publication. Many of the
scenes in Part I are based on episodes from his second

* Here as elsewhere, I quote *Inferno* in Mary Sandbach's admirable
translation (Hutchinson, 1962).

marriage. Those by the seashore stem from his honeymoon on
Heligoland. The visit to the Lady's parents is a more or less
straight account of the visit which Strindberg and Frida paid
to her grandparents in the village of Dornach in Austria,
when they arrived so destitute that, like the characters in the
play, they lacked the money to pay the ferryman. Frida's
grandfather had been a noted lawyer who now devoted
himself mainly to hunting; her grandmother, once a
celebrated beauty, greeted Strindberg with suspicion from the
start, and the superstitious locals crossed themselves when
they met him on the road along the Danube, which was lined
with Calvaries.

The scene in the Abbey of Good Hope was based on
Strindberg's experiences in the Hôpital de St Louis in Paris,
where he had spent three weeks suffering from the painful
skin disease of psoriasis, and from consequent blood
poisoning. In *Inferno* he gives a vivid description of the place:

'The bell sounded for lunch and I found myself among a
company of spectres. Faces like death's-heads, faces of the
dying. A nose missing here, an eye there, a third with a
dangling lip, another with a crumbling cheek . . . In the
midst . . . moved our kind mother, the Matron . . . She
taught us to smile at our sufferings, as if they had been so
many joys, for she know how salutary pain can be.'

The origin of the scene in the gorge is likewise explained in
Inferno:

'When I took a walk in the outskirts of the village
[Dornach], the little stream led me towards the gorge
between the two hills. The truly magnificent entrance to it,
between masses of fallen rocks, lured me on with a strange
and irresistible fascination. The perpendicular side of the
rock, upon which the ruined castle stood, came down right
to the bottom and formed a gateway to the ravine itself at
the spot where the stream became the mill-race. By a freak
of nature the top of the rock looked like the head of a Turk,
so like, that everyone in the district had noticed it.

'Under it, nestling against the wall of rock, was the miller's wagon shed. On the door handle hung a goat's horn, containing the grease for lubricating the wagons, and, close by, leaning against the wall, was a broom.

'In spite of the fact that all this was perfectly natural and just as it should be, I could not help asking myself what demon it was who had put those two insignia of witches, the goat's horn and the broom, just there and right in my way on this particular morning.

'I walked on along the dark, damp path, feeling decidedly uneasy, and pulled up sharply before a wooden building of unusual appearance. It was a low, oblong shed with six oven doors. Ovens! . . . The image of Dante's Hell rose up before me, the sinners being baked red hot . . . and the six oven doors. Was it a nightmare? No, it was a commonplace reality, that was made perfectly plain by a horrible stink, a stream of mire, and a chorus of grunts coming from the pig-sty . . .

'The waterfall and the mill-wheel made a noise that was just like the humming in my ears that had been with me ever since those first nights of agitation in Paris. The mill-hands, white as false angels, handled the machinery like executioners, and the great paddle-wheel performed its Sisyphean task of sending the water running down ceaselessly, over and over again.

'Further on was the smithy, with the begrimed, naked smiths armed with fire-tongs, pincers, sledge-hammers, standing in the midst of fire and sparks and glowing iron and melted lead and a din that made my head whirl and my heart thump against my ribs . . .

'I returned the way I had come, lost in contemplation of a sequence of accidental circumstances which, taken together, formed one great whole, awe-inspiring but by no means supernatural.'

To Damascus also contains, inevitably, several of Strindberg's
more or less permanent obsessions: his old sense of guilt at
being unable to support the three children of his first
marriage, his fear that they might acquire an unsympathetic,
even a cruel stepfather, his lack of recognition as a scientist
(which seems to have bothered him much more than his lack
of recognition as a writer), his agoraphobia, his fear of
darkness (especially now that he was living alone), and his
fear of madness. His interest in the occult also left its mark; in
Paris he had maintained close contact with the French
occultists, and had been much impressed by their experiments
in hypnosis, telepathy and black magic. Dreams, as always,
fascinated him; as did the idea of the Doppelgänger, the
dream self that each of us has in addition to our 'real' self
(hence the character of the Beggar). He noted in *Inferno*:

> 'A stranger . . . was put into the room adjacent to my
> writing desk. This unknown man never uttered a word; he
> seemed to be occupied in writing something behind the
> wooden partition that separated us. All the same, it was
> odd that he should push back his chair every time I moved
> mine. He repeated my every movement . . . When I went to
> bed the man in the room next to my desk went to bed too.'

The occultists confirmed his suspicion that a man has the
power to revenge himself on another, even at a distance. In
Berlin he had had an affair with the Norwegian Dagny Juel,
famous as the model of Edvard Munch. After Strindberg,
Dagny (who was later murdered by another lover) had
become the wife of Przybyszewski, and in Paris Strindberg
became convinced that Przybyszewski (now, according to
Munch, in France) was trying to kill him by, among other
methods, projecting electricity into him. He kept on hearing
the Pole's favourite melody, Schumann's *Aufschwung*, and
hastily changed to another hotel, whither it pursued him. The
plays of the Belgian symbolist Maurice Maeterlinck, whom
Strindberg had read and admired, may have influenced the
method and structure of the drama.

'My play [Part I] creeps beautifully forward', Strindberg

wrote to the author Gustaf af Geijerstam on 2 March 1898
from Paris, 'and gives me good hopes now that I am over the
brow.' By 8 March he had finished it. 'Here is a play of whose
value I have no idea,' he informed Geijerstam that day,
enclosing it. 'If you find it good, chuck it in at the theatre. If
you find it impossible, hide it away.' Two days later he wrote
a cryptic yet revealing letter to Axel Herrlin (a young
academic who had written to him describing some Inferno-
like experiences he had recently had and with whom
Strindberg had had many conversations about the occult
during his stay in Lund the previous year):

'Who stages these performances for us, and with what
purpose? Are they real? Is there a hell apart from this? Or
is it to frighten children? My own crisis, which lasted
nearly seven months, has given me no further certainty,
except regarding certain points. I know what is demanded
of me ethically, but the demands seem gradually to be
intensified. Alchemy and occultism, divination and
exploring what is hidden, are absolutely forbidden, but not
speculative chemistry. On the other hand, I seem to have
been granted again the grace of being able to write for the
theatre, and have just completed a big play which I am
grateful to have been permitted to write. But I admit that it
is a gift which can be taken from one if one misuses it.'

He goes on to speak of his religion, and of his fear lest he
might

'be punished with religious fanaticism and led astray.
But I'm not sure whether this is a trial which one must
withstand or a calling which must be obeyed. My earlier
fatalism has been translated into a belief in Providence, and
I fully realize that standing alone I have nothing and can
achieve nothing. But I shall not attain complete humility,
for my conscience will not permit me to commit suicide as
an individual.'

On 1 April he tried to comfort a newspaper editor,
Waldemar Bülow, who had written to Strindberg that he felt

persecuted. 'It is not people who persecute you; people are too lazy and self-occupied to waste time persecuting others. No, it is Someone else, the Invisible One, Whom you have challenged.' On 23 April, in Lund, he wrote a moving letter to another correspondent who suffered from a conviction that she was persecuted, his sister Elisabeth, to whom he was deeply attached and who later that year was to be admitted to a mental home. 'As regards your feelings that you are persecuted, they are like the ones I had when I was ill; and they lack any foundation; though not wholly so, since one is said to persecute oneself. If you have read my book *Inferno*, you can see the causes of my delusions of persecution, arising mainly from self-reproach . . . Whether your case resembles mine I don't know and have no right to ask or demand; but one piece of advice I can give you; try to search out the purpose of Providence in punishing you with these torments.' And on 12 May he wrote to Geijerstam: 'I wonder where the grass grows where some time I may rest my weary bones; my Colonus, where the wild hunt of my Eumenides will cease!'

On 24 May, in a letter to his three children with Siri, he described Part I of *To Damascus* as 'the best play I have written, and one which gives me and my friends who have read it great hopes'. On 5 June, still in Lund, he addressed a long letter to the Swedish poet Gustaf Fröding, who suffered so violently from hallucinations that he, like Elisabeth, was admitted that year to an asylum:

'Don't use the word hallucination (or even delirium) as though it stood for something unreal. Hallucinations and delirium possess a certain kind of reality – or they are phantasmagoria consciously designed by the Invisible One to frighten us. They all have a symbolic meaning. For example, the projections of alcoholic delirium are always the same: flies and rats. The direct progeny of filth . . . I am sure that your visions are to be found in Swedenborg, and if you could write them down from memory you would do yourself, me and many people a great service. I would interpret them for you; you would see that there is a

consistency in them, a meaning and a good intent. When I
chanced to find my hallucinations described in
Swedenborg, I was freed. Now, when in the night they
attack me, I lie and balance these torments against the evil
things I have thought and done. I at once think: "Serve you
right! Take note and don't do that again!" And so I regain
peace; till I sin again. But don't suppose that I am
punished just for wine and women; no, every harsh word I
have spoken of others, even if it is true and well known;
hubristic thoughts; and much besides, all come under
scrutiny. I don't believe in any Hell but this, though I
don't know. And Swedenborg's Hell is an exact description
of life on earth; I don't think we leave this world until we
have had our ration of suffering. But we, we seem to have a
task to fulfil, and it is no use throwing oneself like Jonah
into the sea to escape one's calling. We must stand forth
and prophesy, and risk being disavowed like Jonah. My
development is not as absurd as it appears. "Pull down!"
said the Spirit, and I pulled down. "Now build!" says the
Spirit . . . And now I shall try to build.'

To Damascus, Part I received its stage première at Dramaten
in Stockholm on 19 November 1900. It does not seem to have
been a good production, and the reception was muted;
Strindberg's old friend Pehr Staaff suggested in *Dagens Nyheter*
that the play was of greater interest to Strindberg himself
than to the public, and *Aftonbladet* thought 'this oppressive
fever-fantasy of a sick and tormented soul . . . is not suited to
the stage', though *Social-Demokraten* regretted that the
audience reacted with 'a notable lack of understanding' to this
'gripping and fascinating drama'. However, it achieved the
respectable run, for so demanding a play, of 20 performances.
A 22 year old Norwegian actress, Harriet Bosse, played the
Lady, and on the day of the première Strindberg wrote her a
letter of advice: '. . . I had imagined the character as a little
lighter, with hints of mischief and more outgoing. A little of
Puck! . . . A smile in the midst of misery suggests the
existence of hope, and the situation does not turn out to be

hopeless – words that might be heeded by any actress playing any of Strindberg's tragic heroines. The following year Harriet became Strindberg's third wife.

To Damascus, Part I was first staged in Britain on 2 May 1937 by the Stage Society at the Westminster Theatre in London, with Francis James and Wanda Rotha under the direction of Carl H. Jaffé. It was not seen again until 3 April 1975, when Michael Ockrent and David Gothard directed it at the Traverse Theatre in Edinburgh, with Roy Marsden and Katherine Schofield. This production was rightly acclaimed; Allen Wright in the *Scotsman* summed it up as 'a play so packed with ideas and invective that it makes most contemporary dramas seem trivial'. It has been heard twice on BBC radio, on 13 December 1953 (Valentine Dyall and Catherine Salkeld; directed by Peter Watts), and on 4 July 1971 (Stephen Murray and Zena Walker; directed by Charles Lefeaux).

To Damascus (Part I)

(1898)

This translation of *To Damascus* was commissioned by the
BBC. Part I was broadcast, in a shortened form, on Radio 3
on 4 July 1971 (and repeated on 10 October 1971) with the
following cast:

NARRATOR	Martin Friend
THE STRANGER	Stephen Murray
THE LADY	Zena Walker
THE BEGGAR	Edward Kelsey
A MOURNER	Patrick Tull
A LANDLORD	Anthony Higginson
THE DOCTOR	John Rye
A MADMAN	Brian Hewlett
A HOTEL PORTER	Patrick Tull
THE MOTHER	Eva Stuart
THE GRANDFATHER	John Ruddock
THE ABBESS	Sheila Grant

Special sound and music by Malcolm Clarke of the BBC
Radiophonic Workshop.

Directed by Charles Lefeaux

On 3 April 1975, Part I was performed at the Traverse
Theatre, Edinburgh. The cast was:

THE STRANGER	Roy Marsden
THE LADY	Katharine Schofield
THE BEGGAR	Christopher Ryan
THE DOCTOR	Christopher Malcolm
THE SISTER ⎫ THE ABBESS ⎬	Meg Davies
A MADMAN	David Bedard
THE MOTHER	Susan Carpenter
THE OLD MAN	John Young
THE DOMINICAN	Finlay Welsh

Designed by Poppy Mitchell
Directed by Michael Ockrent and David Gothard

CHARACTERS

THE STRANGER
THE LADY
THE BEGGAR
A LANDLORD
FIRST FUNERAL GUEST
SECOND FUNERAL GUEST
THIRD FUNERAL GUEST
THE DOCTOR
THE SISTER
A MADMAN
A HOTEL PORTER
THE SMITH
THE MILLER'S WIFE
THE OLD MAN
THE LADY'S MOTHER
THE ABBESS
THE CONFESSOR
MINOR CHARACTERS AND SHADOWS

This is the actual list of characters, and differs considerably from Strindberg's own list as prefaced to the play. He names only the Stranger, the Lady, the Beggar, the Doctor, the Sister, the Old Man, the Mother, the Abbess, the Confessor, and 'Minor Characters and Shadows'. This is by no means the only instance of Strindberg's 'List of Characters' differing from the actual list. (Translator's note)

SCENES

Act 1. At the street corner
        At the Doctor's

Act 2. A hotel room
        By the sea
        On the highway
        At the gorge
        In the kitchen

Act 3. The rose room
        The asylum
        The rose room
        The kitchen

Act 4. At the gorge
        On the highway
        By the sea
        The hotel room

Act 5. At the Doctor's
        The street corner

ACT ONE

Scene 1

At the street corner.

A street corner with a bench beneath a tree. The side-portals of a small Gothic church, a post-office and a café with chairs outside. The post-office and the café are shut.

The sound of a funeral march approaches, then fades into the distance.

The STRANGER stands on the edge of the pavement, seeming to wonder which way to go. A church clock strikes; first four notes, the quarters, in a highish tone, then three o'clock, in a lower.

The LADY enters, inclines her head to the STRANGER, is about to pass him, but stops.

STRANGER: So there you are. I thought you would come.

LADY: You called me, then? Yes, I felt it. But why do you stand here, on the street corner?

STRANGER: I don't know. I must stand somewhere while I wait.

LADY: What are you waiting for?

STRANGER: If I only knew. For forty years I have been waiting for something. I believe it is called happiness; or it may just be the end of sorrow. Listen to that dreadful music again. Listen! Don't go, please don't go. I shall be frightened if you go.

LADY: We met yesterday for the first time. And talked alone for four hours. I felt sorry for you, but that doesn't mean you may take advantage of my kindness.

STRANGER: That's true, I shouldn't. But, I beg you: don't leave me alone. I am in a strange city, I haven't a friend,

and the few people I know seem worse than strangers –
almost enemies.

LADY: Enemies everywhere, alone everywhere. Why did you
leave your wife and child?

STRANGER: If I only knew. If I only knew why I exist, why I
stand here, where I must go, what I must do. Do you think
some people are damned before they die?

LADY: No, I don't think that.

STRANGER: Look at me.

LADY: Have you never found any happiness in life?

STRANGER: No. And when I thought I had, it was just a ruse
to tempt me to prolong my misery. Whenever the golden
fruit fell into my hand, it was always poisoned or rotten.

LADY: What is your religion?

STRANGER: Only this: that when life becomes too much to
bear, I shall go my way.

LADY: Where?

STRANGER: Into annihilation. This knowledge that I hold
death in my hand gives me an incredible feeling of power –

LADY: Good God, you speak of death like a toy.

STRANGER: Well, life is a toy – to us writers. I was born
melancholy, yet I've never been able to take anything
seriously, even my own sorrows. And there are moments
when I doubt whether life has any more reality than the
things I write. [*The funeral march is heard: psalm tunes;* De
Profundis.] Here they come again. Why must they march
round the streets like this?

LADY: Are you afraid of them?

STRANGER: No. But it irritates me, it's as though it had
happened before. I don't fear death. Only solitude. Because
when one's alone there's always someone else. I don't know

whether it's myself or someone else, but in solitude one is never alone. The air grows thicker, it begins to sprout, to grow things which you can't see but which are there, and alive.

LADY: You've noticed that?

STRANGER: Yes. I've been noticing everything lately. Not just things and incidents, forms and colours – now I see thoughts and what things signify. Life used to be just a great nonsense. Now it has a meaning, and I see a purpose in it where before I saw only a game of chance. So when I met you yesterday I thought you had been sent, either to save me or to destroy me.

LADY: Why should I destroy you?

STRANGER: Because it was your destiny.

LADY: I don't want to destroy you. I pity you. I've never seen anyone before whose mere appearance made me want to weep. What's on your conscience? Have you done something that hasn't been found out, or punished?

STRANGER: You may well ask that. I've no more crimes on my conscience than many who go free. Yes, one thing. I wasn't willing to be life's fool.

LADY: One must let oneself be betrayed in some degree to be able to live.

STRANGER: It seems almost to be a duty, and one I'd gladly be relieved of. Or there must be some other secret in my life that I don't know about. There's a story in my family that I'm a changeling.

LADY: What's that?

STRANGER: A child the fairies have left in exchange for a human one.

LADY: And you believe that?

STRANGER: No. But there must be something in it. When I

was a child I cried continuously and felt I didn't belong to this life. I hated my parents as much as they hated me. I resented discipline and convention. I only longed for the forest and the sea.

LADY: Have you ever seen visions?

STRANGER: Never. But I've often felt that two powers rule my life. One gives me everything I want, while the other stands there and smears every gift with filth, so that it's worthless and I don't want to touch it. I've had everything I wanted in this life, and it has all seemed worthless.

LADY: You have had everything and yet are discontented?

STRANGER: That's what I call being cursed.

LADY: Don't blaspheme! But why didn't you look for something beyond this life, in a place where no dirt is?

STRANGER: Because I've never believed in anything outside it.

LADY: What about those fairies?

STRANGER: Oh, that was just a fantasy. Shall we sit down?

LADY: All right. But what are you waiting for?

STRANGER: Really for the post-office to open. There's a letter waiting for me which keeps on chasing me without ever finding me. [*They sit.*] Tell me a little about yourself.

LADY [*starts knitting*]: There's nothing to tell.

STRANGER: It's strange, but I'd like to think of you as something without a name. I only know your surname. I'd like to name you myself. Let me think. What shall I call you? Yes. I shall call you Eve. [*With a gesture to the wings.*] Trumpets! [*The funeral march is heard.*] That funeral march again! I shall give you an age too, for I don't know how old you are. You are thirty-four – which means you were born in 1864. And a character, because I don't know what kind of person you are. A good one, I think; your voice is like my

dead mother's. I mean my idea of a mother – my own
mother never kissed me, but I remember she hit me. I was
reared in hatred. Hatred – a blow for a blow, an eye for an
eye. You see this scar on my forehead? My brother did that
with an axe, because I'd knocked his tooth out with a
stone, I didn't go to my father's funeral, because he had me
thrown out from my sister's wedding. And I was born
illegitimate, the son of a bankrupt, while the family was in
mourning for an uncle who'd committed suicide. Now you
know my family. As is the tree, so is the fruit. I managed
with difficulty to escape fourteen years hard labour, so I
suppose I ought really to be grateful if not exactly happy.
To the powers.

LADY: I like to hear you speak, but you mustn't meddle with
the powers. It troubles me. Please.

STRANGER: To be honest I don't believe in them, yet they
keep returning to my thoughts. Don't you think there are
lost souls that have failed to find peace? I think so. Then I
must be one too. Once I thought I would find peace,
through a woman. But that turned out the worst hell of all.

LADY: You say such strange things. Yes, you are a lost soul.
But you will find peace.

STRANGER: Through the sound of bells and holy water? I've
tried that. But it was like when the Devil sees a crucifix.
Let's talk about you.

LADY: There's no need. Have you never been accused of
misusing your talents?

STRANGER: I've been accused of everything. No man was
ever so hated, or so lonely. I went alone, and I came alone.
When I entered a public place, people moved away from
me. When I wanted to rent a room, it was always taken.
The priests cursed me from the pulpits, the scholars from
their lecture platforms, my parents in my home. Once the
church committee tried to take my children from me. Then
I raised my fist to heaven and reviled God.

LADY: Why are you so hated?

STRANGER: I don't know. Yes – I couldn't see people suffer.
And I said so, and I wrote: 'Free yourselves and I will help
you!' And I said to the poor: 'Don't let the rich exploit
you'. And to the women: 'Don't let men crush you'. And –
which I suppose was the worst – I said to children: 'Do not
obey your father and mother when they are unjust.' The
result was, everyone united against me, rich and poor, men
and women, parents and children. I became sick, poor,
beggared, dishonoured, divorced, denounced, exiled, alone,
and now – ! Do you think I am mad?

LADY: No.

STRANGER: You're the only one who doesn't. I like you for
that.

LADY [gets up]: I must leave you now.

STRANGER: You too!

LADY: You mustn't stay here.

STRANGER: Where shall I go?

LADY: Home, to work.

STRANGER: I'm not a worker. I'm a writer.

LADY: I didn't mean to hurt you. But writing is a gift which
can be taken away. Don't forfeit it.

STRANGER: Where are you going?

LADY: There's something I must do.

STRANGER: Are you religious?

LADY: I am nothing.

STRANGER: All the better, then you can become something.
Oh, I wish I was your old blind father, whom you could
lead to the market place to sing, but my tragedy is that I
can't grow old – that's the way with children who've been

left by the fairies, they don't grow old, they just get
enormous heads and scream. I wish I was someone's dog
whom I could follow so that I'd never be alone – a little
food now and then, a kick now and then, a pat now and
then, a whipping –

LADY: Now I must go. Goodbye.

STRANGER [*absently*]: Goodbye.

*She leaves him sitting on the bench. He takes off his hat, wipes his
forehead. Then he draws with his stick in the dust. The* BEGGAR
enters. His appearance is very strange. He rummages in the gutter.

STRANGER: What are you scrabbling for, beggar?

BEGGAR: I don't know what you mean. Anyway, I'm not a
beggar. Have I asked you for anything?

STRANGER: I beg your pardon. One shouldn't judge by
appearances.

BEGGAR: No, you shouldn't. Can you guess who I am?

STRANGER: It doesn't interest me.

BEGGAR: How can one tell in advance? People never get
interested until it's too late. *Virtus post nummos!*

STRANGER: You know Latin?

BEGGAR: You see. You're interested already. *Omne tulit
punctum qui miscuit utile dulci.* I've succeeded in everything
I've attempted, because I've never attempted anything. I
call myself Polycrates, that fellow with the ring. I've got
everything I wanted in life. But I never really wanted
anything, and, bored with success, I threw my ring away.
Now I'm old I miss it and rummage for it in the gutters.
But if I don't find a gold ring, I don't turn my nose up at
the odd cigar butt.

STRANGER: I'm not sure if that's wisdom or rubbish.

BEGGAR: Neither am I.

STRANGER: Do you know who I am?

BEGGAR: Doesn't interest me.

STRANGER: People never get interested until – no, damn it, you're turning me into a parrot. It's as bad as picking up other men's cigar butts. Be off with you!

BEGGAR [*raises his hat*]: And you don't want to pick up mine?

STRANGER: What's that scar on your forehead?

BEGGAR: I got that from a close relative.

STRANGER: No, now you're frightening me. May I feel you and see if you're real? [*Touches the* BEGGAR *on the arm.*] Yes, you're real. Will you condescend, my dear sir, to accept a small coin in return for a promise to look for Polycrates' ring in some other suburb? *Post nummos virtus* – no, there I go again. Be off with you!

BEGGAR: I'll go. But you've given me too much. Here's three-quarters back. Then it's just a loan between friends.

STRANGER: Am I your friend?

BEGGAR: At least I am yours. And when a man's alone in the world, he can't be choosy.

STRANGER: Would you be offended if I called that impertinent?

BEGGAR: Not at all, not at all. When we meet again, I'll have an epithet for you. [*Goes.*]

STRANGER [*sits and draws with his stick*]: Sunday afternoon. Long, grey, gloomy Sunday afternoon. Everyone digesting roast beef and cabbage and boiled potatoes. The old are sleeping, the young smoking and playing chess – the servants have gone to evensong and the shops are shut. Oh, this long, murderous afternoon, the day of rest, when the pulse ceases to beat, when it's as impossible to meet a friendly face as to get into a pub –

The LADY *enters. She now wears a flower in her bosom.*

STRANGER: Hullo! I can't open my mouth today without being proved a liar.

LADY: Are you still sitting here?

STRANGER: What does it matter whether I draw in the sand here or elsewhere, as long as I draw in the sand?

LADY: What are you writing? Let me look.

STRANGER: I seem to have written: Eve, 1864. No, don't walk on it.

LADY: What would happen?

STRANGER: Bad luck. For you and me.

LADY: You know that?

STRANGER: Yes. And I also know that that rose you are wearing in your breast is a Mandragora. That symbolizes malice and slander, though it used to be used as a medicine to cure madness. Will you give it to me?

LADY [*hesitates*]: As a medicine?

STRANGER: Of course. Have you read my books?

LADY: You know I have. I have you to thank for teaching me freedom and belief in human rights and human dignity.

STRANGER: Then you haven't read my last books.

LADY: No. And if they're different from your first books, I don't want to.

STRANGER: Promise me you will never open any of my books again.

LADY: Let me think first. Yes, I promise.

STRANGER: Good. But don't break that promise. Remember Bluebeard's wife when curiosity tempted her to unlock the forbidden room –

LADY: You're already beginning to talk like a Bluebeard. Have you forgotten that I am married, that my husband is a doctor and that he admires your work, so that his house stands open any time you wish to enter it?

STRANGER: I have done my best to forget it. I've so wiped it from my mind that it has ceased to have any reality for me.

LADY: In that case, will you come home with me?

STRANGER: No. Will you come home with me?

LADY: Where?

STRANGER: Anywhere. I have no home. Money sometimes, but seldom. It's the only thing life didn't jib at giving me, perhaps because I never really wanted it.

LADY: Hm!

STRANGER: What are you thinking?

LADY: I'm surprised I'm not offended by your sense of humour.

STRANGER: Humour and earnestness are the same thing to me. Ah! Now the organ has begun to play, which means the cafés are going to open.

LADY: Is it true that you drink?

STRANGER: A great deal. Wine helps my soul to leave its cell, I escape into space, I see what no man has seen and hear what no man has heard –

LADY: And the day after?

STRANGER: I have beautiful pangs of conscience, a liberating sense of guilt and remorse, a pleasure in the body's torment while the soul hovers like smoke about my brow. It is like a limbo between life and death, when the spirit feels it has stretched its wings and could if it wished take flight.

LADY: Come with me into the church for a moment. You won't hear a sermon, only the music of evensong.

STRANGER: No, not the church. It makes me feel I'm unclean, and can never belong there, any more than I can become a child again.

LADY: You feel this already?

STRANGER: That's how far I have come; and it seems to me as though I lay chopped to pieces in Medea's cauldron, being slowly boiled; I shall either dissolve into nothing, or arise renewed. It all depends on Medea's skill.

LADY: You talk like an oracle. Couldn't you become a child again?

STRANGER: I'd have to start at the cradle. And I'd have to be the right child this time.

LADY: Exactly. But wait while I go into St Elizabeth's chapel. If the café was open, I should beg you not to drink. But luckily it's shut.

The STRANGER *sits down again and draws in the sand. Six mourners dressed in brown enter, with funeral guests. One carries a banner with the insignia of the Carpenters' Guild, and brown crêpe; another, a large axe decorated with spruce twigs; a third carries a cushion with a speaker's gavel on it. They stand outside the café and wait.*

STRANGER: Excuse me. Whose funeral was this?

FIRST GUEST: A carpenter. [*Makes a noise like a clock ticking.*]

STRANGER: A real carpenter? Or the insect kind that lives in walls and goes tick-tock?

SECOND GUEST: Both. But mostly the insect kind. What did you say it was called?

STRANGER [*to himself*]: The rogue! He's trying to trick me into saying death-watch beetle. But I'll say something else to annoy him. [*Aloud.*] You mean a goldsmith?

SECOND GUEST: No, I didn't mean that. [*Makes the ticking sound again.*]

STRANGER: Are you trying to frighten me? Or is the dead man working miracles? I'm not afraid and I don't believe in miracles. Strange, though, that you mourners are wearing brown. Why not black? It's cheap, looks good and is practical.

THIRD GUEST: To our foolish eyes it is black, but if Your Honour so commands, it is brown.

STRANGER: You seem a strange company, and I feel an unease which I'd like to attribute to that wine I drank last night. But if I say those are spruce-twigs around that axe, I suppose you'll tell me they're – well, what are they?

FIRST GUEST: That's a grape-vine.

STRANGER: I guessed they wouldn't be spruce-twigs. Look, now the café's opening. At last.

The café is opened. The STRANGER *sits down at a table and is served with wine. The* GUESTS *sit at the empty tables.*

STRANGER: You must have been glad to see the back of your late companion, since you make haste to wet your throats.

FIRST GUEST: Well, he was a good-for-nothing. Couldn't take life seriously.

STRANGER: And drank, no doubt?

SECOND GUEST: He did.

THIRD GUEST: And let others support his wife and children.

STRANGER: Ah, that was wicked of him. But no doubt that's why such fine words are being spoken over his coffin. Would you mind not pushing my table while I'm drinking?

FIRST GUEST: I've a right to when I'm drinking.

STRANGER: When you are, yes. There's a big difference between you and me.

The Mourners murmur. The BEGGAR *enters.*

STRANGER: Hullo, here's that beggar picking around again.

BEGGAR [*sits at a table*]: Landlord! A bottle of hock!

LANDLORD [*comes out with a document*]: Off! You'll get nothing here. You haven't paid your taxes. Here's the court finding, your name, your age and your character.

BEGGAR: *Omnia serviliter pro dominatione*. I'm a free man, with a University education and I have refused to pay taxes because I don't wish to be conscripted into society. A bottle of hock!

LANDLORD: If you don't clear off, you'll get a free trip to jail.

STRANGER: Can't you two settle this matter somewhere else? You're disturbing your customers.

LANDLORD: Well, I want you as a witness that I'm acting within the law –

STRANGER: I think the whole thing's idiotic. Can't a man enjoy the small pleasures of life simply because he hasn't paid his taxes?

LANDLORD: I see! You're one of those fellows who go round telling people to ignore their responsibilities.

STRANGER: No, this is going too far. Do you realize that I am a famous man?

The LANDLORD *and Mourners laugh.*

LANDLORD: Notorious, more like! Wait a moment. Let me see. This description could fit. [*Reads from the document.*] Thirty-eight years old, brown hair, blue eyes, no fixed occupation, abandoned his wife and children, holds subversive views on social questions, and gives the impression of not being in full command of his senses. Doesn't it fit?

STRANGER [*gets up, pale and crushed*]: What is this?

LANDLORD: Bless my soul, but it does fit!

BEGGAR: Perhaps it is him and not me.

LANDLORD: Looks like it. Now why don't you two trot along?

BEGGAR [*to* STRANGER]: We'd better go.

STRANGER: We? This is beginning to look like a plot.

The church bells ring. The sun breaks through and lights up the coloured rose windows above the church door, which opens and reveals the interior of the church. Organ music: Ave Maris Stella *is sung.*

LADY [*comes out of church*]: Where are you, what are you doing? Why did you call me again? Must you hang on to a woman's skirts like a child?

STRANGER: Yes, now I am afraid. Things are happening here which can't be explained naturally.

LADY: I thought you weren't afraid of anything, even death.

STRANGER: No, not of death. But of – the other thing. The unknown.

LADY: Listen, my friend. Give me your hand and I'll take you to a doctor. You're ill. Come.

STRANGER: Perhaps. But first tell me one thing. Is all this a carnival, or – are these people real?

LADY: They seem to be real –

STRANGER: But that beggar. He's a horrible creature. Does he really look like me?

LADY: If you go on drinking, you'll become like him. Go into the post-office now and collect your letter. Then come with me.

STRANGER: No, I won't go into the post-office. It's probably only a summons.

LADY: But suppose it isn't?

STRANGER: It'll be bad news of some kind.

LADY: Do as you please, but no one can escape his destiny. I feel as though higher powers had conferred about us, and decided our fate.

STRANGER: You too? Do you know, just now I heard the gavel fall, the chairs pushed back and the servants sent out. Oh, this torture! No, I won't go with you.

LADY: What have you done to me? When I went into that chapel, I couldn't pray. A candle went out on the altar and a cold wind blew on my face just as I heard you call me.

STRANGER: I didn't call. I just longed for you.

LADY: You're not the weak child you pretend to be. Your power is extraordinary. I'm frightened of you.

STRANGER: When I'm alone I'm as weak as a paralytic, but once I have hold of someone I become strong. Now I want to be strong, so I will go with you.

LADY: Perhaps you can free me from my ogre.

STRANGER: Are there such things?

LADY: I call him that.

STRANGER: Good. Then I will go with you; to fight with trolls, to liberate princesses, to kill ogres – that is to live!

LADY: Come, my liberator.

She draws the veil from her face, kisses him swiftly on the mouth and hastens out. The STRANGER stands for a moment bewildered and dazed. A high-pitched chorus of women's voices approaching a shriek is heard from the church. The illuminated rose window suddenly becomes dark; the tree above the bench stirs; the Mourners rise from their places and look up at the sky, as though seeing something unusual and alarming. The STRANGER hurries out after the LADY.

Scene 2

At the DOCTOR's.

A courtyard enclosed by three rows of houses – single-storeyed wooden buildings with tiled roofs and small windows. To the right, glass doors and a verandah. Left, outside the windows, a rose-hedge and beehives. In the centre of the yard is a heap of wood, shaped like an oriental cupola; beside it, a well. Over the centre of the middle wall rises the top of a tall walnut tree. In the right-hand corner is the gate to the garden. By the well is a large tortoise. Right, the entrance down to the cellar. An ice-chest and a rubbish-bin. Outside the verandah, tables and chairs.

SISTER [*enters from the verandah with a telegram*]: Here is bad news, brother.

DOCTOR: When wasn't there?

SISTER: But this time! Ingeborg is coming home, with – guess whom?

DOCTOR: Wait a moment. I know, because I have long sensed that this would happen, and longed for it. This writer – I have admired him, learned from him and wished to know him. Now he is coming, you say. Where did Ingeborg meet him?

SISTER: In town, it seems. Probably in that literary salon she frequents.

DOCTOR: I have often wondered if this man can be someone I was at school with. The name is the same. I hope so – that boy had something fateful about him, and now that he's a man, he should have fulfilled those tendencies.

SISTER: Don't let him enter your house. Go away, pretend you have to see someone.

DOCTOR: No. One cannot run from one's fate –

SISTER: You never shrank from anything. Are you going to grovel before this imaginary monster that you call Fate?

DOCTOR: Life has taught me to. I have wasted much time and strength struggling against the inevitable.

SISTER: But why do you let your wife go round compromising herself, and you?

DOCTOR: You know why. Because, when I released her from her vows, I offered her a life of freedom, in contrast to what she regarded as a prison. Anyway, I couldn't love her if she obeyed me or if I was able to command her.

SISTER: So you make a friend of your enemy.

DOCTOR: Now, now.

SISTER: And you let her bring into your house the man who will destroy you. Oh, if you knew how boundlessly I hate that man!

DOCTOR: I know, I know. His latest book is loathsome. But it suggests that he suffers from some mental sickness.

SISTER: Then they should have put him away.

DOCTOR: Some people say that, but I do not feel he has gone that far –

SISTER: That's because you're so eccentric yourself, and have a wife who is raving mad.

DOCTOR: I can't deny that mad people have always exercised a strong attraction for me. At least eccentricity is never banal. [*A steamer's whistle is heard.*] What was that? Someone cried out!

SISTER: You're nervous. It was only the steamer. But I beg you – please go!

DOCTOR: I think I'd like to – but I can't. Do you know, when I stand here, I see his portrait there in my study. And the sunshine casts a shadow which makes him look like – it's horrible! Do you see who he looks like?

SISTER: He looks like the Evil One. Go!

DOCTOR: I can't.

SISTER: At least defend yourself –

DOCTOR: I usually do. But this time it's like an approaching storm. How many times have I not wished to run away but been unable to! It's as though the earth was of iron and I a magnet. If disaster strikes, it's not of my choice. They've just come in through the gate.

SISTER: I heard nothing.

DOCTOR: But I, I hear them. And now I see them too. It is he, my old schoolfriend. He did something once in school – I was blamed, and punished for it. But he acquired the nickname Caesar, I don't know why.

SISTER: And this man –

DOCTOR: Yes, such is life. Caesar!

LADY [enters]: Good afternoon, husband. I've a nice surprise for you.

DOCTOR: So I've heard. He is welcome.

LADY: He's in the guest room changing his collar.

DOCTOR: Are you happy with your capture?

LADY: He is certainly the unhappiest person I have ever met in my life.

DOCTOR: That's saying a lot.

LADY: Yes; he suffers for all mankind.

DOCTOR: I'm sure. Go to him, sister, and show him down to us.

SISTER goes.

DOCTOR: You've had an interesting journey?

LADY: Yes; I've met many strange people. Have you had any patients?

DOCTOR: No, the surgery's been empty all morning. My practice seems to be declining.

LADY [*sympathetically*]: I'm sorry. I say, aren't you going to bring the wood-pile in? It'll get damp out there.

DOCTOR [*without reproach*]: I know. And I should kill the bees and pick the fruit in the garden, but I can't seem to care about anything –

LADY: You're tired.

DOCTOR: Tired of everything.

LADY [*without bitterness*]: And you have a bad wife, who can't be of any help to you.

DOCTOR [*gently*]: You mustn't say such things, when I don't say them.

LADY [*turns to the verandah*]: Here he is.

The STRANGER *enters, dressed more youthfully than in the opening scene. He steps in from the verandah with a forced ease; seems to recognize the* DOCTOR, *cringes and stumbles forward, but recovers himself.*

DOCTOR: Welcome to my house.

STRANGER: Thank you.

DOCTOR: You bring good weather. We need it – it's been raining here for six weeks –

STRANGER: Not seven? It usually rains for seven weeks after St Swithin's Day. But I'd forgotten, that hasn't come yet. How stupid I am! Hm!

DOCTOR: I'm afraid our simple way of life in this small town will seem dull to you who are used to the pleasures of the capital.

STRANGER: Oh, no – I am as little at home there as here. Forgive my asking, but haven't we met before? When we were young?

DOCTOR: Never.

The LADY *has seated herself at the table, and is knitting.*

STRANGER: You're sure?

DOCTOR: Quite sure. I have followed your literary career from its beginning and, as I know my wife has told you, with the greatest interest, so that if we had met I should have remembered it, at any rate your name. However – here you see how a country doctor lives.

STRANGER: If you knew how a so-called liberator lives, you wouldn't envy him.

DOCTOR: I can imagine – I've seen how people love the chains that bind them. Perhaps it is ordained, since it is so.

STRANGER [*listens*]: That's strange. Who is playing the piano next door?

DOCTOR: I don't know who it can be. Do you know, Ingeborg?

LADY: No.

STRANGER: It's Mendelssohn's Funeral March. It follows me everywhere. I don't know if it's only in my head, or –

DOCTOR: Do you have auditory hallucinations?

STRANGER: Not hallucinations, but little things that have actually happened persecute me. Can't you hear music?

DOCTOR *and* LADY: Yes, of course.

LADY: And it is Mendelssohn.

DOCTOR: He's very fashionable now.

STRANGER: Yes, I know, but that someone should be playing it just now, here – [*Gets up.*]

DOCTOR: If it will reassure you, I'll go and enquire. [*Goes out on to the verandah.*]

STRANGER [*to* LADY]: I'm stifling here. I can't spend a night under this roof. Your husband looks like an ogre, and in his presence you turn into a pillar of salt. Murder has been committed in this house. There are ghosts here, and I shall leave as soon as I get the chance.

DOCTOR [*from outside*]: Yes, the postmistress is playing the piano.

STRANGER [*nervously*]: Oh. That's all right, then. This is a strange home you have here, Doctor. Everything is unusual. That wood-pile, for instance –

DOCTOR: Yes. It's been struck by lightning twice –

STRANGER: How horrible. But you still keep it there?

DOCTOR: Yes, just because of that. And this year I've raised it six feet. But also because it gives me shade in the summer. Like Jonah's gourd. But when autumn comes, he'll go into the woodshed –

STRANGER [*looks around*]: And you have Christmas roses – which flower in summer. Where did you get them? Everything here is as though time was going backwards –

DOCTOR: Oh, those. Well, I have a patient here who's a little mentally disturbed –

STRANGER: In this house?

DOCTOR: Yes, but he's a quiet fellow. He simply broods over the aimlessness of Nature, and thinks it stupid that Christmas roses should freeze in the snow, so he puts them in the cellar and plants them in the spring.

STRANGER: You have a madman in the house? That's disagreeable.

DOCTOR: He's very peaceable.

STRANGER: How did he become mad?

DOCTOR: Who can tell? Mental illness is not like bodily illness.

STRANGER: Is he – around?

DOCTOR: The madman? Yes, he's walking in the garden arranging the universe. But if he bothers you, we'll lock him in the cellar.

STRANGER: Why do they allow such wretches to live?

DOCTOR: One never knows if they're ready –

STRANGER: For what?

DOCTOR: For what follows.

STRANGER: Nothing follows life.

Pause.

DOCTOR: Who knows?

STRANGER: It's horrible here. Do you have corpses too?

DOCTOR: Yes. In the ice-chest here. Some nice bits and pieces, which I must send along to the medical board. [*Takes out a leg and arm.*] Look.

STRANGER: It's like Bluebeard's castle.

DOCTOR [*sharply*]: What do you mean by that? [*Glances sharply at the* LADY.] You think I murder my wives? Eh?

STRANGER: Good heavens, no, I can see that you don't. But – you do have ghosts here, don't you?

DOCTOR: I should say we do! Ask my wife.

He moves behind the wood-pile, so that he is invisible to the LADY *and the* STRANGER.

LADY [*to* STRANGER]: You can speak normally. My husband is a little deaf, though he can lip-read.

STRANGER: Then I'll take the opportunity to say that I've never had a more agonizing half-hour in my life. We stand

here talking the most utter nonsense, simply because no
one has the courage to speak his thoughts. I was in such a
state just now that I was seriously thinking of taking out
my knife and opening a vein to cool myself down, but now
I feel inclined to speak plainly and blow him to blazes.
Shall we tell him straight out that we intend to go away
together, and that you've had enough of his lunacy?

LADY: If you talk like that, I shall come to hate you. One
should always behave like a gentleman.

STRANGER: How nicely you've been brought up.

The DOCTOR *moves into their view. They continue.*

STRANGER: Will you run away with me, before the sun goes
down?

LADY: Sir –

STRANGER: Why did you kiss me yesterday?

LADY: Sir –

STRANGER: Imagine if he can hear us! He looks so sly –

DOCTOR: Well, Ingeborg, how shall we amuse our guest?

LADY: Our guest doesn't expect to be amused. He is not
accustomed to pleasure –

The DOCTOR *blows a whistle. The* MADMAN *comes into sight in
the garden. He wears a laurel wreath on his head and is curiously
dressed.*

DOCTOR: Caesar! Come here!

STRANGER [*disturbed*]: Is his name Caesar?

DOCTOR: No, that's a nickname I gave him after a boy who
was at school with me –

STRANGER [*uneasily*]: What is this?

DOCTOR: Well, it's a strange story. But I got the blame.

LADY [*to* STRANGER]: Who ever heard of a child being destroyed by that?

The STRANGER *winces. The* MADMAN *enters.*

DOCTOR: Come in and bow to the great writer, Caesar.

MADMAN: Is that the great writer?

LADY [*to* DOCTOR]: Why must you bring the madman in, when it upsets our guest?

DOCTOR: Now, Caesar, don't be rude, or you'll be whipped.

MADMAN: He's Caesar, all right, but he isn't great. He doesn't know which came first, the chicken or the egg. But I know.

STRANGER [*to* LADY]: I'm going. Have you tempted me into an ambush, or what am I to believe? In a moment he'll probably let out the bees to amuse me.

LADY: You must trust me implicitly, however things may appear. And don't talk so loud.

STRANGER: But he'll never leave us, this frightful ogre. Never.

DOCTOR [*looks at his watch*]: Well, if you'll excuse me, I must go and visit a patient. I'll be back in an hour. I hope you won't get bored waiting.

STRANGER: I'm used to waiting for what never comes.

DOCTOR [*to* MADMAN]: Caesar, you scoundrel, come here. I'll shut you in the cellar. [*Goes out with the* MADMAN.]

STRANGER [*to* LADY]: What is this? Who is persecuting me? You assure me that your husband feels friendly towards me; I believe you, and yet he can't open his mouth without wounding me. Every word he spoke pierced me like a needle. And there's that funeral march again – it really is being played. And that Christmas rose again. Why does everything recur? Dead men and beggars and madmen and human destinies and childhood memories. Come away. Let me liberate you from this hell.

LADY: That was why I brought you here. And also so that no one would be able to say that you had stolen another man's wife. But I must ask you one thing. Can I trust you?

STRANGER: You mean my feelings?

LADY: We won't speak of them; we have excluded them. And they'll last as long as they will last.

STRANGER: You mean, for material support, then? Yes, I've a lot of money due to me. I need only write or send a telegram –

LADY: Then I trust you. Very well. [*Puts her knitting in her pocket.*] Go out through that gate. Follow the lilac hedge and you'll see a wooden door. Open it and you'll find yourself on the high road. Meet me in the next village.

STRANGER [*hesitates*]: I don't like back doors. I'd rather have fought him in the open –

LADY [*with a gesture*]: Hurry!

STRANGER: Come with me.

LADY: Very well. But then I'll go first. [*Turns and blows a kiss towards the verandah.*] My poor ogre!

ACT TWO

Scene 1

A hotel room.

The STRANGER. *A* PORTER. *The* LADY.

STRANGER [*with a travelling bag in his hand*]: You have no other room?

PORTER: None at all.

STRANGER: But I don't want to sleep in this one.

LADY: They haven't another, dearest, and all the other hotels are full.

STRANGER [*to* PORTER]: Leave us.

The LADY *falls into a chair without removing her overcoat or hat.*

STRANGER: Is there anything you'd like?

LADY: Yes. For you to kill me.

STRANGER: I can understand that. Refused everywhere because we're not married, the police after us, and now we find ourselves in this hotel, the last in the world I'd choose – and this room, number eight. There's someone fighting against me. There's someone.

LADY: Is this number eight?

STRANGER: You've been here before too?

LADY: And you?

STRANGER: Yes.

LADY: Let's get out of here – on to the street, into the forest, anywhere –

STRANGER: I'd like to. But I'm as tired as you are, after this dreadful chase. Do you know, I felt our journey would end here – I resisted, I tried to go somewhere else, but the trains were late, they didn't come, and we had to come here, to this room. It's the Devil's work; but we'll get to grips, he and I!

LADY: It seems we shall never find peace, on this earth.

STRANGER: It's amazing how nothing has changed here. That permanently withering Christmas rose – there it is again. And that picture, the Hotel Breuer in Montreux. I've stayed there too.

LADY: Did you go to the post-office?

STRANGER: I was waiting for you to ask that. Yes, I went. In reply to five letters and three telegrams I'd sent, there was just a telegram saying my publisher had gone abroad for a fortnight.

LADY: Then we're finished.

STRANGER: Pretty well.

LADY: And in five minutes the porter will come to ask for our passports, and then the manager will ask us to leave.

STRANGER: Then there'll be only one thing left –

LADY: Two.

STRANGER: But the other's impossible.

LADY: What is the other?

STRANGER: To go to your parents, in the country.

LADY: You read my thoughts already.

STRANGER: We can no longer have any secrets from each other.

LADY: Then our dream is finished.

STRANGER: Perhaps.

LADY: Go and send one more telegram.

STRANGER: I should, but I can't do anything any more. I don't any longer believe in any future to my labours. Someone has paralysed me.

LADY: And me. We had decided never to talk about the past, but we drag it with us. Look at this wallpaper. Do you see the picture those flowers make?

STRANGER: Yes, it's him. Everywhere, everywhere! How many times – ! But I see someone else in the pattern of that tablecloth – ! Is this real? No, it must be a delusion. I'll be hearing that funeral march any moment, and then it'll be complete. [*Listens.*] There it is!

LADY: I hear nothing.

STRANGER: Then – I'm going –

LADY: Shall we go home?

STRANGER: The last and worst resort. To come as vagabonds, as beggars – no, that's impossible.

LADY: But it's – no, it's too much. To come in shame and dishonour, and bring grief to them – for me to see you humiliated, and you me. We could never respect each other again.

STRANGER: It's true, it would be worse than death. And yet – somehow I feel it's inevitable, and I begin to long for it, to get it over with, since it must be.

LADY [*takes out her knitting*]: But I have no wish to be insulted in your presence. There must be some other way. If we were married – we could do it quickly, my other marriage isn't strictly legal according to the laws of the country where it happened. We only need to go and get ourselves married by the same priest who – but this is humiliating for you –

STRANGER: It's like everything else. This honeymoon is beginning to be like a pilgrimage – or a gauntlet –

LADY: You're right. And in five minutes the manager will come and turn us out. The only way to end these humiliations is to swallow the final – hush! I hear footsteps.

STRANGER: I feel you're right. Well, I'm ready. I'm ready for everything now, and since I can't fight the invisible I'll show how long I can endure it. Lend me your jewellery – I'll redeem them when my publisher gets back, if he hasn't got drowned bathing or been killed in a railway accident. When one's as ambitious for honour as I am, the first thing one must be ready to sacrifice is one's honour.

LADY: Since we're agreed, don't you think we'd better leave this room voluntarily? Oh, God! Here he comes. The manager.

STRANGER: Let us go. The gauntlet of the waiters, the chambermaids, the bootboys and the porter – the blush of shame and the pallor of anger. The beasts of the forest have their holes, but we must flaunt our shame. At least lower your veil.

LADY: This is freedom.

STRANGER: And I the liberator.

They go.

Scene 2

By the sea.

A hut on a cliff by the sea. Outside, a table with chairs. The STRANGER *and the* LADY *are in light-coloured clothes and look younger than in the previous scene. The* LADY *is knitting.*

STRANGER: Three days of happiness and peace with my wife. Now the old unease returns.

LADY: What are you afraid of?

STRANGER: That this won't last.

LADY: Why do you think that?

STRANGER: I don't know. I feel it must end, suddenly,
horribly. There's something false in this sunshine and calm.
And I feel that happiness is not part of my destiny.

LADY: But everything's settled. My parents accept the
situation, my husband has written to say he understands –

STRANGER: What's the use, what's the use? Fate spins her
web, I hear again the gavel fall, the chairs pushed back
from the table. The sentence is pronounced, but it must
have been decided before I was born, because I began to
serve my punishment even in childhood. There isn't a
moment in my life on which I can look back with joy –

LADY: And you got everything you asked from life.

STRANGER: Everything. But I forgot to ask for gold.

LADY: Are you back there again?

STRANGER: Do you wonder?

LADY: Hush!

STRANGER: Why do you always knit? You look like one of
the Fates, drawing that wool through your fingers. No,
don't stop. The most beautiful sight I know is a woman
bent over her work, or her child. What are you knitting?

LADY: Only a shawl.

STRANGER: It looks like a net of nerves and knots: your
thoughts. I imagine the inside of your brain must look like
that –

LADY: If I had half the thoughts you think I have. But I have
none at all.

STRANGER: Perhaps that's why I find such contentment with
you. I find you complete. I can't imagine life without you.
The clouds have gone, the sky is blue, the breeze warm –

feel how it strokes your face! This is life; yes, now I am alive, just now! I feel myself swell and stretch, rarefy, become boundless; I am everywhere, in the sea which is my blood, in the mountains which are my skeleton, in the trees, in the flowers. And my head reaches to heaven. I look out over the Universe which is I, I feel the strength of the Creator within me, for I am the Creator. I should like to take this globe into my hand and knead it into something completer, more lasting, more beautiful. I should like to see all creation happy – born without pain, living without grief, and dying calmly joyful. Eve, will you die with me, now, this moment, for in another moment the agony will return?

LADY: No, I'm not ready to die.

STRANGER: Why?

LADY: I think I still have something left undone. Perhaps I have not suffered enough –

STRANGER: You think that is the purpose of life?

LADY: It seems so. But please do one thing for me.

STRANGER: Well?

LADY: Don't blaspheme like you did just now, and don't liken yourself to God. When you do, you remind me of Caesar in his cellar at home –

STRANGER [*disturbed*]: Caesar? How can you know? Tell me!

LADY: If I hurt you, I didn't mean it. I was stupid to say 'home'. Forgive me.

STRANGER: Were you only thinking of blasphemy when you likened me to Caesar?

LADY: Yes.

STRANGER: It's strange, I believe you when you say you don't want to wound me. And yet you do, like everyone else I meet. Why?

LADY: Because you're hyper-sensitive.

STRANGER: There you are again. You mean I'm paranoiac?

LADY: I swear I didn't mean that. Now the demons of discord and suspicion have come between us. Drive them away while there's time!

STRANGER: You mustn't say I blaspheme when I say what so many have said: 'Look, we are gods!'

LADY: Oh, if it's true, why can't you help yourself and us?

STRANGER: Can't I? Wait. We are only beginning.

LADY: If the end is like the beginning, Heaven help us!

STRANGER: I know what you are afraid of. I had a surprise I meant to keep for you, but I won't torment you any longer. [*Takes out a registered, unopened letter.*] Look.

LADY: The money has come!

STRANGER: This morning. Who can destroy me now?

LADY: Don't talk like that. You know who can destroy us.

STRANGER: Who?

LADY: He Who punishes human pride.

STRANGER: And courage. Especially courage. This was my Achilles' heel, and I have borne everything except this damned lack of money, which always trapped me.

LADY: Forgive my asking, but how much have you received?

STRANGER: I don't know, I haven't opened it yet. But I know roughly how much there should be. Let me see. [*Opens letter.*] What is this? No money, only a note from the bank to say I have nothing in my account. Can this be right?

LADY: I begin to believe what you said just now.

STRANGER: That I am damned? Yes. But I fling my

damnation back where it came from. You up there! I curse
You!

LADY: Don't! You frighten me.

STRANGER: Fear me if you like, but don't despise me. Now
the gauntlet is down, and you'll see a bout between
champions. [*Opens his coat and waistcoat and gazes threateningly
upwards.*] Come on! Strike me with Your lightning, if You
dare! Scare me with Your thunder, if You can!

LADY: Don't talk like that!

STRANGER: Yes! Just like that! Who dares to wake me from
my dream of love? Who snatches the beaker from my
mouth, and women from my arms? Jealous powers, be they
gods or devils. Petty-bourgeois gods, who answer an honest
challenge with pinpricks from the rear; who refuse to meet
a man on his own ground, but taunt him with unpaid bills
and sneak in through the back door to humiliate him before
his servants; who won't fight with honest weapons, but
must hoot and spit; I defy them! These mighty powers and
masters, I defy them!

LADY: May Heaven forgive you!

STRANGER: The sky is still blue and silent, the sea still blue
and foolish. Hush; I hear a poem coming. I call it that
when a theme begins to stir in my head. First I hear the
rhythm. This time it is like the tramping of hooves, the
jingle of spurs; the clash of swords; but a fluttering too, as
when a sail bellies. Banners!

LADY: No, it is only the wind in the trees –

STRANGER: Hush! Now they are riding over a bridge – a
wooden bridge, and there is no water in the river, only
stones. Wait! Now they are reading a prayer, men and
women. A *Te Deum*. Now I see – do you know where? – in
your shawl – a big kitchen, white, with lime-washed walls;
three small windows, deep-set, with lattices and flowers. In

the left-hand corner stands a stove, in the right a dining-table with pine benches; and over the table in the corner hangs a black crucifix. Beneath it burns a lamp. But the ceiling is of sooty brown beams – and on the walls hangs mistletoe, rather withered –

LADY [*frightened*]: Where do you see all this? Where?

STRANGER: In your shawl.

LADY: Do you see any people there?

STRANGER: I see an old, a very old man sitting at the kitchen table. With a hunting-bag. But his hands are clasped in prayer. And on the floor an old woman is kneeling. Now I hear the prayer again. It seems to come from outside, on the verandah. But the two in the kitchen look as though they were made of white wax or honey. And over it all lies a veil. No, this is no poem. [*Awakes.*] This is something else.

LADY: It is reality. It is the kitchen in my parents' home, where you have never been. The old man was my grandfather, the forester; the woman, my mother. She was praying – for us. It is six o'clock – when the servants read prayers on the verandah –

STRANGER: It's horrible. Am I seeing into the future too? Yet it was beautiful. The room, snow-white, with mistletoe and flowers. But why are they praying for us?

LADY: Yes, why? Have we done wrong?

STRANGER: What is wrong?

LADY: I have read that Wrong does not exist, and yet – ! I so long to see my mother again. Not my father, he disowned me, as he disowned my mother –

STRANGER: Why did he disown her?

LADY: Who knows such things? The children least of all. Let us go home. I long to.

STRANGER: To the lion's den, the snake pit. One more or less, why not? For your sake I will do it, but not as a prodigal son. For your sake I will go through fire and water –

LADY: You cannot know that.

STRANGER: But I can usually guess.

LADY: It is a hard journey. They live on a mountain. The house can only be reached on foot.

STRANGER: It sounds like a fairy tale. But I seem to have read or dreamed something like this.

LADY: Perhaps you have. But everything you will see is real – a little strange, perhaps, but people are sometimes strange. Are you ready?

STRANGER: Quite ready, for whatever may happen.

LADY [*kisses him on the forehead and makes the sign of the cross, simply and shyly, without affectation*]: Come!

Scene 3

On the highway.

A mountain landscape. Rear right, on a peak, stands a chapel. The highway, lined by fruit-trees, winds downstage. Between the trees can be seen Calvaries, small chapels of expiation, and crosses commemorating accidents. Downstage a signpost with a notice: 'Begging is forbidden in this parish'.

The STRANGER. *The* LADY.

LADY: You are tired.

STRANGER: I won't deny it. But what humiliates me is that I am hungry, because our money is finished. I never thought that would happen to me.

LADY: It seems we must be ready for everything, for I think

we are fallen from grace. Look, my boot has split. We shall
look like beggars.

STRANGER [*points at the signpost*]: And begging is forbidden in
this parish. Why do they have to write it in such big letters?

LADY: It's been there for as long as I can remember. I
haven't been here since I was a child. The road seemed
quite short then, the mountains less high, the trees smaller.
And I think we used to hear birds sing.

STRANGER: Birds sang for you all the year round, poor child.
Now they sing only in the spring – and it is nearly autumn.
But then you danced down this endless road of Calvaries,
picking flowers at the foot of the crosses – [*A distant hunting-
horn is heard.*] What's that?

LADY: It's Grandfather coming back from hunting. The good
old man. Let's hurry and get there before dark.

STRANGER: Is it far?

LADY: Not very. We have only the mountain to cross, and
then the river.

STRANGER: That's the river I hear, then?

LADY: Yes. That's where I was born and brought up. I was
eighteen before I crossed to this shore, to see what made
the distance so blue. Now I have seen it.

STRANGER: You're crying.

LADY: The good old man! When I stepped into the boat, he
said: 'There lies the world, child. When you have seen
enough, come back to your mountain. The mountains
hide.' I have seen enough. Enough!

STRANGER: Let us go. The road is long, and it is beginning
to grow dark.

They take up their things and go.

Scene 4

At the gorge.

The narrow entry to a gorge. It is lined by steep mountains covered with pine forests. Downstage a hovel. Against its door stands a broom, on the shaft of which hangs a buck's horn. Left, a smithy, the open door of which emits a red glow. Right, a flour mill. In the background, the gorge, with a millstream and bridge. The mountains form gigantic human profiles.

As the curtain rises the SMITH *is standing in the door of the smithy and the* MILLER'S WIFE *in the door of the mill. As the* LADY *enters they make a gesture to each other and disappear through their doorways. The* LADY *and* STRANGER *have ragged clothes. The* LADY *goes towards the smithy.*

STRANGER [*enters*]: They hid. Because of us, I suppose.

LADY: I don't believe that.

STRANGER: What a strange landscape this is! And how disquieting! Why is that broom there, and that greasehorn? Probably because it's their normal place, but they make me think of witches. Why is the smithy black and the mill white? Because one is sooty and the other floury, but just now when I saw the blacksmith standing in the glow of his fire facing the white miller's wife, I thought of an old poem. But do you see those giants up there? No, it's intolerable. Can't you see your ogre, whom I saved you from? It's his profile. Look! There!

LADY: It's only the mountain –

STRANGER: It is the mountain, but it's still him.

LADY: Don't ask me why we see him.

STRANGER: Conscience pricks when one is hungry and tired, it sleeps when one is full and rested. Isn't it like a curse that we have to arrive like beggars? Do you see how ragged we are after climbing through these thorn bushes? I think someone is fighting me –

LADY: Why did you challenge God?

STRANGER: Because I want to fight openly, not with unpaid bills and empty purses. Even so; here is my last shilling. Let the god of the river take it, if he exists. [*Throws a coin into the stream.*]

LADY: We needed that for the ferryman. When we enter the house now we must first ask for money –

STRANGER: When did we talk about anything else?

LADY: You despise money –

STRANGER: Like everything else.

LADY: Everything is not contemptible. There are good things –

STRANGER: I haven't noticed them.

LADY: Come with me and you'll see.

STRANGER: Very well. I'll come.

He shrinks as he is about to pass the smithy.

LADY [*who has gone ahead*]: Are you afraid of the fire?

STRANGER: No. But –

The hunting-horn is heard distantly. He runs past the smithy after her.

Scene 5

In the kitchen.

A large kitchen with whitewashed walls. Three windows in the right-hand corner (two in the rear wall, one in the right wall). The windows are small and set in deep niches containing flower pots. The roof is sooty brown, with beams. In the left corner, a stove with pots, etc., of copper, iron, pewter and wood. In the right corner, a crucifix with a lamp.

Beneath it a square table with benches against the wall. Sprigs of
mistletoe hang here and there. A door upstage. Outside can be seen the
workhouse; through the rear windows, the church. By the stove are
baskets for the dogs, and the beggars' table.

The OLD MAN *is seated at the table under the crucifix with his hands*
clasped. His hunting-bag lies in front of him. He is in his eighties,
strongly built with white hair and a full beard, and is dressed as a
forester. The MOTHER *is kneeling in the centre of the room. She is*
grey-haired, approaching fifty, dressed in black and white. From outside
can be clearly heard the voices of men, women and children singing the
final bars of the prayer: 'Holy Mary, Mother of God, pray for us poor
sinners, now and at the hour of our death. Amen'.

OLD MAN *and* MOTHER: *Amen.*

MOTHER: Father. Two tramps have been seen by the river.
They were ragged and dirty and had been in the water.
When the boatman asked for their fare they had nothing.
Now they're sitting in the sheep-hut drying their clothes.

OLD MAN: Let them sit.

MOTHER: Never close your door to a beggar. It may be an
angel.

OLD MAN: That is true. Let them come.

MOTHER: I'll put some food out here on the beggars' table, if
it won't disturb you.

OLD MAN: By all means.

MOTHER: Shall I give them some of the cider?

OLD MAN: Yes. You can light a fire. They'll be frozen.

MOTHER: It's a little late to make up a fire. But if you wish
it, Father –

OLD MAN [*looks out through the windows*]: Yes, do it.

MOTHER: What are you looking at, Father?

OLD MAN: The river has risen. I'm wondering what I've

wondered for seventy-five years. When shall I reach the sea?

MOTHER: Are you sad this evening, Father?

OLD MAN: *Et introibo ad altarem Dei; ad Deum qui laetificat juventutem meam.* Yes, I am sad. *Deus, Deus meus; quare tristis est anima mea, et quare conturbas me?*

MOTHER: Put your trust in God.

The MAID *enters and makes a sign to the* MOTHER, *who goes over to her. They whisper. The* MAID *goes.*

OLD MAN: I heard you. My God! Must I endure this too!

MOTHER: You don't have to meet them. You can go up to your room.

OLD MAN: No, I shall accept them as a penitence. But why do they come like this, as tramps?

MOTHER: I expect they lost their way and had an accident. Do you think – ?

OLD MAN: But that she should bring her – her husband here, with her! It's shameless.

MOTHER: You know Ingeborg. She always thinks everything she does is right and proper. Have you ever known her be ashamed of anything she's done, or suffer correction? Yet she's not shameless, quite the reverse. And everything she does, however tasteless, somehow seems right for her.

OLD MAN: Yes. And somehow one can't be angry with her. She always feels she's not responsible, isn't even touched by insults; it's as though she denied her own existence, or was two women, one sinning, the other absolving. But this man! I've never hated anyone as much as I do him. He sees nothing but evil everywhere. And I've never heard as much evil of any man as I have of him.

MOTHER: I know, Father. But perhaps Ingeborg has some

destiny to fulfil in this man's life, and he in hers. Perhaps they have to torment each other until they find peace –

OLD MAN: You may be right. But I don't want to have any share in something I find shameless. Must I have this man under my roof? But I must endure it, like everything else. I've deserved it.

MOTHER: In God's name, then.

The LADY *and the* STRANGER *enter.*

MOTHER: Welcome to you both.

LADY: Thank you, Mother.

The OLD MAN *rises and studies the* STRANGER.

LADY: God's peace be with you, Grandfather. This is my husband. Give him your hand.

OLD MAN: I want to look at him first. [*Approaches the* STRANGER, *places his hands on his shoulders and looks him in the eyes.*] Why have you come to my house?

STRANGER [*simply*]: Only to keep my wife company at her request.

OLD MAN: If that is true, you are welcome. I have had a long and stormy life, and have at last found, in solitude, a certain peace. I beg you not to disturb it.

STRANGER: I do not come to beg for anything, and I shall take nothing with me when I go.

OLD MAN: That answer displeases me; we all need each other. I may even need you. One never knows, young man.

LADY: Grandfather!

OLD MAN: Yes, child. I do not wish your happiness, for there is no such thing, but I wish you strength to endure your fate. Now I shall leave you. Your mother will see to your needs. [*Goes.*]

LADY [*to* MOTHER]: Did you put that food out for us, Mother?

MOTHER: On the beggars' table? No, no – I didn't realize –

LADY: Yes, we must look like beggars. We got lost on the mountain. If Grandfather hadn't sounded his horn –

MOTHER: Grandfather gave up hunting long ago.

LADY: Then it must have been someone else. Well, Mother, I'll go to the rose room and make it ready.

MOTHER: Go, child. I'll follow you.

The LADY *wants to say something, but cannot. She goes.*

STRANGER [*to* MOTHER]: I've seen this room before.

MOTHER: And I've seen you. I've been waiting for you.

STRANGER: As one who awaits misfortune?

MOTHER: Why do you say that?

STRANGER: Because I usually bring misfortune with me. But since I must be somewhere, and cannot change my fate, I have no scruples –

MOTHER: Then you're like my daughter. She has no scruples, and no conscience –

STRANGER: Oh?

MOTHER: You thought I meant ill; but I can't stand here and speak ill of my child. I only made the comparison because I assumed you knew her character as I do.

STRANGER: I haven't noticed those characteristics in Eve.

MOTHER: Why do you call Ingeborg Eve?

STRANGER: By inventing a name for her I made her mine. I shall recreate her as I wish her to be –

MOTHER: In your own image? [*Smiles.*] Country witches

carve an image of the one they want to destroy and give it the name of their intended victim. So you calculate through this new Eve of yours to destroy her whole sex?

STRANGER [*looks at the* MOTHER *in amazement*]: Damn it – ! Forgive me, you are my wife's mother, but I know you to be religious. How can you have such thoughts?

MOTHER: They are yours.

STRANGER: This is beginning to be interesting. I came expecting a country idyll and find myself in a witch's kitchen.

MOTHER: Not quite. But you forgot, or didn't know, that I am a woman who was shamefully abandoned by a man, and that you are a man who shamefully abandoned a woman.

STRANGER: That's plain speaking. Well, now I know where I am.

MOTHER: And I'd like to know where I am. Can you support two families?

STRANGER: Yes, if all goes well.

MOTHER: All doesn't go well in this life. Money can vanish.

STRANGER: But my talent is a capital asset which will not vanish.

MOTHER: It's been known to happen.

STRANGER: I've never met anyone who so knew how to drain a man's courage –

MOTHER: Arrogance needs to be drained. Your last book wasn't so good.

STRANGER: You've read that too?

MOTHER: And know your secrets. So don't try to fool me. One small thing which bothers me. Why didn't you pay the boatman?

STRANGER: My Achilles' heel again! I threw away my last shilling. Can't you talk about anything but money here?

MOTHER: Oh, we can. But in this house we do our duties first and take our pleasures afterwards. So you came on foot because you hadn't any money?

STRANGER: Yes.

MOTHER [*smiles*]: And perhaps you haven't eaten, either?

STRANGER: No.

MOTHER: You're a schoolboy, a lazy good-for-nothing –

STRANGER: I've been through a lot in my life, but I never found myself in a situation like this –

MOTHER: I almost pity you. I'd be inclined to laugh if you weren't so pathetic. You'll be the cause of many tears. Now you've got what you want, stick to the woman who loves you. If you throw her over you'll never smile again. You'll forget what happiness was.

STRANGER: Is that a threat?

MOTHER: No. A warning. Now go and eat your supper.

STRANGER [*indicates the beggars' table*]: At that table?

MOTHER: You mock poverty; you may not always do so. I've known it happen before.

STRANGER: I'll soon believe nothing is impossible. This is the worst I've ever known.

MOTHER: Oh, no. There's worse possible. Just you wait.

STRANGER [*miserably*]: Yes. I expect anything now.

He goes. The MOTHER *is left alone. The* OLD MAN *enters.*

OLD MAN: Well. That was no angel.

MOTHER: Not a good one, anyway.

OLD MAN: Ssh! You know how superstitious the people are

around here. Well, as I was going down to the river, I heard some of them talking. One said that his horse shied at 'him'; another that his dogs flew at him, so that he had to tie them up; the ferryman swore that his boat rose in the water when 'he' stepped into it. Of course it's just superstition, but –

MOTHER: But?

OLD MAN: Well, only that a magpie flew in through the window, and it was shut, through the glass, into their room. But perhaps I didn't see right.

MOTHER: I expect not. But why does one sometimes see wrong – and in the right place?

OLD MAN: That man's very presence makes me ill. I feel a tightness in my chest when he looks at me.

MOTHER: We must get rid of him. I don't think he'll be happy here.

OLD MAN: No, I don't see him growing old here. I got a letter last night warning me against him. For one thing, the police are after him –

MOTHER: The police? In your house!

OLD MAN: Yes, it's some question of money. But I beg you – the laws of hospitality, even towards beggars, even towards enemies, are sacred. Leave him in peace for a few days till he has recovered from this mad chase. You see how Providence has got her claws into him. His soul must be ground in the bruising-mill before he goes into the sieve!

MOTHER: I wouldn't mind being the instrument of Providence in this case.

OLD MAN: Don't confuse Providence with revenge.

MOTHER: I'll try not to. If it's possible.

OLD MAN: Good night.

MOTHER: Do you think Ingeborg has read his latest book?

OLD MAN: Hardly. How could she bind herself to a man with such views?

MOTHER: You're right. She can't have. Well. Now she shall.

ACT THREE

Scene 1

The rose room.

A room in the forester's house, furnished in a simple but homely manner. The walls are washed in rose-pink; the curtains are of thin rose-red muslin. Flowers stand in the small latticed windows. Right, a desk and bookshelf. Left, an ottoman with a canopy of rose-red curtains above. Chairs and tables in old German style. Upstage, a door; outside, a landscape and the workhouse, a dark gloomy building with uncurtained windows. The sun is shining brightly.

The LADY *is seated on the ottoman, knitting. The* MOTHER *is standing with a red-bound book in her hand.*

MOTHER: You don't want to read your husband's book?

LADY: No, not that book. I promised him not to.

MOTHER: Don't you want to know the man to whom you've entrusted your destiny?

LADY: What purpose would it serve? We're happy as we are.

MOTHER: You don't make great demands of life.

LADY: Why should I? Demands never get satisfied.

MOTHER: I can never decide whether you're wiser than any of us, or just stupid.

LADY: I don't know anything about myself either.

MOTHER: As long as the sun shines and you've enough to eat, you're content.

LADY: Yes. And when the sun doesn't shine, I think: 'It is ordained so.'

MOTHER: To change the subject, do you know he's being
  sued for debt?

LADY: What poet isn't?

MOTHER: Which is he, a fool or a knave?

LADY: Mother, he's neither. He's – different. The only
  tiresome thing is, I can never say anything that he hasn't
  heard before. It means we don't talk much, but he's happy
  just to have me with him. And I'm happy to have him.

MOTHER: So? You've reached calm waters already. Then it
  won't be long before you hit the rapids. But don't you think
  if you read his new book it might give you something to
  talk about with him?

LADY: Perhaps. You can leave it there if you like.

MOTHER: Take it and hide it. It'll be a nice surprise for him
  when you quote something from his latest masterpiece.

LADY [*puts the book in her pocket*]: Here he comes. He seems to
  know when anyone's talking about him. Even at a distance.

MOTHER: If only he knew when others were suffering for
  him. Even at a distance.

She goes. The LADY *is left alone for a few moments. She opens the
book and glances at it; seems amazed; and puts it back in her
pocket.*

STRANGER [*enters*]: Your mother's been here. And you were
  talking about me. I can almost hear the echo of her voice. I
  can feel her words poison the air and see them darken the
  sunlight. I think I can even see the impress of her body in
  the air – there! She leaves a smell after her like a dead
  snake.

LADY: How nervous you are today.

STRANGER: Terribly. Some bungler has overtuned my
  nerves, and now he's playing on them with a horsehair
  bow, so that they scream like a partridge – you don't know

what it's like. There's someone here who is stronger than I.
Someone who goes round with a lantern and searches me
out wherever I am. Do you have witches in this part of the
country?

LADY: Don't turn your back on the sunshine. Look at the
beautiful landscape, and you'll feel calmer.

STRANGER: No. I can't look at that workhouse. I feel it was
built there just for my sake. And there's always a
madwoman standing there, waving at me.

LADY: Do you think you've been badly treated here?

STRANGER: In a way. No – but they stuff me with delicacies,
as though I was being fattened for slaughter, and yet
everything rankles, because it isn't well wished. I feel their
hatred like – like when you open an ice-chest. Can you
imagine, I feel a cold wind everywhere, although the air's
quite still and it's terribly hot! And I keep hearing that
damned mill –

LADY: But it isn't grinding now.

STRANGER: Yes. It grinds, it grinds –

LADY: My dear, there is no hatred here. Only infinite
compassion –

STRANGER: And there's something else. Why do people cross
themselves when I walk on the road?

LADY: That's only because the people here pray silently as
they walk. It's their custom. What was in that letter you
got this morning?

STRANGER: Enough to make my hair stand on end, and
make me want to spit in the face of destiny. I'm being sued
for alimony by my children's guardians. Have you ever
seen anyone in such a humiliating situation? It's not my
fault; I've money due to me, but I can't get it. I can do
what's asked of me, I want to, but I'm not allowed to. Is

that my fault? No. But I get the shame. This is not the work of nature, but of the devil.

LADY: But why?

STRANGER: Exactly! Why? Why is man born into this world an ignorant being, ignorant of laws, customs and conventions, which through his ignorance he breaks and is therefore punished? Why does one enter manhood full of noble intentions, only to be driven into every kind of contemptible action which one loathes? Why, why?

LADY [*who, unnoticed by him, has been reading the book and not listening*]: It must have some purpose, though we cannot fathom it.

STRANGER: If it is to make us humble, as some assert, it's a bad way to do it, for it only makes me proud. Eve!

LADY: You mustn't call me that.

STRANGER [*starts*]: Why not?

LADY: I don't like it. It's as though I were to call you Caesar –

STRANGER: Are we there now?

LADY: Where? What do you mean?

STRANGER: Did you mean something else by that name?

LADY: Caesar? No, I didn't. Now I'm beginning to understand.

STRANGER: Good. Then allow me to drive the knife home myself. I am Caesar, the schoolboy who did something for which another boy got the blame. That other boy was your husband – the ogre. Thus it amuses Fate to spin her web. A noble pleasure! [*The* LADY *hesitates and is silent.*] Say something!

LADY: I can't.

STRANGER: Say that he became an ogre because as a child he

lost faith in the existence of divine justice, through being innocently punished for someone else's crime. Say it, and I shall say how I suffered twenty times over for that crime, and emerged from the religious crisis which it caused so chastened that I have never since committed a similar act.

LADY: It isn't that. It isn't that.

STRANGER: What, then? Is it that you can no longer respect me?

LADY: Not that either.

STRANGER: Then it is because I shall always feel ashamed in your presence, and then it will be finished between us.

LADY: No!

STRANGER: Eve!

LADY: Don't! You wake evil thoughts in me –

STRANGER: You have broken your promise. You have been reading my book.

LADY: Yes.

STRANGER: That was foolish. You should not have done that.

LADY: I meant well, only well.

STRANGER: Good intentions may have evil consequences. Now I am trapped, though I set the trap myself. Why must everything recur, everything? Childish follies and adult crimes. That one should reap evil where one has sown evil is fair enough; but when does a good act have its reward? What kind of being is He Who writes down every misdeed, large or small? No human being does that. Men may forgive, but the gods, never.

LADY: Don't talk like that, please? Say that you can forgive.

STRANGER: I am not petty, I think you know that; but what have I to forgive you?

LADY: Oh – more than I can say –

STRANGER: Say, and then perhaps we shall be quits.

LADY: He and I used to read the curse of Deuteronomy over you – because you had destroyed his life.

STRANGER: What curse is that?

LADY: In the Bible, the one the priests read in chorus at the beginning of Lent.

STRANGER: I don't remember it. But what matter, one more or less?

LADY: In our family, it is a tradition that whomever we curse, the curse comes home.

STRANGER: I don't believe in that. Though I don't doubt that evil goes out from this house. But may it return on the heads of those who send it! That is my prayer. According to the laws of the land it should be my duty to put a bullet through my head. But I can't while I have not fulfilled my duties. Imagine – I can't even die! And my right to do that was the last religious belief I'd retained. The powers are cunning. I have heard that a man can wrestle with God and have some hope of success, but even Job couldn't fight with Satan. Shall we have a little talk about you now?

LADY: Not yet. Soon, perhaps. Reading your dreadful book – I've only glanced at it, a few lines here and there – has been like eating of the tree of knowledge. My eyes are opened, and I know now what evil is and what good is. I didn't before. And now I see how evil you are. Now I know why you wanted to call me Eve. But if sin came into the world through the first mother, forgiveness came through another mother. We were cursed for the one, redeemed for the other. You will not destroy my sex through me, but I may have another purpose to serve in your life. We shall see.

STRANGER: You *have* eaten of the tree of knowledge. Goodbye.

LADY: Are you leaving?

STRANGER: What else can I do? I can't stay here.

LADY: Don't go.

STRANGER: I must. To clear up my affairs. I'll go and say goodbye to the old people, then I'll come back to you. I won't be a minute. [*Goes.*]

LADY [*stands for some seconds as though frozen; then goes to the door and looks out*]: No. He's gone. Gone.

She sinks brokenly to her knees.

Scene 2

The asylum.

The refectory of an old abbey. It resembles a simple, whitewashed semi-circular church, but the walls show stains of damp which resemble curious figures.

Eating tables with food bowls. At the end of each table, a lectern for the reader. Upstage, the door to the chapel. Candles burn on the tables. On the left, a painting of Michael slaying Satan.

At a long eating-table on the left sits the STRANGER in a white invalid's dress, alone with his food bowl. At a table to the right sit the Mourners in Brown from Act One; the BEGGAR, a WOMAN IN MOURNING with Two Children; a WOMAN who resembles the LADY but is not the LADY, and who knits instead of eating; a man who resembles the DOCTOR but is not he; others who resemble the MADMAN, the GRANDFATHER, the MOTHER and the BROTHER; the Parents of the 'Prodigal', etc. All are dressed in white, over which they wear gauze habits of different colours. Their faces are waxen yellow and white like those of corpses, and they all look and move like ghosts.

As the curtain rises, all except the STRANGER *are concluding the Lord's Prayer.*

STRANGER [*rises and goes to the* ABBESS, *who is standing at the serving table*]: Mother, let me speak to you for a moment.

ABBESS [*in a black and white Augustine dress*]: Yes, my son.

They come downstage.

STRANGER: First of all; where am I?

ABBESS: In the Abbey of Good Hope. We found you on the mountain above the gorge, with a cross you had broken from a wayside Calvary, with which you were threatening someone in the clouds whom you imagined you saw. You were in a fever and had fallen down a precipice. We found you unhurt but in a delirium; we brought you here to the hospital and put you to bed. You have been in a delirium ever since, and though you complained of a pain in one of your hips we could find no wound.

STRANGER: What did I say in my delirium?

ABBESS: The usual things men say in fevers. You reproached yourself with everything imaginable, and thought you saw your victims, as you called them.

STRANGER: And then?

ABBESS: You talked mainly of money. You wanted to pay for your treatment. I tried to assure you that we take no payment here, but do all for charity –

STRANGER: I want no charity. I don't need that.

ABBESS: It is indeed more blessed to give than to receive. But it takes a noble spirit to receive and be grateful.

STRANGER: I don't need to receive anything and I don't ask anything. I will not be forced into gratitude.

ABBESS: Hm! Hm! Hm!

STRANGER: Tell me, why will none of these people sit at the same table with me? They get up and go away.

ABBESS: They are afraid of you.

STRANGER: Why?

ABBESS: The way you look.

STRANGER: The – way I look? But how do they look? Are they real?

ABBESS: If you mean, do they exist – yes, in that sense they are terrifyingly real. They may look strange to you because you still have a fever. Or there may be another reason.

STRANGER: But I seem to know them all. I see them as though in a mirror. And they're only pretending to eat. Those two over there are like my parents – at first sight, that is. I've never feared anything before, because life meant nothing to me, but now I begin to be frightened.

ABBESS: If you don't believe they are real, let us ask the Confessor to introduce them to you.

She makes a sign to the CONFESSOR, *who approaches.*

CONFESSOR [*in Dominican dress, black and white*]: Sister!

ABBESS: Tell our invalid who these people are.

CONFESSOR: That won't take long.

STRANGER: May I ask you something first? Haven't we met before?

CONFESSOR: Yes. I sat by your sick-bed while you were in a fever, and heard your confession –

STRANGER: My confession!

CONFESSOR: Yes. But I could not grant you absolution, for my impression was that what you were telling me were hallucinations.

STRANGER: How do you mean?

CONFESSOR: There was hardly a crime or a vice to which you
did not plead guilty, including some so terrible that we
require the strictest penitence before we can grant
absolution. Now that you have regained consciousness, I
must ask if there is any ground for these self-accusations.

The ABBESS *moves away.*

STRANGER: Have you any right to ask that?

CONFESSOR: No, I have not. You are right. But you wanted
to know who these people are? Well, they are not the
happiest of mankind. There, for example, we have a
madman called Caesar, who lost his reason through
reading the books of a certain author whose notoriety is
greater than his fame. And there a Beggar, who won't
admit that he is a Beggar because he can read Latin and
claims that he has been liberated. And there a Doctor, also
called an ogre; his story is well known. And a father and
mother who grieved to death for a depraved son who raised
his hand against them. He did not follow his father's bier to
the churchyard and in a state of drunkenness profaned his
mother's grave; for that he must answer himself. There sits
his poor sister, whom he drove out into the winter snow,
according to his own account. And there an abandoned
wife with two neglected children. And there a woman who
knits. You know them all. Go and greet them.

During this speech the STRANGER *has turned his back on the
company. Now he goes and sits at the table left, still with his back
towards them. When he raises his head he sees the picture of Michael
and drops his eyes. The* CONFESSOR *goes over and stands behind
the* STRANGER. *A Catholic requiem is heard from the chapel.*

CONFESSOR [*whispers to the* STRANGER *as the music is heard
softly*]:
Quantus tremor est futurus
Quando judex est venturus
Cuncta stricte discussurus.
Tuba mirum spargens sonum

Per sepulchra regionum
Coget omnes ante thronum.
Mors stupebit et natura
Cum resurget creatura
Judicanti responsura
Liber scriptus proferetur
In quo totum continetur
Unde mundus judicetur.
Judex ergo cum sedebit
Quidquid latet apparebit
Nil inultum remanebit.

He goes to the lectern by the table right. He opens the breviary. The music ceases.

CONFESSOR: Now let us continue with our reading. 'But it shall come to pass, if thou wilt not hearken unto the voice of the Lord thy God, to observe to do all His commandments and His statutes which I command thee this day; that all these curses shall come upon thee and overtake thee. Cursed shalt thou be in the city and cursed shalt thou be in the field. Cursed shall be thy basket and thy store. Cursed shalt thou be when thou comest in and cursed shalt thou be when thou goest out.'

OTHERS [*whisper*]: Cursed!

CONFESSOR: 'The Lord shall send upon thee cursing, vexation and rebuke, in all that thou settest thine hand unto for to do, until thou be destroyed and until thou perish quickly; because of the wickedness of the doings, whereby thou has forsaken Me.'

OTHERS [*aloud*]: Cursed!

CONFESSOR: 'The Lord shall cause thee to be smitten before thine enemies; thou shalt go out one way against them, and flee seven ways before them; and shall be removed into all the kingdoms of the earth. And thy carcase shall be meat unto all fowls of the air, and unto the beasts of the earth, and no man shall fray them away. Thou shalt betroth a

wife, and another man shall lie with her; thou shalt build
an house, and thou shalt not dwell therein; thou shalt plant
a vineyard and shalt not gather the grapes thereof. Thy
sons and thy daughters shall be given to other people, and
thine eyes shall look and fail with longing for them all the
day long; and there shall be no might in thy hand. And
among the nations shalt thou find no ease, neither shall the
sole of thy foot have rest; but the Lord shall give thee a
trembling heart, and failing of eyes and sorrow of mind.
And thy life shall hang in doubt before thee; and thou shalt
fear day and night, and shalt have none assurance of thy
life. In the morning shalt thou say: "Would God it were
even!" And at even shalt thou say: "Would God it were
morning!" And because thou servest not the Lord thy God
with joyfulness, and with gladness of heart, for the
abundance of all things; therefore shalt thou serve Him in
hunger and in thirst, and in nakedness and in want of all
things; and He shall put a yoke of iron upon thy neck, until
He have destroyed thee.'

OTHERS: Amen!

The CONFESSOR *has been reading quickly and loudly, without
addressing himself to the* STRANGER. *The Others, except the*
LADY, *who is knitting, have listened and cursed, without seeming to
notice the* STRANGER, *who has been sitting with his back to them,
quiet and hunched. He rises to go. The* CONFESSOR *goes towards
him.*

STRANGER: What was that?

CONFESSOR: The curse of Deuteronomy.

STRANGER: Oh – it was that! I seem to remember it
contained a blessing too.

CONFESSOR: For those who keep His commandments.

STRANGER: I see. I can't deny it shook me a little, for a
moment. I don't know whether this is a trial to test me, or

a warning to heed. However, my fever still seems to be with me, so I'll go and find a real doctor.

CONFESSOR: As you please. But make sure it's the right one.

STRANGER: Of course, of course.

CONFESSOR: One who can cure these 'beautiful pangs of conscience'.

ABBESS: If you ever need charity, you know where it can be found.

STRANGER: No, I don't.

ABBESS [*softly*]: I will tell you. In a rose-red room, by a broad, flowing river.

STRANGER: Yes! In a rose-red room – ! Let me see. How long have I been lying here?

ABBESS: Three months.

STRANGER: Three months? Ah! Have I been sleeping, or where have I been? [*Looks out through the window.*] Yes, it's autumn. The trees are bare, the clouds wear their cold colour. Memories begin to awake. Do you hear a mill turning, a horn calling, a river rushing, a forest whispering, and – a woman crying? Yes, you are right. Only there is charity. Goodbye! [*Runs out.*]

CONFESSOR [*to* ABBESS]: The madman! The madman!

Scene 3

The rose room.

The curtains have been removed and the windows gape like brown holes at the darkness outside. The furniture is covered with brown dustsheets and is pushed forward into the middle of the room. The flowers are gone and the big, black iron stove is lit.

The MOTHER *stands ironing white curtains by the light of a single candle. There is a knock on the door.*

MOTHER: Come in.

STRANGER [*enters*]: Good evening. Where is my wife?

MOTHER: Oh, it's you. Where have you come from?

STRANGER: I think from Hell. But where is my wife?

MOTHER: Which one?

STRANGER: That question is justified. Everything is justified, except me.

MOTHER: There's a reason; and it's good you've noticed it. But where have you been?

STRANGER: Whether it was a poorhouse, a madhouse or an ordinary hospital, I don't know. I like to think it was a hallucination. I've been ill and lost my memory. I can't believe three months have gone. But where is my wife?

MOTHER: I should ask you that. When you left her she went away. To look for you. Whether she's tired of looking, I don't know.

STRANGER: It looks terrible here. Where's the old man?

MOTHER: Where no griefs torment him.

STRANGER: Dead?

MOTHER: Yes. He is dead.

STRANGER: You speak as though I were to blame for that too.

MOTHER: Perhaps.

STRANGER: He didn't look that sensitive. And showed himself capable of strong hatred.

MOTHER: No. He could only hate evil, in himself and others.

STRANGER: Then I am blamed unjustly. For that too.

Pause.

MOTHER: What are you looking for here?

STRANGER: Charity.

MOTHER: At last. But tell me. What happened after you left here?

STRANGER: I fell on the mountain and hurt my hip. I lost consciousness. If you talk sensibly to me I'll tell you the rest.

MOTHER: I'll talk sensibly.

STRANGER: Well, then. I woke in a bed of red steel bars, and three men were pulling on a rope which ran between two blocks, and each time they pulled it felt as though I was being stretched a yard longer –

MOTHER: You'd dislocated your hip, and they were trying to re-set it.

STRANGER: You're right. I hadn't thought of that. But then – yes, then I lay there and saw my whole life unreel in a kind of panorama from my childhood, through my youth, right up to . . . And when it was finished, it began to unreel again – and the whole time, I heard a mill turning – and I hear it still. Yes, now it's here too!

MOTHER: It can't have been a pretty spectacle.

STRANGER: No. And in the end I came to the conclusion that – I was a dreadful blackguard.

MOTHER: Why do you use that expression?

STRANGER: I know you'd rather I said 'an evil person'. But anyone who says that about himself seems to me to be bragging, and there's a kind of cocksureness about it that I haven't yet attained to.

MOTHER: You still have doubts?

STRANGER: Yes. About many things. But I begin to believe one thing –

MOTHER: Yes?

STRANGER: That there are things – and powers – that I didn't believe in before.

MOTHER: Have you also realized that neither you nor any other human being controls your curious destiny?

STRANGER: I – think I did realize that.

MOTHER: Then you've got somewhere.

STRANGER: But there's something else. I'm – bankrupt. I've lost the power to create. And I can't sleep at night –

MOTHER: Oh?

STRANGER: What people call – night mares. And the worst is, I no longer dare to die, because I'm no longer sure that death puts an end to misery.

MOTHER: I see.

STRANGER: But the worst thing of all is that I've developed such a loathing for myself that I'd gladly get rid of that self, but I can't see any possibility of doing so. If I were a Christian, I couldn't obey the commandment to love my neighbour as myself, because that would mean I would hate my neighbour, which I do. I know it's true that I am a great blackguard, and I've always suspected it, but because I didn't want to be life's fool I've always kept a wary eye on 'the others' – and when I saw that they weren't any better than myself, I became angry when they tried to master me.

MOTHER: Yes, but you've got it wrong. You thought it was just a matter between yourself and the rest of mankind. It's between you and Him –

STRANGER: Who?

MOTHER: The Invisible One Who steers our destiny.

STRANGER: May I see Him?

MOTHER: You will be dying when you do.

STRANGER: No!

MOTHER: Where did you get this accursed spirit of rebelliousness? If you won't bend like the rest of us, you must be broken like a straw.

STRANGER: I don't know where I got this damned obstinacy. I tremble when I see an unpaid bill, but if I could climb Mount Sinai and confront the Almighty, I wouldn't cover my face.

MOTHER: Blessed Jesus! To talk like that! I think you are a child of the Evil One.

STRANGER: That seems to be the general opinion of me around here. But I've heard that those who are close to the Evil One are usually favoured with honour, possessions and gold, especially gold. Do you think I come into that category?

MOTHER: You will bring a curse on my house.

STRANGER: Then I will leave your house.

MOTHER: Tonight? No. Where will you go?

STRANGER: In search of the one person whom I do not hate.

MOTHER: Are you sure she will receive you?

STRANGER: Quite sure.

MOTHER: I'm not.

STRANGER: But I am.

MOTHER: Then I must make you unsure.

STRANGER: You can't do that.

MOTHER: I can.

STRANGER: You're lying.

MOTHER: Now we're not speaking sensibly any longer, so we'll stop. Can you sleep in the attic?

STRANGER: Anywhere. But I shan't sleep.

MOTHER: Then I'll wish you a good night; whether you think I mean it or not.

STRANGER: There aren't rats in the attic, are there? I'm not afraid of ghosts, but I don't like rats.

MOTHER: It's lucky you're not afraid of ghosts, because – no one's ever stayed a whole night up there. Whatever it is.

STRANGER [*hesitates a moment, then*]: You are the most malignant person I've ever met. But that's because you're religious.

MOTHER: Good night.

Scene 4

The kitchen.

It is dark, but the moon outside casts restless shadows on the floor from the window lattices as the storm clouds run by.

In the corner, right, beneath the crucifix, where the OLD MAN *used to sit, his hunting-horn, gun and hunting-bag hang on the wall. A stuffed bird of prey stands on the table. The windows are open and the curtains flap; and dishcloths, aprons and hand-towels hanging on a line flutter in the wind, the soughing of which can be heard. In the distance a waterfall roars; now and then the wooden floor bangs.*

STRANGER [*enters, half-dressed, with a candle in his hand*]: Is there anyone there? No one. [*Comes in with the candle, which renders the shadow-play less distinct.*] What's that moving on the floor? Is there anyone here? [*Goes towards the table, but stops as though petrified when he sees the bird of prey.*] Jesus Christ!

MOTHER [*enters, dressed, with a candle*]: Are you still up?

STRANGER: Yes, I couldn't sleep.

MOTHER [*gently*]: Why, my son?

STRANGER: There was someone walking upstairs.

MOTHER: Impossible. There's no room above that one.

STRANGER: That's what disturbed me. But what's that moving on the floor like snakes?

MOTHER: The moonlight.

STRANGER: Yes, it's the moonlight. And there is a stuffed bird. And there are kitchen cloths. Everything's normal and natural – it's just that that disturbs me. Who's that knocking? Has someone been shut out?

MOTHER: No, it's a horse kicking in the stable.

STRANGER: Really?

MOTHER: Yes, there are horses that suffer from the night mare.

STRANGER: What is a night mare?

MOTHER: Who knows?

STRANGER: Let me sit down for a moment.

MOTHER: Sit down and let me talk seriously to you. I was cruel to you last night, and I ask you to forgive me. But because I am so cruel, I use religion as I use a hair shirt and a stone floor. If it will ease your mind, I will tell you what the night mare is; it is my evil conscience. Whether it is I or somebody else that punishes me, I don't know, and I don't think I have the right to ask. Now tell me what happened to you in that room.

STRANGER: I really don't know. I didn't see anything, but when I went in I felt someone was there. I looked with my candle, but found no one. Then I went to bed. And then someone began to walk with heavy steps above my head. Do you believe in ghosts and spirits?

MOTHER: No. My religion forbids that. But I believe in the power of conscience to create means of chastisement.

STRANGER: Well . . . After a moment I felt an icy stream of air against my breast, groping until it found my heart. Then my heart went cold, and I had to get out of bed –

MOTHER: And then?

STRANGER: Then I found myself pinned to the floor, and I saw the whole panorama of my life unroll before me, everything, everything. And that was the worst.

MOTHER: Yes. I know all that. I have been through it. There's no name for that sickness, and only one cure –

STRANGER: What?

MOTHER: You know. You know what children have to do when they've done wrong.

STRANGER: What must they do?

MOTHER: First, ask for forgiveness.

STRANGER: And then?

MOTHER: Try to make things right.

STRANGER: Isn't it enough to suffer according to one's deserts?

MOTHER: No. That's just revenge.

STRANGER: Well, what else?

MOTHER: Can you make good a life you've destroyed? Can you undo a wicked deed?

STRANGER: No, that's true. But I was forced to do that deed. I was forced to take, because nobody gave me. But shame on Him Who forced me! Ah! [*Puts his hand to his breast.*] Ah!

Now He's here, in this room! He's tearing the heart from my breast! Ah!

MOTHER: Humble yourself.

STRANGER: I can't!

MOTHER: On your knees!

STRANGER: I won't.

MOTHER: Christ have mercy upon you. Lord have mercy! [*To the* STRANGER.] On your knees to Him Who was crucified for us! Only He can undo what has been done.

STRANGER: No, not to Him! Not to Him! And if I'm forced to do it, I'll take it back – later.

MOTHER: On your knees! My son!

STRANGER: I can't kneel! I can't! Help me, Eternal God!

Pause.

MOTHER [*mutters a swift prayer, then*]: Well. Do you feel better?

STRANGER [*collects himself*]: Yes. But do you know what that was? It wasn't death. It was annihilation.

MOTHER: Annihilation of the godhead in you. We call that spiritual death.

STRANGER [*earnestly, without irony*]: I see. Now I begin to understand.

MOTHER: My son. You have left Jerusalem and are on the road to Damascus. Go there; by the same road you came. And plant a cross at every station, but stop at the seventh. You don't have to suffer fourteen, like Him.

STRANGER: You speak in riddles.

MOTHER: Well . . . Get up. Go and search out those to whom you have something to say. First your wife.

STRANGER: Where?

MOTHER: Search. But don't forget the one you call the ogre –

STRANGER: Never!

MOTHER: I hear you said that when it was suggested that you should come here. But, as I told you, I was expecting you.

STRANGER: Why?

MOTHER: For no reason that you would call rational –

STRANGER: Just as I saw this kitchen – in – an ecstasy, if you like –

MOTHER: I regret now that I tried to part you from Ingeborg. You and she were meant to meet. Go now, and search her out. If you find her, good. If not, perhaps it was intended so. It is beginning to grow light. The dawn is here. The night is over.

STRANGER: And what a night!

MOTHER: You will remember it.

STRANGER: Not all of it. But I shall remember some.

MOTHER [*looks out through window; as though to herself*]: O morning star, why hast thou fallen so far from heaven?

Pause.

STRANGER: Have you noticed that before the sun rises we mortals shiver? Are we children of darkness, that we tremble before the coming of the light?

MOTHER: Do you never tire of asking questions?

STRANGER: Never. You see – I long for the light.

MOTHER: Go now. And peace be with you.

ACT FOUR

Scene 1

At the gorge.

The landscape is as before, but it is autumn and the trees are bare. There is a noise of hammering from the smithy, and the mill is turning. The SMITH *stands in his doorway, left; the* MILLER'S WIFE *right. The* LADY *is dressed in a jacket and a patent-leather hat, but is in mourning. The* STRANGER *wears Tyrolean Alpine dress – a woollen jacket, knee-breeches, mountain boots, a staff, and a green huntsman's hat with a blackcock's feather in it. Over his clothes he wears a brown 'Kaiser's cloak', with a cape and hood.*

LADY [*enters in travelling clothes, tired and distressed*]: Has a gentleman in travelling clothes passed this way?

The SMITH *and* MILLER'S WIFE *shake their heads.*

LADY: Can you give me shelter for the night?

They shake their heads again.

LADY [*to* SMITH]: May I stand in your doorway and warm myself for a moment?

The SMITH *pushes her back.*

LADY: May God reward you as you deserve!

She goes; is seen a moment later on the bridge; then disappears.

STRANGER [*enters in travelling clothes*]: Has a lady in travelling dress gone across the river? [*They shake their heads. To the* MILLER'S WIFE] Can you sell me a crust of bread? I have money. [*She rejects the money.*] Have you no charity?

An echo in the distance imitates his voice: 'Charity!' The SMITH *and the* MILLER'S WIFE *utter a long and high-pitched laugh, which is answered by the echo.*

STRANGER: I like that. An eye for an eye, a tooth for a tooth. That always helped to ease my conscience.

He enters the gorge.

Scene 2

On the highway.

Again, the landscape is as before, but it is autumn. The BEGGAR *is sitting outside a chapel of expiation with a lime-twig and a starling in a cage.*

STRANGER [*enters dressed as in the preceding scene*]: Tell me, beggar. Have you seen a lady in travelling dress pass this way?

BEGGAR: I've seen five hundred. And I'd be obliged if you'd stop calling me beggar. I work now.

STRANGER: Oh, it's you.

BEGGAR: *Ille ego qui quondam* –

STRANGER: What work do you do?

BEGGAR: I keep a starling. He whistles and talks –

STRANGER: He's the one who works, then?

BEGGAR: Yes. I've become independent.

STRANGER: Do you catch birds, too?

BEGGAR: Oh, the lime-twig. No, that's just for appearances.

STRANGER: You care about appearances?

BEGGAR: What else matters? Who cares about what's inside?

STRANGER: Is that your philosophy?

BEGGAR: My whole metaphysical system. It may seem rather an outdated viewpoint, but –

STRANGER: Say something serious. Tell me your history.

BEGGAR: Oh, what's the use of rooting in dunghills? Forget the past, friend, forget it. Do you think I'm always as merry as this? No, it's only when I meet you. You're so bloody funny.

STRANGER: How can you laugh with a whole life wasted behind you?

BEGGAR: Now you're being personal. But if a man can't laugh at adversity, even other people's, how's he to go on living? Listen. If you follow these wheel-tracks in the mud, you'll come to the sea, and there the road ends. Sit down there and rest for a while, and you'll see things differently. You get so many accidents on this road – religious worries, painful memories – they keep your mind from the rose room. But just follow the tracks. If it gets a bit muddy now and then, just stretch your wings and try to fly. Talking of flying, I once heard a bird singing something about Polycrates' ring. How he'd got all the glory of the world but didn't know what to do with it. So he went round proclaiming the worthlessness of the life he'd managed to create out of the emptiness he'd found in riches. I wouldn't say it was you if I couldn't swear to it. And once when I asked you if you knew who I was, you replied that you weren't interested. I offered you my friendship, but you refused it and said: 'Be off!' But I don't take offence or bear grudges, so I'll just give you this good advice. Follow the tracks.

STRANGER [shrinks aside]: No, you won't fool me again.

BEGGAR: Sir! You only think bad of people, so you only get bad in return. Try to think good for once. Try.

STRANGER: I'll try. But if people betray me, I have the right to –

BEGGAR: You never have that right.

STRANGER [as though to himself]: Who reads my secret

thoughts, who turns my soul inside out, who persecutes
me? Why do you persecute me?

BEGGAR: Saul, Saul, why persecutest thou me?

The STRANGER, *with a gesture of horror, goes. The sound of the
funeral march is heard, as before. The* LADY *enters.*

LADY: Have you seen a gentleman pass this way?

BEGGAR: Yes, there was a poor chap here just now, hobbling
along.

LADY: The man I am looking for isn't lame.

BEGGAR: This one wasn't exactly that. But he seemed to
have hurt his hip, so he couldn't walk properly. Well, I
won't be hard. Look there in the mud.

LADY: Where?

BEGGAR [*points*]: There. See that wheeltrack? Beside it there's
a heavy footprint –

LADY [*looks at it*]: It's him. Yes, they are heavy. Shall I be
able to catch him up?

BEGGAR: Follow the tracks.

LADY [*takes his hand and kisses it*]: Thank you, my friend.
[*Goes.*]

Scene 3

By the sea.

*The same landscape as before, but winter. The sea is blue-black; on the
horizon clouds tower like giant heads. In the distance three white,
dismantled masts of a wrecked ship, like three crosses, project from the
water. The table and bench still stand under the tree, but the chairs are
gone. There is snow on the ground. Now and then a bell-buoy sounds.*

The STRANGER *enters left, stops for a moment and looks out to sea.
Then he goes out right, behind the hut. The* LADY *enters left; seems to
follow the* STRANGER'S *footprints in the snow and goes out right, in
front of the hut. The* STRANGER *re-enters right, goes left, finds the*
LADY'S *footprints, stops and looks back right. The* LADY *enters, runs
to embrace him, but staggers back.*

LADY: Are you pushing me away?

STRANGER: No. But someone seems to stand between us.

LADY: Someone does. So; I've found you. But –

STRANGER: Yes. It is winter now, as you see.

LADY: And I feel the cold stream out of you.

STRANGER: I got frozen there. In the mountains.

LADY: Will it never be spring again?

STRANGER: Not for us. We have been driven from Paradise
    and must wander among stones and thistles. And when our
    feet and hands are bleeding we must rub salt in one
    another's wounds. And that mill is turning; and it will
    never stop, for the stream will never run dry.

LADY: I suppose you are right.

STRANGER: But I don't want to yield to the inevitable. I
    don't want us to tear each other apart. I shall offer myself
    to the gods as a placatory sacrifice. I shall say: 'I am the
    guilty one.' It was I who taught you to loose your bonds, I
    who tempted you. You can blame me for everything. What
    we did, and the consequences –

LADY: You can't bear it alone.

STRANGER: There are moments when I feel I can bear all the
    world's sin and grief and dirt and shame. There are
    moments when I believe that my sins and crimes are
    themselves my ordained punishment. Do you know, a little
    while ago I lay in a fever and among other things – there
    were so many things – I dreamed that I saw a crucifix with

Him on it. And when I asked the Dominican – there was a
Dominican there, among many others – I asked him what
this might mean, and he replied: 'You will not let Him
suffer for you, so suffer yourself.' That is why mankind has
grown so sensitive to its own agonies.

LADY: And why our consciences become so heavy, now that
we must bear the burden alone.

STRANGER: Have you reached that point too?

LADY: Not yet. But I am on the way.

STRANGER: Put your hand in mine and let us go together.

LADY: Where?

STRANGER: Back – the way we came. Are you tired?

LADY: Not any longer.

STRANGER: Several times I fell. But then I met a strange
beggar – perhaps you remember him? – the one they said
was like me. And he told me to try to think good of his
intentions. I tried – just to see – and –

LADY: Yes?

STRANGER: Things got better. Since then I have found the
strength to go on.

LADY: Let's go together.

STRANGER [*turns to the sea*]: It's growing dark, and the clouds
are gathering.

LADY: Don't look at the clouds.

STRANGER: And down there. What's that?

LADY: Only a wrecked ship.

STRANGER [*whispers*]: Three crosses! What new Golgotha
awaits us?

LADY: They are white. That means good.

STRANGER: Can any good ever happen to us again?

LADY: Yes. But not yet.

STRANGER: Let us go.

Scene 4

The hotel room.

As before. The LADY *is seated knitting beside the* STRANGER.

LADY: Say something.

STRANGER: No. I've only had evil thoughts since we came back here.

LADY: Why did we have to come back to this dreadful room?

STRANGER: I don't know. It was the last thing I wanted to do. So I began to long to come here – to suffer.

LADY: And you have suffered.

STRANGER: Yes. I no longer hear any songs, or have good visions. Each day I hear the mill grind, and see that dreadful panorama, which grows and grows. And at night –

LADY: Why did you cry in your sleep?

STRANGER: I had a dream –

LADY: A real dream?

STRANGER: Terrifyingly real. Now you see my curse – I *must* talk about it, and whom can I tell but you? But I mustn't tell you, because then I shall touch the door to that closed room –

LADY: The past.

STRANGER: Yes.

LADY [*simply*]: There is always something trivial in those sealed rooms.

STRANGER: I suppose so.

Pause.

LADY: Tell me.

STRANGER: I fear I must. Well, I dreamed I saw – your former husband married to my former wife. So that my children had him for their father –

LADY: Only you could imagine that.

STRANGER: I hope you're right. [*Sighs.*] But I saw him maltreat them. [*Gets up.*] Then I strangled him, of course, and – no, I can't go on. But I shall have no peace until I know. And to do that I must go and see him, in his own home.

LADY: Has it come to that?

STRANGER: I've felt on the verge of it for a long time, and now there's no help for it. I must see him.

LADY: Suppose he won't see you?

STRANGER: I shall go as a patient, and tell him about my illness.

LADY [*frightened*]: You mustn't do that.

STRANGER: I understand. You mean he might have me put away? Well, I must risk that. I *need* to risk everything – my freedom, my life, my well-being. I must suffer enough to bring my soul up into the daylight; I long for a torture to restore my sense of feeling equal with society, so that I don't have to go on feeling in debt. So; down into the snake pit, and the sooner the better.

LADY: If I could go with you –

STRANGER: You don't need to. My sufferings will suffice for both of us.

LADY: Then I shall call you my liberator, and the curse I once invoked on you shall become a blessing. Do you see that it is spring again?

STRANGER: I noticed it in that Christmas rose. It's beginning to wither.

LADY: But don't you feel that there is spring in the air?

STRANGER: Yes. I think that chill is beginning to leave my heart.

LADY: Perhaps the ogre will be able to cure you completely.

STRANGER: We'll see. He may not be so dangerous after all.

LADY: He is certainly not so cruel as you.

STRANGER: But my dream! Imagine –

LADY: – if it was only a dream! My wool is finished now, and my useless task. It has got dirty –

STRANGER: But it can be washed.

LADY: Or dyed a new colour.

STRANGER: Rose-red.

LADY: Never!

STRANGER: It is like a scroll –

LADY: With our saga on it.

STRANGER: Written in mud, and tears, and blood.

LADY: Our saga will soon be done. Go and write the last chapter.

STRANGER: Then we shall meet at the seventh station. Where we started.

ACT FIVE

Scene 1

At the DOCTOR's.

The scene is as before, except that the wood-pile is half its former size, and on the verandah stands a bench with surgical instruments – knives, saws, forceps, etc. The DOCTOR *is busy polishing his instruments.*

SISTER [*enters from the verandah*]: There's a patient asking for you.

DOCTOR: Do you know him?

SISTER: I haven't seen him, but here's his card.

DOCTOR [*reads it*]: Well! This goes beyond anything I've ever – !

SISTER: Is it he?

DOCTOR: Yes. I respect courage, but such brazenness as this I find cynical. It's almost like a challenge. However, show him in.

SISTER: Are you serious?

DOCTOR: Absolutely. But if you wish, you can talk to him a little. In your brazen way.

SISTER: I'd already decided to.

DOCTOR: Good. You do the ground work. I'll add the veneer.

SISTER: Never you fear! I'll tell him everything you're too kind to say.

DOCTOR: Never you mind my kindness. And hurry up, so I don't start feeling unkind. But shut the doors!

The SISTER *goes.*

DOCTOR: What are you doing by that rubbish bin again, Caesar? [*The* MADMAN *enters.*] Tell me, Caesar. If your enemy comes and rests his head on your knees, what would you do?

MADMAN: Cut it off.

DOCTOR: That is not what I taught you.

MADMAN: No, you say I should heap coals of fire on it. But I think that's wicked.

DOCTOR: I think so too, really. It's crueller, and more cunning. Better to take some small revenge, then he feels he has made amends and his debt is settled.

MADMAN: If you understand these things better than I do, why ask me?

DOCTOR: Shut up, I'm not talking to you. Right; we'll take his head off. And then, we'll see.

MADMAN: It depends on how he behaves.

DOCTOR: Quite right. How he behaves! Hush! Be off, now.

STRANGER [*enters from verandah, disturbed but with a certain air of resignation*]: Doctor.

DOCTOR: Yes.

STRANGER: You are doubtless surprised to see me here –

DOCTOR [*earnestly*]: I gave up being surprised a long time ago. But I see I must start again.

STRANGER: Will you grant me a private conversation?

DOCTOR: On any subject regarded as proper among civilized people. Are you ill?

STRANGER [*hesitantly*]: Yes.

DOCTOR: Why do you come to me?

STRANGER: You should be able to guess.

DOCTOR: I do not wish to. What is wrong with you?

STRANGER [*hesitantly*]: I can't sleep.

DOCTOR: That's not an illness, it's a symptom. Have you been to a doctor about it before?

STRANGER: I was a patient in – an institution. I had a fever – but it was a very strange fever.

DOCTOR: What was strange about it?

STRANGER: May I ask you – can one walk in a delirium?

DOCTOR: Yes, if one is mad. But only then.

The STRANGER *gets up, but sits down again.*

DOCTOR: What was the name of the hospital?

STRANGER: The House of Good Hope.

DOCTOR: There is no hospital of that name.

STRANGER: Is it a monastery, then?

DOCTOR: No. A madhouse.

The STRANGER *gets up.*

DOCTOR [*gets up and calls*]: Sister! Shut the front door. And the little door to the main road. [*To the* STRANGER.] Please sit down. I have to shut these doors for fear of tramps. The district's full of them.

STRANGER [*calms himself*]: Doctor; a straight question. Do you think I am mad?

DOCTOR: One never gets an honest answer to that question, you know – or believes it, if the answer is yes. So it doesn't matter what I say. But if you think your soul is sick, go and find a priest.

STRANGER: Wouldn't you care to take on that job for a minute?

DOCTOR: No. I lack the calling.

STRANGER: If –

DOCTOR [*interrupts*]: Anyway, I haven't the time. I'm about to get married.

STRANGER: My dream.

DOCTOR: I thought it might help you to know that I've consoled myself, as the saying is – might even make you happy – it's the usual reaction – but I see it increases your sense of suffering. There must be some reason for that. I must investigate. How can it trouble you that I am marrying a widow?

STRANGER: With two children?

DOCTOR: One moment. One moment. Ah, I see! What a hellish notion, just like you. If there is a hell, you ought to be in charge of it. Your inventiveness in finding new methods of punishment exceeds my wildest imaginings – and people call me the ogre!

STRANGER: But it could happen.

DOCTOR [*interrupts*]: For a long time I hated you, as you perhaps know, because you did something unforgivable which destroyed my good name. But as I grew older and wiser, I realized that if my punishment was unjustified at the time, I had nevertheless deserved it for other things which had not been found out. And anyway you were a child and had enough of a conscience to punish yourself, so that needn't worry you either. Was that why you came?

STRANGER: Yes.

DOCTOR: Then will it content you if I say: 'Go in peace'? [*The* STRANGER *looks at him questioningly.*] Or did you think I was going to have you put away, or saw you up with that instrument over there? Or kill you, perhaps? What was it you once said, 'Why do they allow such wretches to live'? [*The* STRANGER *looks at his watch.*] You'll have time to catch the boat.

STRANGER: Will you give me your hand?

DOCTOR: No, I can't do that. I mustn't. Anyway, what help
will it be if I forgive you, if you haven't the strength to
forgive yourself? There are situations when the only help is
to undo what has been done; and in this case there is no
help, or hope.

STRANGER: 'The Good Hope'.

DOCTOR: Things haven't been that bad. You challenged
Fate, and you were broken. There's no shame in a good
fight. I did the same, but as you see I've cut down my
wood-pile. I don't want to have lightning in my house. I
don't play with that kind of thing any longer.

STRANGER: One more station, and my journey will be done.

DOCTOR: Never, sir. Goodbye.

STRANGER: Goodbye.

Scene 2

The street corner.

As in Act One. The STRANGER *is seated on the bench under the tree,
drawing in the sand.*

LADY [*enters*]: What are you doing?

STRANGER: I am drawing in the sand. Still.

LADY: Don't you hear any songs?

STRANGER [*points to the church*]: Yes, but from in there.
There's someone I wronged without knowing it.

LADY: I thought our wandering was near our end, now that
we are back here.

STRANGER: Where we started. In the street, between the café

and the church. And the post-office. The post-office! P, o, s, t – I say, didn't I leave a registered letter here, uncollected?

LADY: Yes, because it contained something bad –

STRANGER: Or a writ. [*Strikes himself on the forehead.*] There it is again!

LADY: Go and fetch it. And believe it may contain something good.

STRANGER [*ironically*]: Good?

LADY: Believe it. Try to imagine it.

STRANGER [*goes into the post-office*]: I'll try.

The LADY *walks up and down, waiting. The* STRANGER *comes out with a letter.*

LADY: Well?

STRANGER: I am ashamed. It was money.

LADY: You see. All this misery, all these tears – for nothing.

STRANGER: Not for nothing. It seems horrible, this game, but perhaps it's not. I wronged the Invisible One when I suspected Him of –

LADY: Hush! Don't try to shift the blame.

STRANGER: No. It was my own stupidity. Or wickedness. I didn't want to become life's fool, and so I became it. But the powers –

LADY: Have returned the changeling. Let us go.

STRANGER: Yes. Let us return to your mountains and hide ourselves with our griefs.

LADY: Yes. The mountains hide. But first I must light a candle to my blessed Saint Elizabeth. [*The* STRANGER *shakes his head, deprecatingly.*] Come.

STRANGER: Well. I can always go in with you. But I won't stay.

LADY: You don't know. Come. In there you will hear new songs.

STRANGER [*goes after her to the church door*]: Perhaps.

LADY: Come.